Gunplays

Gunplays

Five Plays on Inner City Violence and Guns

By William Electric Black
aka Ian Ellis James

APPLAUSE
THEATRE & CINEMA BOOKS

Essex, Connecticut

APPLAUSE
THEATRE & CINEMA BOOKS

An imprint of Globe Pequot, the trade division of
The Rowman & Littlefield Publishing Group, Inc.
4501 Forbes Blvd., Ste. 200
Lanham, MD 20706
www.rowman.com

Distributed by NATIONAL BOOK NETWORK

Library of Congress Cataloging-in-Publication Data Available

ISBN 978-1-4930-7480-8 (pbk.: alk. paper)
ISBN 978-1-4930-7481-5 (electronic)

♾™ The paper used in this publication meets the minimum requirements of American National Standard for Information Sciences—Permanence of Paper for Printed Library Materials, ANSI/NISO Z39.48-1992

This book is dedicated to my beautiful electric family—Lucille, Erikka, Carllee, and Skyye—my parents Carlos and Virginia, my brothers Carlos and Kevin and their beautiful families, and to everyone who is trying to stop and prevent gun violence, a public health crisis that is destroying too many precious lives, families, and communities of color

Acknowledgments

All 5 Gunplays premiered at Theater for the New City, New York, New York, Crystal Field, Executive Director. Thank you, Crystal, for your continued support of my creative visions.

Contents

Welcome Home Sonny T.
Designer Sharon Jacobs, Urban Circle Design, NYC

Welcome Home Sonny T

a play by

William Electric Black

CAST

LASHON WALKER: 16-years-old, lean, attractive, runs track, street smart, precocious, wants to go to college, African American.

RODNEY WALKER (RD): 19-years-old, LaShon's older brother, unemployed, angry teen, needs direction, hangs with Big Boy, African American.

FUNKYGOOD: early 60s, quick witted, not afraid to speak his mind, helps out at the Harriet Tubman Center, loves to do his signature James Brown spin, African American.

REVEREND MILLER: early 60s, civil rights activist, community leader, founder of The Black Radical Society, having doubts about his leadership abilities, African American.

BIG BOY: 19-years-old, large, tall teen, thug mentality, troublemaker, packs a gun, out of work, bitter, his brother is doing prison time, African American.

CARLOS MENDEZ: early 20s, Mexican, delivery boy, illegal citizen, recently lost his brother, speaks up for what is right, wants justice and equality for his people.

MAY WALKER: early 60s, large, dynamic woman, mother of Sonny T, Rodney, and LaShon, very elated to have her child Sonny T return from duty in Iraq, single mom, would do anything for her kids, African American.

ACT I
Scene I

In the darkness we hear a SAXOPHONE (live if possible). The sax line begins to blend in with the faint sound of gunshots until finally the gunshots ring louder than the pulsating beat. The gunshots turn into the sound of high caliber military fire, rumbling humvees, then army helicopter noises. The sound swells and SWELLS then, ABRUPT SILENCE. Back to saxophone, a cool sound.

A spotlight suddenly illuminates REVEREND MILLER, early 60s, seated behind a small desk, cluttered with books, at a small college radio station. He is a broad shouldered, statuesque man dressed in a suit and tie. He seems tired as he speaks into the studio mic on top of the desk. The bare bones station is raised up above the main set, SL. It should rest atop a scaffolding. A neon sign—REVOLUTION RADIO—hangs above the station.

REV MILLER

(into the mic) Always like to end my mornin' radio show with a reflection of the way life used to be. Ain't that what Diana Ross sang about . . . reflections of the way life used to be! On the steps of Danton College in the late 60s, The Black Radical Society was formed. I was a foundin' member who wanted the campus, the lily white campus, to wake up and smell the revolution. *(beat)* See, there was a great storm just beyond the main campus gate. Like Hurricane Sandy that just come our way. Bringin' more inner-city blues than Marvin Gaye ever dreamt about. What the hell is goin' on? That's what we would ask ourselves 'cause there were no Black professors at Danton that we could ask. *(beat)* Sure, we could sit in the classroom but there was no reflection of us standing up at the podium to quote Marcus Garvey, Malcolm X, Eldridge Cleaver, Sojourner Truth or Angela Davis. Had to do somethin' so somethin' we did. Took over the campus. Locked arms, embraced hope, and did not move until we removed the chains from the closed mind of the President of Danton College and got him to hire a dozen Black professors. This is Reverend Wallace Miller here at Revolution Radio, Staten Island Community College . . . it's time to wake up and smell the revolution! *(beat)* And keep dropping those groceries off for hurricane victims still in need.

The James Brown tune I'M BLACK AND I'M PROUD kicks in as the stage lights fade. Same day. LIGHTS UP on the main hall of the Harriet Tubman Community Center, Port

Richmond, Staten Island, NY. The old hall has been around for many years and its faded, cracked pale blue walls are a testimony to that fact. The door to the hall is located on the SR wall. A few feet from the door, on the same wall, is a window facing the street. USC, along another wall, is another wooden door that leads to a storage room. On the SL wall are various paintings of well-known African Americans—Harriet Tubman, Shirley Chisholm, Malcolm X, A. Philip Randolph, Rosa Parks, Dr. Martin Luther King Jr., W. E. B. Du Bois, etc.

The hall is slowly being filled up with worn, faded tan, metal folding chairs by a thin, scrappy gray-haired 60-year-old man, FUNKYGOOD. FUNKYGOOD sports a blue shark skin suit, a black shirt, and a thin red tie. He pauses briefly to examine a LARGE, 3-by-2-foot PHOTO of US Army Specialist Sonny T Walker. The photo sits DSR on an easel facing the audience. He takes a second to adjust the angle of the photo. On the floor there are SEVERAL boxes and bags filled with assorted groceries.

Behind FUNKYGOOD, high atop one of the two 6-FOOT A-FRAMED LADDERS, some ten feet apart, is LASHON WALKER, a sweet 15-year-old, who wears orange sweatpants with a matching top. LASHON is lean and attractive. The banner she struggles to hang reads—"WELCOME HOME SONNY T."

LASHON
Funkygood, you know what time it is?

FUNKYGOOD
Time for you to be puttin' up that welcome home banner. (*beat*) Better get on the good foot!

FUNKYGOOD does a James Brown spin.

LASHON
I told Rodney to meet me here at nine and help me.

FUNKYGOOD
You told 'im, but I see he ain't the listenin' type.

LASHON
Now I'm gonna have to run home and get him.

FUNKYGOOD
You the runnin'est child I ever done seen. Why you always in such a hurry?

LASHON

Gotta practice so I can get me one of them track scholarships. If I get a scholarship then Momma won't have to pay for me to go to college.

FUNKYGOOD

They pay folks to go to college and run? What happened to goin' to college to learn something?

LASHON

Got to get there first. Once I'm there I might become a lawyer or maybe a doctor. What do you think?

FUNKYGOOD

I think you ain't there yet so get back to hangin' up that banner.

LASHON

But I need Rodney!

FUNKYGOOD

Well, stop wastin' your time talkin' and go find his butt.

LASHON climbs down the ladder and heads towards the main door.

FUNKYGOOD

If ya momma got some fried chicken ready bring me a piece.

LASHON

Funkygood, that chicken is for Sonny T's party.

FUNKYGOOD

Sonny T ain't gonna miss one piece. Now go on with ya bad self, Miss Wilma Rudolph!

LASHON

Miss who?

FUNKYGOOD

You a track star wannabee and you ain't never heard of Wilma Rudolph? (*beat*) What they teaching you in school?

LASHON

Algebra . . . The Scarlet Letter . . . chemistry . . . Spanish . . .

FUNKYGOOD

No Black History? See if I was runnin' these here schools . . .

REVEREND MILLER enters.

REV MILLER

But you ain't. So, leave the girl be.

LASHON

Hey, Reverend Miller.

REV MILLER

Hey, right back at ya!

LASHON

I woke up to hear the revolution this mornin'.

REV MILLER

How was my flow?

LASHON

It was mad nice.

REV MILLER

You hear that? LaShon said my flow was mad nice.

FUNKYGOOD

She's just being kind 'cause you an old man with an old revolution.

LASHON

You seen Rodney? He's supposed to be here helping me with Sonny T's banner.

REV MILLER

Better go find him. We got to get that banner up and do some more decorating.

LASHON

I'm gonna run all the way.

REV MILLER

You do that!

LASHON bolts out of the Community Center. FUNKYGOOD takes the opportunity to stare at REVEREND MILLER.

REV MILLER

What . . . is my zipper open?

FUNKYGOOD

No, but your mouth always is. One day you're gonna say somethin' on that radio show of yours that's finally the truth.

REV MILLER

What? Danton College was a lie?

FUNKYGOOD

No, I was right there with you. Me, LaShon's momma . . . we was all there.

REV MILLER

So, what's the problem?

FUNKYGOOD

The revolution came, went, and faded away just like afros and bell bottoms. And you let it.

REV MILLER

Me? I kept marchin' after Danton College. Kept sittin' in, gettin' called niggah, spit at, arrested . . . (*beat*) Damn, I sang "we shall overcome" so many times, during one march, lost my voice but not my nerve. And when you got drafted, I went down to the draft board. Me, May and a hundred others to get your butt out.

FUNKYGOOD

Yeah, you did. But I still had to go. If not, I was goin' to jail.

REV MILLER

That was your choice. Told ya to get your behind up to Canada. The BRS would think of something while you was in hidin'.

FUNKYGOOD

I ain't the hidin' type.

REV MILLER

But when ya came back there was this here center. A place to organize people's minds, bodies, and spirits. A home for Black folks to keep their heads up even when they was gettin' cracked open by social and economic injustice.

FUNKYGOOD

Look around. Ain't nobody home.

REV MILLER

Sonny T's coming home. That's good enough for me. That's good enough for today.

FUNKYGOOD

Well, it ain't good enough for me.

REV MILLER

What do you want, Funkygood? What the hell do you want from me?

FUNKYGOOD

Just want you to tell the truth one mornin' on that radio show.

REV MILLER

You want the truth? Truth is that I'm tired. Truth is I can't take no more fire hoses, no more fists raised, no more chantin' integration not segregation or . . . we shall not be moved. I'm on the radio every mornin' looking for help. I'm the last man standing in a cesspool of corrupt, vile, bigoted, tea sippin', NRA card carryin' folks still tryin' to be slave masters while allowin' a Black man in the big house, but still holdin' on tight to the keys that unlock all the doors. (*beat*) Truth is I'm hopin' Sonny T comes home to resurrect Black soldiers from Watts to Harlem, from Homewood to Compton. I'm hopin' he's the chosen one that we, up in the hood, pray for each night before we sip on that Black Label or take a hit on that crack pipe. The one little Black boys want to be like more than LeBron or Jay Z. I'm hopin' for Sonny T be the man I can no longer be. (*beat*) Is that truth enough for ya?

FUNKYGOOD

You helped him so he's gonna help you. Is that what you counting on?

REV MILLER

Need some new warriors. Sonny T is a good man. I know that, I feel that . . .

FUNKYGOOD

You got a lot ridin' on this boy, ain't ya? Just like when I come back from 'Nam. But I wasn't the one, was I? Didn't have the fight no more. Taste for the revolution was just dry spit in my mouth. Yours, too.

REV MILLER

Now there's no spit at all. Guess my faith is washed away just like them homes Hurricane Sandy done swallowed. Hear what I'm sayin'?

SILENCE. The two men stare at one another again until RODNEY enters causing them to act busy. RODNEY WALKER, 19-years-old, is a lanky teen full of anger. He wears blue jeans, a black hoodie and a black BROOKLYN NETS hat cocked to the side.

FUNKYGOOD

Boy, where you been? Your sista' went lookin' for ya.

RODNEY

Boy? I ain't no boy.

FUNKYGOOD

You get mad if I call you boy but when your homies call you niggah that's okay?

RODNEY

Man, go on with your stupid self!

FUNKYGOOD

Stupid? Can you spell erudite, fool?

RODNEY

Huh?

FUNKYGOOD

Exactly my point. (*beat*) How about penicillin 'cause you gonna need some after I put a whuppin on your ass! (*beat*) Yeah, give it up turn me loose!

FUNKYGOOD does a James Brown spin then raises his fists, ready to fight.

REV MILLER

Funkygood, take these here groceries to the storage room and bring back some more chairs 'fore ya hurt yourself. Go on, now!

FUNKYGOOD lowers his hands, grabs a box of food then exits to the storage room.

RODNEY

YO, he's trippin'!

> REV MILLER

Living hard makes you do crazy things. It ain't easy being green . . . or Black.

> RODNEY

What?

> REV MILLER

Sesame Street? Never mind. Get on up that there ladder. Need that banner hung up.

RODNEY heads up the ladder.

> RODNEY

Where's LaShon? Woke me up tellin' me to get on down here and she ain't even around!

FUNKYGOOD emerges from the storage room holding two folding chairs.

> REV MILLER

She was here. She run off lookin' for you.

> FUNKYGOOD

Did you get lost?

FUNKYGOOD opens the two folding chairs.

> RODNEY

Went to the corner store. Played me some Lotto.

RODNEY, now at the top of the ladder, fiddles with the banner.

> FUNKYGOOD

Ain't gonna win! The man gets you playin' and playin', thinkin' you gonna win. But ya never do.

> REV MILLER

Kind of like life. Cuts ya when you ain't lookin' then leaves you for dead.

> FUNKYGOOD

Amen!

> RODNEY

But when I do win y'all be beggin' me for a ride in my Bentley. But there ain't gonna be no room 'cause my rides gonna be over flowin' with fly honeys.

FUNKYGOOD

And I thought Martin Luther King Jr. had a dream.

RODNEY

Dollar and a dream. That's all it takes.

FUNKYGOOD

Only way you gonna get a Bentley is steal one.

RODNEY

YO, you'd better shut up old man unless you wanna get hurt.

REV MILLER

He's just playin' with you.

RODNEY

Just 'cause Vietnam messed with his head don't mean he can say whatever the hell he wants to.

FUNKYGOOD

Just talkin' loud and sayin' nothin'. Old men do that. It's a privilege one gets for being Black, beautiful and still alive. May the honor be yours one day.

FUNKYGOOD grabs another box of groceries then exits to the storage room to get more chairs. A moment, then LASHON enters.

LASHON

Rodney, where you been? Momma said if you don't help me . . .

RODNEY

I'm here, ain't I? So, let's get busy 'cause I gotta bounce soon.

LASHON

But you just got here.

LASHON climbs up the other ladder grabbing her end of the banner.

RODNEY

No, you just got here.

LASHON

(*angrily*) I been here!

RODNEY

If you been here then why you just gettin' here now?

LASHON

Fool, I was here at nine o'clock!

RODNEY

Who you callin' fool?

REVEREND MILLER approaches the bottom of LASHON's ladder and calls up to the teens, interrupting their feud.

REV MILLER

(*calling*) Okay . . . okay! Can we focus on what we have to do and not on how much you two dislike each other? We are supposed to be here gettin' things ready for Sonny T's party.

RODNEY

YO, I got mad things to do.

LASHON

Like what, go shoot somebody?

RODNEY abruptly stops hanging the banner.

RODNEY

What did you say?

FUNKYGOOD enters from the storage room with another metal chair.

FUNKYGOOD

I heard her. She said, "Like what, go shoot . . ."

RODNEY

Shut up, fool! Or I just might shoot your dumb ass!

LASHON

You think I'm dumb? Don't know what you're up to? I'm smart. Get straight A's. And I'm gettin' me a track scholarship so I can go to NC State.

FUNKYGOOD

Girl, you got it all figured out. (*beat*) What you got figured out, Rodney?

RODNEY climbs down the ladder and gets all up in FUNKYGOOD's face.

RODNEY

The name ain't Rodney. It's RD! And what I got figured out is there ain't a hell of a lot out here for me. (*beat*) Driving a bus, a cab . . . setting up chairs in a community center? Ain't gotta go to college to do that.

LASHON

You graduated last year. Momma wanted you to go to college.

RODNEY

(*to LaShon*) Why? So, I could owe a lot of money when I get out?

LASHON addresses RODNEY from atop her ladder.

LASHON

We poor. They give you money if you're poor so you can go to college.

RODNEY

World don't give you a damn thing if you're poor. Just heartaches.

RODNEY (CONT'D)

You see what the storm did? Took what little shit people had and destroyed it. Rich folks, they got their power back, they got their clothes, got their food, their homes. Poor people just got poorer.

REV MILLER

You been on this earth for 19 years and ain't learned a damn thing.

FUNKYGOOD

See, I told you! Ain't learnin' nothing 'bout nothin' in these here schools.

RODNEY

I'm outta here. You can celebrate without me.

RODNEY heads for the door.

REV MILLER

Without you? Your brother's comin' home. One of our very own who grew up on these streets. Off to Iraq to fight for us. For our country, our freedom . . . and you too busy to be here? When you gonna grow up?

RODNEY

Our country? Our freedom?

RODNEY (CONT'D)

What you been smokin', Rev? 'Cause I damn sure want some of that.

FUNKYGOOD

You couldn't handle it.

REV MILLER

Don't need to get high to see things clearly. This is a good country. A good land. Sure, it's filled with a sea of hatred, mountains of bigotry, rivers of violence but also filled with valleys of love, sunsets of compassion, and rainbows painted by God's own hands . . .

FUNKYGOOD

And music by James Brown!
(*spins*) Good God!!!

RODNEY

Sonny T ain't no angel. So, don't you believe goin' off to the army changed him. He ran the streets before and he's gonna run 'em when he gets back.

REV MILLER

You sure about that? People change.

RODNEY

Do they? (*beat*) When he comes through that door in a few hours y'all will be singin' and shoutin' his name for a week or two, maybe even a month. But what happens when Sonny T's back for six months, a year? When Sonny T starts hangin' over at Freddy Mack's drinkin' 'til four in the morning. So stressed out from the war he shoots himself in the damn head.

LASHON

Rodney, why you gotta be hatin' on Sonny T?

RODNEY

I said call me RD.

LASHON

RD ain't ya name. Nobody calls you that 'cept Big Boy.

CARLOS MENDEZ, late 20s, a Mexican man wearing a bike helmet and reflecting vest, enters <u>carrying a box</u> of groceries. He is greeted by FUNKYGOOD as he removes his helmet.

FUNKYGOOD

Can I help you, young man?

CARLOS

I . . . I have come with some food. Food for the hurricane victims.

RODNEY

Beans and rice?

REV MILLER

Show some respect, Rodney.

LASHON

See, Reverend Miller calls you Rodney.

RODNEY

Shut up, girl!

CARLOS

You are the Reverend Miller?

REV MILLER

Do I owe you money?

CARLOS

Sorry . . . ?

REV MILLER

Just a joke. I am Reverend Miller. And thank you for the food. (*beat*) Rodney, please take the young man's box.

RODNEY gets in CARLOS' face.

RODNEY

Man? He's migrant trash not no man. Move to our hood, hangin' on the corners like flies hangin' on garbage. Taking what little jobs we got. Real men don't do that to other men.

CARLOS

You and your homies don't want to deliver pizza but I do. What is wrong with that?

RODNEY

Didn't you get the hint last week?

CARLOS

Were you responsible for shootin' my brother?
(*angrily*) I asked you a question.

RODNEY knocks CARLOS' box of food to the floor.

RODNEY

I wish I did shoot him.

REV MILLER

That's enough! It's time for you to leave!

RODNEY

Thought you wanted me here for the celebration?

REV MILLER

It ain't until tonight, so get.

RODNEY glares at CARLOS, then exits.

LASHON

Ah man, now Momma's gonna be mad the banner ain't up.

REV MILLER

I'll help you, LaShon. Just give me a few minutes to speak with this young man.
(*beat*) Run on up to the house and see if your mother needs you.

LASHON

I just ran up there.

REV MILLER

Well, run on back. Ain't gonna be citywide champ if you don't keep training.

LASHON

You think I'm gonna be an all-city champ this year?

REV MILLER

What do you think, Funkygood? Do we got us a city champion?

FUNKYGOOD

Girl got it going on! Say it loud—I'm fast and I'm proud!

Beat. LASHON heads towards the door but suddenly turns back.

LASHON

Why they shootin' up his people, Reverend Miller? Don't make any sense. Ain't one storm enough?

CARLOS

This girl . . . she is very smart, no?

LASHON

Get straight A's! And I'm gettin' me a track scholarship.

REV MILLER

Go on, LaShon. Sonny T will be gettin' here around six and I'm sure your momma got plenty more things for you to do 'fore he gets here.

LASHON

I'm going. I'M GOING!

LASHON exits. FUNKYGOOD picks up the spilled groceries while offering CARLOS a chair.

FUNKYGOOD

Would you like a seat, amigo?

CARLOS sits.

CARLOS

Thank you.

REV MILLER

So, your brother was Hector. The boy who got shot near the corner store?

FUNKYGOOD places CARLOS' box of groceries on the floor.

CARLOS

Si! (*beat*) He recently came to live with me. He's got nothing back in Mexico. The drug cartels want him to kill for them. If he sez no, they kill him. My family had to get him out.

FUNKYGOOD

Out of the fire and into the hot grease.

REV MILLER

How did you get to this country?

CARLOS

You want to know if I am illegal?

REV MILLER

I want to know your story.

CARLOS

Does it matter? We are all guilty of crossing into territory that doesn't belong to us.

CARLOS looks at Sonny T's photo.

CARLOS (CONT'D)

Just ask the soldier in that picture?

REV MILLER

He's not here right now so I'm askin' you. (*beat*) And this ain't about him.

CARLOS

It's about all of us, no? Is not America one big pot filled with white, black, brown and yellow beans?

FUNKYGOOD

Beans give me gas.

REV MILLER

America is a melting pot but there's a lot of people who think the pot is overflowing. (*beat*) The country can't take care of those who were born and raised here. How can it deal with the thousands that sneak in year after year?

CARLOS

So that justifies the hatred?

REV MILLER

Hatred can never be justified.

CARLOS

What happened to giving a fellow man a chance, a helping hand?

FUNKYGOOD

Been asking myself that very same question, amigo.

FUNKYGOOD pulls up a chair next to CARLOS. He GRINS at CARLOS.

REV MILLER

Crabs in a barrel. Pulling each other back. That's what we've become. But we just don't pull. We steal, lie, shoot, murder, rape, cheat, drop the bomb, drop a name, drop our pants. Our reality has become blurred by reality TV. Done lost ourselves within ourselves.

FUNKYGOOD

Reverend, you one deep man. Damn if I understood a word of what you just said! Did you get that, ah . . . ?

CARLOS

Carlos. And I understand. We are not that different.

FUNKYGOOD

You kind of deep, too, Carlos.

REV MILLER

People are mad, outraged. And there ain't no magic pills, no soft words, no amusing op eds from the New York Times magazine section to ease the pain. Tune it out if you can. Or discuss it later via email or a text. If that don't work try and google the answer to your problems.

CARLOS

So that is why you didn't come to my house after Hector was attacked by those thugs? You had no kind words? No answers?

REV MILLER

I called the mayor. It was the second attack in three weeks so I spoke to him about it. We want to have a community meeting soon.

CARLOS

Meeting? What happened to the man everyone talks about around here? The man who marched, gave speeches? Who stopped traffic when the police put dozens of

CARLOS (CONT'D)

bullets into a boy, a Black kid who they said brought a gun onto the ferry, but he had no weapon on him. I heard you did these great things.

REV MILLER

I'll do whatever it takes when I feel the time is right.

CARLOS

I guess now is not the right time, no? You are too busy reflecting on the radio.

CARLOS stands, heads for the door.

FUNKYGOOD

I think this young man just spit on you. (*takes out hanky*) You want my handkerchief to wipe it off?

CARLOS

We are marchin' tonight, Reverend Miller. We will march from our homes right by this center, right to the corner store where my brother got shot.

FUNKYGOOD

Ya gonna march right past this here center? But tonight we's having a welcome home party for a war hero. (*beat*) Tell him, Rev. Tonight ain't a good night.

REV MILLER

It's a free country.

FUNKYGOOD

Don't they got to get a permit or somethin'?

CARLOS

We got one, Señor.

REV MILLER

(*to Funkygood*) He's got one. Now let it be, Funkygood. Let it be.

CARLOS

Perhaps you will leave your celebration for a few minutes and march with us?

REV MILLER

Perhaps I will.

REVEREND MILLER shakes CARLOS' hand then walks him toward the exit door.

CARLOS

Well, thank you for your time. It was a pleasure to meet you.

CARLOS pauses, putting his helmet back on.

CARLOS

I hope your celebration is a success.

CARLOS gazes at the photo.

CARLOS

He looks very brave.

REV MILLER

How do you know what a brave man looks like?

CARLOS

Sometimes . . . you just know. (*beat*) Am I right?

SILENCE. CARLOS exits.

FUNKYGOOD

Well, I knows me a foolish young man when I sees one. And he just walked out that door!

REV MILLER

Quiet, now. He might hear you.

FUNKYGOOD

Good! I hope he does. Maybe I should say it louder. (*loudly*) FOOLISH YOUNG MAN! FOOLISH YOUNG MAN!

REV MILLER

Think the whole damn neighborhood done heard ya!

FUNKYGOOD

Does you think marchin' right in front of our center tonight is a good idea or a foolish one? (*beat*) Answer me that!

REV MILLER

To him, it's a good idea.

FUNKYGOOD

I ain't askin' him. I'm askin' you!

REV MILLER

A man's got the right to march. We marched. Don't you remember?

FUNKYGOOD

I remember lots of things. Do you?

LASHON enters, slightly winded.

LASHON

Momma said come by this afternoon and help her bring over the fried chicken, potato salad, green beans, mac and cheese, biscuits, ribs, baked ham, rice, cornbread, rice puddin', yams, mustard greens, beets, sweet potatoes, and chocolate cake.

FUNKYGOOD

Does your momma think Sonny T's bringin' the whole United States Army with him?

LASHON

I think she does!

FUNKYGOOD

Well then, I'm gonna go get my fried chicken right now.

FUNKYGOOD quickly exits the center.

REV MILLER

Okay, LaShon, climb back up on the ladder and let's get that banner up. What good is a welcome home party without a welcome home sign?

LASHON climbs up one ladder and REVEREND MILLER climbs up the other one.

LASHON

Reverend Miller, can I tell you something?

REV MILLER

Anything you want.

LASHON

But you won't tell Momma?

REV MILLER

If you don't want me to.

LASHON

Don't want you to tell anyone.

REV MILLER

Not a soul. You have my word.

LASHON climbs down the ladder and heads toward REVEREND MILLER, still atop his ladder.

LASHON

(*hesitates, then . . .*) I . . . I think Rodney and Big Boy got somethin' to do with all this.

REV MILLER

(*holding banner*) All of what?

LASHON

Them attacks against the Mexican boys. Everyone knows Black kids are doin' it.

REV MILLER

Got a lot of Black teenagers here on Staten Island. Black, white, brown . . .

LASHON

He be hangin' out with Big Boy. And I heard them sayin' how the Mexicans are ruinin' everything here in Port Richmond.

REV MILLER

I think you're getting worked up over nothin'.

SILENCE.

LASHON

He's got a gun. Is that nothin'?

REV MILLER

(*concerned*) Big Boy?

LASHON

Rodney! I seen it. I was lookin' for a shoe box to put my babysittin' money in and found it.

REV MILLER

(*concerned*) You sure about this?

REVEREND MILLER makes his way down the ladder and approaches LASHON at center stage.

LASHON

Ain't mine and it ain't Momma's. Don't have to be no Einstein to figure out who it belongs to.

REV MILLER

(*thinking*) Could be holding it for someone.

LASHON

And he could be waiting to shoot someone. (*upset*) What are we gonna do, Reverend?

REV MILLER

We? You stay out of this. I'll handle things.

LASHON

Like you did for Sonny T three years ago? You won't let Rodney go to jail either? Promise me?

REV MILLER

Sonny T was runnin' with a rough crew when he got arrested for that shootin' some years back, but I got him a deal so he could join the army instead of going to jail. Didn't pull the trigger, didn't even go inside the corner store. Now if Rodney ain't used that gun you got nothin' to worry about.

LASHON

Ya ever wonder why so many Black kids have guns. Guess they think they have to save themselves.

REV MILLER

A gun don't save no one. Just kills. Now I will handle this. Is that clear?

LASHON

Yes, Reverend Miller.

REV MILLER

Good, now let's finish these here decorations.

REVEREND MILLER and LASHON climb back up their ladders.

LASHON

Think Sonny T ever killed anyone in Iraq?

REV MILLER

Don't really know.

LASHON

He did. Told me in one of his letters. I saved all of 'em.

REV MILLER

I'm sure you did.

LASHON

He didn't like killing. Said it made him feel sick.

REV MILLER

When a man kills another man, it destroys part of his soul. And nine times out of ten . . . he don't ever get that part of his soul back.

STAGE LIGHTS fade to black.

End Scene I

ACT I
Scene II

Lights up on REVOLUTION RADIO, late afternoon. A spotlight once again illuminates REV-EREND MILLER. The SAXOPHONE is heard.

REV MILLER

(*into mic*) You may be wonderin' why I'm back at Revolution Radio this afternoon. Well, we got another storm blowin' towards Port Richmond. Blowin' harder than any Coltrane solo. Mightier than August Wilson's Joe Turner who come, but ain't about to be goin'. (*beat*) There's been blood in our streets. Precious blood spilled by Mexican and Black teenagers over what? If you ask them, they probably don't even know. Funny thing is the kids I'm tryin' to reach are not even listening to me right now. Why should they? What have I got to say that means any damn thing to them. Do I have to be a P. Diddy or a Jennifer Lopez to get through to y'all? Do I have to be a Marvel super hero to stop you from hatin' one another. A hatred that's spreadin' far beyond our little town. And how do you cure this hatred? Well, we all gonna have to get involved. Biggie Smalls once asked, who you be with? Now I ask that same question to you? (*beat*) I'd like to thank Staten Island Community College for lettin' me have these few minutes to speak to y'all. See you in the mornin' when we wake up and smell the revolution.

Lights fade on the RADIO STATION as the SAXOPHONE fades. LIGHTS UP in the main hall of the Community Center. Several hours have passed. The boxes of donated food have been put away. The banner is now strung between the two ladders. A dozen metal chairs now fill the open room. Red, white, and blue balloons have been attached to radiators along the faded, blue cracked walls. A long folding table is now situated right between the two ladders. On top of the table, covered by a white tablecloth, are several PANS and TRAYS covered by foil. The pans and trays are filled with assorted foods. A large chocolate layer cake is also visible.

BIG BOY, a heavy-set, rather large 19-year-old teen sporting a "MIAMI HEAT" basketball jersey, LOW RIDING JEANS that show his underwear, high top sneakers, and a "MIAMI HEAT" basketball cap enters the hall with RODNEY, who sports a NETS jersey and cap.

BIG BOY

YO, RD . . . what we come by here for? We got mad business to take care of.

RODNEY

I'm hungry and my moms spent all day making this crazy ass food for my brother's party.

BIG BOY

For Sonny T?

RODNEY

Can't you read the banner?

BIG BOY

Yeah, I can read. It should say welcome home punk ass Sonny T!

RODNEY heads for the table and looks inside a tray of food.

RODNEY

YO, to the folks 'round here my brother's a damn hero. Someone finally got out of here alive!

BIG BOY

To me, he's the niggah that let my brother Jasper take the rap.

RODNEY

Your brother shot the deli owner. Not Sonny T.

BIG BOY

Sonny T had a piece. But he was such a pussy he didn't even use it.

RODNEY

Maybe he figured the dude was already dead so why bother.

BIG BOY

And maybe he was afraid.

RODNEY

You know Sonny T ain't like that. Niggah could kick anyone's ass. (*beat*) You want some fried chicken?

BIG BOY

Nah, man. I'm tryin' to watch my figure.

RODNEY

You and your big ass? Who you kiddin'?

BIG BOY

Hey, man . . . all that fast food from Wendy's and MickyD's is a plot by the white man to get us all fat and shit.

RODNEY

A plot?

BIG BOY

Get fat . . . and get a fuckin' heart attack! You feel me, dog?

RODNEY sits down on a folding chair and eats a piece of chicken.

RODNEY

You trippin'! (*beat*) Everybody runnin' 'round these tired ass streets with guns and you worried about dyin' from eatin' a double cheeseburger with extra bacon?

BIG BOY

Told you what's up man, I read shit.

RODNEY

Yeah, right . . .

BIG BOY

I can read you, niggah.

RODNEY

You crazy . . .

BIG BOY

I said I can <u>read</u> you.

RODNEY

Then you must be readin' how much I love my momma's fried chicken.

BIG BOY

I'm reading how much you are a <u>chicken</u>! Man, if it wasn't for me, you wouldn't even know how to break into them flooded homes over in South Beach and steal shit.

RODNEY

Thank you, Mista PhD of crime!

BIG BOY

Man, I get you some heat and you ain't never used it.

RODNEY

Don't have to 'cause you always shoot first!

BIG BOY

You a punk just like your brother.

RODNEY

(*standing*) My brother ain't no punk. Kicked your brother's ass right up on Oak Street. Or maybe you forgot about that.

BIG BOY

I ain't forgot shit. Ain't forgot that Jasper is still in the joint and Sonny T got a damn free ride thanks to Reverend Miller.

RODNEY

He tried to help Jasper, too.

BIG BOY

Niggah just out to help himself. Why you think he's lettin' them wetback punk muthers walk right through our part of town? He's just a fake Jessie Jackson, MLK wanna-be. Big Black man who gathered up dope dealers, project dwellers, single moms, and homeless niggahs thirty years ago and gave 'em hope right here at the Tubman Center. (*beat*) Damn he's good. Even I almost fell for his bullshit.

RODNEY

He's alright. Just ain't down with us gang-bangin' taco heads.

BIG BOY

You down, RD? Or are you just frontin'?

RODNEY

You seen me. I was right there swingin' a bat at them rice and bean eaters. I think they got my message.

BIG BOY whips out his 9MM.

BIG BOY

But with this message they don't think, they know. And in a half hour when they come marchin' along like this land is their land and shit, they's gonna get another damn mutherfuckin' message. And this time you ain't gonna be swingin' no fuckin' bat.

RODNEY

Man, I ain't shootin' nobody.

                    BIG BOY

Oh, you gonna shoot somebody.

                    RODNEY

And if I don't?

BIG BOY jams his gun into RODNEY's temple.

                    BIG BOY

Somebody might shoot your ass!

                    RODNEY

Can't shoot nobody 'cause I ain't got no piece.

                    BIG BOY

Like hell you don't! Niggah, I gave you one.

                    RODNEY

Someone took it.

BIG BOY lowers his gun.

                    BIG BOY

What the hell you talkin' 'bout?

                    RODNEY

I was home chillin' 'fore I caught up to you. My crib is jammin' with people 'cause all of this Sonny T business. My Aunt Rudy's there. Mr. and Mrs. Pickett, LaShon and crazy ass Funkygood. I tipped into my room, reached into my Converse shoe box to get my piece and it was gone.

                    BIG BOY

Niggah, go back and look for it. Maybe it fell out.

                    RODNEY

I did look for it. All over!

                    BIG BOY

Maybe your moms took it.

                    RODNEY

Wouldn't be standin' here if my moms found it. She'd cuss my ass out then send me down south to live with my Aunt Rudy.

BIG BOY tucks his gun away.

BIG BOY

You gonna need that piece tonight. You'd better find it.

LASHON, carrying a chocolate cake and a shopping bag, enters now wearing a cute party dress. BIG BOY eyes her young, shapely body as she makes room on the table, placing the cake down.

BIG BOY

What about her?

RODNEY

LaShon? She's smart, not crazy!

BIG BOY

We'll see about that. Ask her.

RODNEY

But if she didn't take it then she'll know I got a piece.

BIG BOY

Probably already does know. Go on, ask the stuck up bitch.

LASHON

Excuse me, but I can hear you two fools!

RODNEY

(to Big Boy) I'll talk to her. Meet me up by the corner store.

BIG BOY

They be marchin' up this way real soon. Don't be playin' me. You hear, RD?

RODNEY

No problem.

BIG BOY

There better not be a problem. *(to LaShon)* YO, LaShon . . . you look all grown up and shit.

LASHON

Yeah, some of us grow up and some of us don't. You get a job, yet?

> BIG BOY

Even lawyers can't find jobs these days.

LASHON strolls over to BIG BOY and looks him dead in the eyes.

> LASHON

Oh, you a lawyer now?

> BIG BOY

You real funny.

> RODNEY

And fast.

> BIG BOY

So, I heard. Real fast and shit. (*beat*) But are you faster than a bullet, like Superman?

> LASHON

Are you?

LASHON and BIG BOY glare at each other.

> RODNEY

(*to Big Boy*) I said I got this.

> BIG BOY

You'd better. (*beat*) Nice legs, LaShon. Real nice.

BIG BOY exits with a grin on his face.

> RODNEY

Ya tryin' to get yourself killed?

> LASHON

Are you?

> RODNEY

You took my gun, didn't you?

> LASHON

You took some fried chicken, didn't you?

> RODNEY

Girl, I ain't got time to be playin'. Big Boy is serious. That gun is his!

LASHON

Don't know what you're talkin' 'bout.

LASHON turns to walk away. RODNEY grabs her arm.

RODNEY

LaShon, where's the damn gun?

LASHON

Ask Reverend Miller. Maybe he got it.

LASHON pulls away from RODNEY.

RODNEY

If he got it, you're the one who gave it to him.

LASHON

You know guns are illegal without a license. Look what happened to that Plaxico guy on the Giants. One day he's a Super Bowl star, the next day he's in jail. Why? 'Cause of some dumb ass gun.

RODNEY heads for the hall door.

RODNEY

Ain't got time for no lecture.

LASHON

Maybe Reverend Miller can work out a deal for you just like he did for Sonny T.

RODNEY stops and turns back.

RODNEY

What are you talkin' 'bout?

LASHON

Said he wanted to talk to you.

RODNEY

I ain't going to no damn army. Rather be jobless and stuck on Staten Island than enlist.

LASHON

Go to jail, then. But don't be expecting me to visit you from college.

LASHON (CONT'D)

NC State's a long way from Rikers Island. And with all my track meets I doubt I'll . . .

RODNEY

Listen, LaShon . . .

FUNKYGOOD, dressed to impress, enters wearing a pair of old, wire-framed glasses. He carries a gift-wrapped bottle of wine.

FUNKYGOOD

Y'all better hush that noise. Your family is supposed to be standing tall tonight. Tall and together.

RODNEY

Says who?

FUNKYGOOD

Go on, then. Act a fool!

LASHON

Won't be too hard for Rodney.

FUNKYGOOD places the bottle of wine on the table.

FUNKYGOOD

RD's okay. He's just confused like most ignoramuses his age.

RODNEY

I ain't confused! And I ain't no ignor . . . whatever the hell you just said.

FUNKYGOOD

Ignoramus.

RODNEY

Told you, ya better watch what you say to me!

FUNKYGOOD

I'm watching, but it don't do no good. See these glasses I'm wearin' are kind of old. Ain't had no new prescription in, well . . . twenty some odd years.

RODNEY

You think you're funny but you ain't.

FUNKYGOOD

I ain't funny. I'm funky. My feet show it and now you knows it! (*spins*) GOOD GOD!

RODNEY

YO, you mad crazy!

MAY WALKER, a no-nonsense woman in her early 60s, enters wearing a flower print jumper.

MAY

Alright now, no one eats a thing until Sonny T walks through that door and has the first bite.

LASHON

Rodney already ate some chicken.

MAY

(*confronting Rodney*) Boy, tell me it ain't true. Tell me you didn't eat some chicken.

RODNEY

I was hungry so I ate a piece!

MAY

Told you not to tell me.

LASHON

Momma, do you like the decorations?

MAY

I don't like 'em, I LOVE 'EM!

FUNKYGOOD

Sonny T's gonna love 'em, too.

LASHON

Ya think so?

FUNKYGOOD

I know so! What do you think, RD?

MAY

RD? Who's that?

LASHON

Rodney's new name!

RODNEY

What's wrong with RD?

MAY

What's right with it?

FUNKYGOOD

Everyone's got a nickname these days. Li'l Wayne, LL Cool J, Snoop Dogg . . .
(*beat*) I wasn't always Funkygood. My dancin' got me this name back in 'Nam.
Kept it since James Brown's "Cold Sweat" made me get on the good foot!

MAY

As long as this child lives under my roof his name is Rodney.

FUNKYGOOD

What's in a name? That which we call a rose by any other name would smell as
sweet.

LASHON

Ain't that a line from Romeo & Juliet? We just read that in English class.

FUNKYGOOD

Shakespeare . . . Langston Hughes, Morrison, I do not discriminate. If you write it,
I will read it.

RODNEY

I go by RD . . . and that's that.

MAY

That's that?

FUNKYGOOD

This is about to get ugly. Better close your eyes, LaShon.

LASHON

No way. I wanna see this!

MAY

Rodney was okay 'til you started hangin' out with that Big Boy. And he ain't
nothin' but trouble. Just like that older brother of his.

RODNEY

Ain't nothin' but trouble out here. Don't believe me? Ask Sonny T when he gets home. He'll tell you.

MAY

You so grown up why don't you tell me?

RODNEY

Won't do no good. You only hear what you wanna hear.

FUNKYGOOD

Maybe I'd hear better if I could afford a hearing aide.

MAY heads to the table and places some serving spoons in one of the trays.

MAY

Your hearin' is fine, Funkygood. And so is Rodney's. He just don't wanna listen. Don't wanna go to college . . . don't wanna work!

LASHON

I know what he wants to do.

RODNEY gives LASHON a threatening look.

MAY

And what is that?

REVEREND MILLER enters.

REV MILLER

Is Sonny T . . . here, yet?

MAY

Called about twenty minutes ago from JFK. He's in a taxi cab and should be here real soon.

REV MILLER

Where you want these cups, May?

MAY

Wherever Rodney put the sodas?

                            RODNEY

That ain't my name.

                            MAY

(*to Reverend Miller*) You hear this? Wants to be called RD.

                            REV MILLER

Yeah, I heard. Kinda has a nice ring to it.

                            MAY

Ring? Sounds more like a thump to me.

                            FUNKYGOOD

Tried to tell May that RD's just keepin' up with the times. Expressing himself.

                            MAY

I wish that he'd express himself with a job.

                            RODNEY

Gonna get paid. Just don't wanna have to be a slave to get mines.

                            FUNKYGOOD

So, you wanna do the whuppin' and not get whupped?

                            RODNEY

For real!

                            MAY

Will somebody please talk some sense into this child. I can't take it no more.

                            REV MILLER

He's just being himself.

                            MAY

Himself?

                            REV MILLER

A rebel! (*beat*) We did the same thing when we was his age. Black berets, dashikis . . .

                            LASHON

Did you do it with a gun?

                            MAY

What gun?

REV MILLER
No one said nothin' about no gun.

FUNKYGOOD
Someone should. Everybody got one these days!

MAY
Who got a gun?

REV MILLER
Know anything about a gun, RD?

RODNEY
Don't know a thing.

REV MILLER
You wanna kill somebody? I know the feelin'.

MAY
Don't go there, Reverend.

FUNKYGOOD
It's all about the truth.

LASHON
You wanted to kill someone, Reverend?

REVEREND MILLER turns away. He takes a seat on a chair and stares off.

REV MILLER
Ain't the leader I was thirty-five years ago. Mr. Mendez is right. Should have gone out there in the streets when his brother and that other Mexican boy got shot. But I didn't. I made a call. Reverend Wallace Miller made a phone call.

REVEREND MILLER ponders his efforts while the others look on.

RODNEY
You kill someone or not, Reverend?

MAY
He ain't kill no one. He's just wish he did.

LASHON
But Rodney wants to. He wants blood. Mexican blood!

MAY

Hush up, LaShon. Ain't no one talkin' about nobody's blood.

RODNEY

(*to Reverend Miller*) Big Boy's right. You just be frontin'. You're a useless community leader who couldn't lead a bunch of girl scouts.

VOICES are heard in the distance, chanting.

MEXICAN CROWD (OFFSTAGE)

(*chanting in Spanish*)
THE VIOLENCE MUST END
WE ARE ALL THE SAME MEN
THE VIOLENCE MUST END
WE ARE ALL THE SAME MEN
THE VIOLENCE . . .

Chanting continues outside. MAY heads to the window and looks out. The others join her.

MAY

What's going on out there?

FUNKYGOOD

There's a protest march tonight. Mexicans is all upset about the recent shootings. Told Reverend Miller it was a bad idea.

MAY

Tonight?

Chanting continues.

REV MILLER

A Mexican boy was shot up on the corner a week ago. Another boy was shot not long before him.

RODNEY

(*from atop ladder*) Welcome to America! Welcome home Sonny T!

The chanting grows nearer as May's CELL PHONE rings.

MEXICAN CROWD (O.S.)

(*chanting in Spanish*)
THE VIOLENCE MUST END
WE ARE ALL THE SAME MEN
THE VIOLENCE MUST END
WE ARE ALL THE SAME MEN
THE VIOLENCE . . .

MAY

(*answering cell phone*) Hello? Sonny T? What, baby? Yeah, I just found out about it.
They got the whole street blocked off? You gonna have to get out and walk?

BIG BOY rushes in.

BIG BOY

(*shouting out*) YO, RD, IT'S TIME. LET'S DO THIS!

RODNEY climbs down from the ladder and heads to the door.

MAY

(*grabs Rodney*) You stay put. (*back to phone*) Not you, Sonny T. I was talkin' to
Rodney. Okay. We's all at the center waitin' for you.

*MAY shuts her cell phone and throws a hard look at RODNEY. The chanting grows CLOSER
and LOUDER "THE VIOLENCE MUST END . . ."*

MAY

Any minute your brother's comin' home from Iraq and you goin' to hang out in
the street?

RODNEY

Got my own war, Momma. Sonny T ain't the only one fightin' for somethin'.

MAY

What war you got? I give you a roof over your head. Pocket change. Put clothes
on your back. Even paid for you to go to two weeks of computer classes.

BIG BOY

(*to Rodney*) You down or what? We got to show 'em they can't just march through
our neighborhood.

MAY

Rodney . . . don't.

RODNEY shakes his head then exits the hall with BIG BOY. MAY, exhausted, sits down.

MAY

That boy is gonna be the death of me. (*beat*) Lawd, where is Sonny T?

LASHON consoles her.

LASHON

He'll be here any second.

FUNKYGOOD

Rev . . . maybe we'd better go look for him.

REV MILLER

Maybe . . .

Suddenly a SHOT rings out causing everyone to drop to the floor.

REV MILLER

(*alarmed*) Everyone, stay down!

MAY, FUNKYGOOD, LASHON, and REVEREND MILLER crouch behind the chairs as ANOTHER SHOT is heard.

MAY

Where are the police?

A BRICK comes through the window of the hall BREAKING THE GLASS, then TWO MORE SHOTS are heard. MAY gets up and starts for the door. REVEREND MILLER stops her.

MAY

My two boys is out there!

LASHON

Momma, it ain't safe!

*CARLOS MENDEZ RUSHES into the hall as POLICE SIRENS are heard approaching.
FLASHING POLICE LIGHTS shine through the window.*

CARLOS

Help! Senors, Senoras, someone has been shot. COME QUICK! PLEASE HELP!

FUNKYGOOD

Damn kids!

REV MILLER

Where?

CARLOS

In the street! Just outside!

MAY

Lawd, not another Mexican boy gunned down?

CARLOS

No, he is not Mexican. (*points to large photo*) It is that man! The one in the uniform.
In the photograph!

MAY

Sonny T?

CARLOS

Come quick! PLEASE, HURRY!

CARLOS rushes out.

MAY

My Sonny T's been shot?

QUICK BLACKOUT.

End of Act I

Rodney holds a gun to Big Boy's head after he discovers that Big Boy killed his brother, Sonny T.
Photo by Jonathan Slaff

May Walker (Verna Hampton) recalls being a member of the Black Radical Society that fought for civil rights during the 60s and 70s.
Photo by Jonathan Slaff

Big Boy confronts Rodney.
Photo by Jonathan Slaff

Richard Pryor Jr. as
Reverend Miller.
Photo by Jonathan Slaff

May comforts her daughter LaShon, local resident Carlos Mendez,
and old BRS friend Funkygood.
Photo by Jonathan Slaff

NEW POLITICAL PLAYS

A reading series curated by Dan Friedman
Artistic director, Castillo Theatre

Mississippi Goddamn
by Jonathan Norton
directed by Imani
Monday, March 23, 7:00 pm

1963. Jackson, Mississippi. Battle lines are drawn —
daughter against father, husband against wife, sister
against sister, and neighbor against neighbor. Set
against the backdrop and changing times of the civil
rights era, Mississippi Goddamn examines the tensions
and complications within families and among
neighbors leading up to the 1963 assassination of
Medgar Evers.

Coming soon...

Welcome Home Sonny T
by William Electric Black
Monday, June 1, 7:00 pm

The older generation of Black radicals comes to terms with their
legacy in the midst of the mounting tensions between the
African American and Mexican communities on Staten Island

CASTILLO THEATRE
543 West 42nd Street, New York City
Tickets $10 • For reservations call: 212-941-1234 • www.castillo.org

NEW POLITICAL PLAYS

ACT II
Scene I

The SAXOPHONE is heard in the darkness and then LIGHTS UP, several hours later in the Harriet Tubman Center. The trays of food and decorations are still visible. REVEREND MILL-ER, all alone, is seen standing in front of Sonny T's large photo. The sound of POLICE RADI-OS can be heard; they fade as the SAX plays.

REV MILLER

(*to Sonny T's photo*) Hospitals can be very lonely places. We forget people who lie there. But I didn't forget you Sonny T. I was by your bedside praying all night long. Prayed hard, I did. Real hard. Even asked the Good Lord if I could trade places with you. But I guess he got no use for a weathered man tossed and turned by a sea of trials and tribulations. (*beat*) Remember when I was in the hospital, Sonny T? You'd come to see me. Asked about my heart, the IV drips. Asked if you could do somethin' for me and I said take over the center. You said one day you would.

And that day was gonna be today. I'm hopin' you get better. I'm hopin' when you wake up, you'll be ready, willing and able. (*beat*) Stayed by your side for a few hours but you didn't say nothin'. You was silent like a Saturday night waitin' for the juke box to crank out some Jackie Wilson! Come back over here to speak to your picture to say I was countin' on you to be the leader, the salvation we need. See there just ain't sickness inside a hospital. It's out here, too.

The sound of the SAXOPHONE fades.
LASHON enters carrying a grocery bag. She is surprised to see REVEREND MILLER.

LASHON
Oh, Reverend Miller I didn't know . . .

REV MILLER
Ain't you supposed to be home?

LASHON
Rodney took me home from the hospital but then he left. Didn't wanna be there by myself so, I come down here.

REV MILLER
Them groceries for the hurricane victims?

LASHON

No, these are letters Sonny T wrote me. Got all of them right here. I was gonna show him how I saved every last one.

She reaches inside the bag and pulls out a handful of Sonny T's letters. Some spill onto the floor in front of Sonny T's photo. LASHON gets on her knees and begins to pick some of them up.

LASHON

(*holding letters*) Letters about humvees being hit by roadside bombs, and mortar attacks. The heat . . . he said it was always so hot . . . so . . .

RODNEY enters. He watches LASHON for a moment, frozen.

RODNEY

LaShon . . . why you leave?

LASHON turns, now standing up.

RODNEY

Momma's lookin' for you. Why ain't you up at the house?

LASHON

'Cause we're still gonna have the party as soon as Sonny T comes through that door. I wanna be the first one to . . .

RODNEY

He's <u>dead</u>, LaShon. Sonny T just died.

LONG SILENCE, and then . . .

LASHON

(*screams*) Nooooooooooooo.

LASHON takes one of the folding chairs and SMASHES it to the floor. She grabs another one and SMASHES it, then another one. She continues grabbing and smashing until a dozen smashed metal chairs surround her. LASHON, exhausted, weeps in the middle of the pile of chairs.

LASHON

How can God do this? First Daddy. Now Sonny T? (*beat*) It . . . it ain't fair.

RODNEY

It damn sure ain't. (*beat*) Reverend Miller, Momma's lookin' for you, too. Needs help with the arrangements. But first, she gotta speak to the military people. Tell them exactly what happened.

REVEREND MILLER approaches LASHON, holding her.

REV MILLER

What did happen?

RODNEY

Don't exactly know. Things just got mad crazy. (*beat*) The Mexicans, they came up the street. And a crowd of us, well . . . we started screamin' at 'em and . . .

LASHON

Us? You mean stupid Black kids?

RODNEY

We ain't stupid kids! And we're tired of . . .

LASHON

Everyone's tired but that's no excuse for what you be doin'!

RODNEY

There was a lot of pushin' and shovin'. Then cans and bricks went flyin' into the air. People starting hittin' one another with bottles and rocks. Then the shit got real tight. I got knocked down. Kicked to the street . . . then I heard gunshots and someone said one of 'em Mexican kids had a piece, then Big Boy said someone got shot and we . . .

LASHON

(*screams*) SONNY T GOT SHOT! SONNY T!!!

REV MILLER

(*still holding her*) Come on, LaShon. Your momma needs you. She needs you to be strong.

LASHON

(*calmly*) Yeah, I'll help Momma. Help her with the funeral plans. There's plenty of food left. We'll invite everyone! The whole neighborhood can come and . . .

LASHON leaves REVEREND MILLER's side and begins picking up the letters. Crying, she starts placing the letters back in the bag.

RODNEY

Leave the letters be, LaShon.

RODNEY grabs the bag and it rips. His GUN spills out, falling to the floor. RODNEY quickly picks it up.

RODNEY

(*angrily*) Knew you took my damn gun!

LASHON

I didn't want you to shoot no body. I was gonna give it to Reverend . . .

RODNEY

What the hell was you thinkin'?

REV MILLER

She was thinking about you. She was tryin' to save you!

RODNEY tucks the gun inside his pants as CARLOS enters.

CARLOS

Excuse me, but I am here to see Reverend Miller.

RODNEY

What the hell do you want?

CARLOS

I have something that I . . .

RODNEY

You got some fuckin' nerve comin' up in here after what you did.

CARLOS

Me?

RODNEY

One of your people killed my brother!

CARLOS

Senor, I do not know . . .

                    RODNEY

You fuckin' liar!

                    CARLOS

I no kill anyone!

                    RODNEY

I hate you! All you damn illegal bastards!

                    CARLOS

Please, Senor . . . let me . . .

                    RODNEY

Big Boy was right! Your kind got to be taught a lesson. This is our fuckin' town!

                    REV MILLER

Now ain't the time, Rodney. (*beat*) Take LaShon back on up to the house!

RODNEY pulls out the gun he tucked inside his pants and points it at CARLOS.

                    LASHON

You gonna kill him?

                    RODNEY

Gotta do this for Sonny T.

                    REV MILLER

Sonny T is dead. Don't matter to him. Now let this boy go!

RODNEY races towards CARLOS. He grabs CARLOS, spinning him into a choke hold.

                    CARLOS

No, no! Please—

RODNEY pushes the gun into CARLOS' head.

                    RODNEY

This is for my brother! This is for movin' to a place you had no damn business comin' to.

                    REV MILLER

You think this is the answer?

RODNEY

This is what you and your bullshit BRS should have done the minute they moved here.

REV MILLER

Shoot them? Burn crosses on their lawns? (*beat*) I know . . . let's lynch them and rape their women. How 'bout that?

RODNEY

They killed Sonny T!

REV MILLER

Put the gun down.

RODNEY

I ain't putting down shit!

CARLOS

But Senor, it wasn't one of us. It was your friend. The very large one.

RODNEY

Big Boy? YOU LYIN'!

CARLOS

There was a witness. The soldier tried to stop the fighting but the tall man shot him. That's why I come here tonight. I wanted to tell the Reverend Miller.

RODNEY

Big Boy killed Sonny T?

LASHON

You know it's true.

RODNEY, bewildered, lowers the gun. LASHON moves CARLOS aside.

REV MILLER

Let the police handle this.

RODNEY

The same police who stopped and frisked me? Who followed a Black kid into his home in the Bronx and shot him. Who shot a brother right before his wedding day? When you gonna wake up and smell your own damn revolution?

RODNEY tucks the gun back inside his pants.

REV MILLER
Big Boy killed Sonny T 'cause Sonny T wasn't like Jasper. Now are you gonna be like Jasper or Sonny T?

RODNEY
I got business to take care of.

RODNEY starts to exit but REVEREND MILLER blocks his path.

REV MILLER
Let me handle this.

RODNEY
Don't think you got killin' in you?

SILENCE.

REV MILLER
At Danton College I killed a man. Don't believe me? Ask your mother, ask Funkygood. (*beat*) So don't stand here and tell me I ain't got killin' in me. I got killin' in me, chokin' me, whuppin' me upside my head from sun up to sun down. (*beat*) And every blessed day I ask God to get this killin' off my back. But it don't go away. No matter how hard I ask it don't go away. (*beat*) It never goes away. You hear me?

REVEREND MILLER gives RODNEY a long, hard look as the stage lights . . .
FADE TO BLACK.

ACT II
Scene II

8 AM. The sound of the SAXOPHONE, ARMY RADIO CHATTER and ARMY HELI-COPTERS fill the darkness. LIGHTS UP on REVOLUTION RADIO. The SAX and ARMY SOUNDS fade. REVEREND MILLER is seated at the station mic.

REV MILLER

(*into mic*) Death ain't nobody's friend. The afterlife is what we long for. And who would not take it, and all its glory, skippin' death entirely. (*sighs*) Last night more death come to Port Richmond. I was expectin' the return of a good soldier. A righteous soul who would take hold of the worn and tethered reins of injustice and lead a gallopin' horse to that mountain top that Dr. King had been to. A horse pullin' a dying country that is slowly losing its way. (*beat*) I had hoped that no one would get lost during this arduous journey. That we would all make it hand in hand. But I know now that is not the case.

For dreamers, like Shakespeare, who can conjure the poetry of Queen Mab can also conjure the darkness of Satan. The evil and ills of a society wielded together by misery, mayhem, and mindless violence. (*beat*) This is Reverend Miller on Staten Island's own WRR . . . wake the hell up and smell the revolution.

LIGHTS FADE on the radio station. LIGHTS UP in the main hall of the Tubman Center where several lit candles, cards and bouquets of flowers now REST BENEATH the large photo of Sonny T. FUNKYGOOD is high atop the USR ladder. He is untying the banner. MAY and LASHON are busy packing up the trays of food and cakes. They place the trays inside several cardboard boxes.

FUNKYGOOD climbs down from untying the banner. He begins to fold up the metal chairs. LASHON starts moving about gathering the red, white and blue balloons then bringing them into the storage room, USC.

FUNKYGOOD

Just don't understand it. Back in the day we used our fists or a switchblade on occasion. But we wasn't tryin' to kill nobody.

MAY

Ain't for us to understand.

FUNKYGOOD

I miss the days when everyone dressed to the nines and headed off to church. Husbands and wives wearin' their finest. Skinny girls with pigtails sportin' fancy dresses. Boys with their heads greased up, faces washed, and spit shined winged-tipped shoes walkin' tall. Walkin' with Jesus!

LASHON returns from the storage room.

LASHON

Is Sonny T with Jesus, Momma?

MAY

Yes, child. He certainly is.

LASHON

And the man Reverend Miller shot?

MAY

Reverend's got a heavy burden on his shoulders. Had it ever since Danton College.

LASHON

How's he get rid of that burden?

MAY

Confess? Ask God for forgiveness? But that don't always work.

LASHON

Why not?

MAY

Depends on the man. Depends on the ones he hurt. And I'm not just talkin' about the man whose life he done took.

LASHON

Are we gonna forgive Big Boy? Are we gonna ask God to forgive him?

MAY

Child, do we have a choice?

FUNKYGOOD stops in front of the cards, candles and flowers that surround Sonny T's photo.

FUNKYGOOD

Flowers and candles. When someone young and innocent passes we's always givin' them flowers and candles. Old habits never die. Just people.

FUNKYGOOD bends down to pick up a PHOTOGRAPH tucked within the flowers.

MAY

What you got there, Funkygood?

FUNKYGOOD hands MAY the photograph.

FUNKYGOOD

Old snapshot of Sonny T with his poppa, James T. Walker.

MAY

Wonder where it come from?

FUNKYGOOD

Don't rightly know. No name on the picture.

LASHON

Maybe one of Sonny T's old friends left it?

MAY

Most of 'em are dead. Now Sonny T's dead. Lord, I tried. I tried so hard to . . .

FUNKYGOOD

Was nothin' you could do. You was always there for him, for all of your children.

MAY

After James died, I did my best. Cancer got him. Smoked them Kools. Two packs a day 'til he died. (*looks at snapshot*) It's a nice picture. Don't Sonny T look happy here?

FUNKYGOOD

Sure do.

MAY

I swear I did my best.

FUNKYGOOD discovers a small photograph hidden under a candle.

FUNKYGOOD

Here go another one.

He bends over and picks up a photo and looks at it.

It's Sonny T in a football uniform. When he played with them Tornadoes.

MAY

That was the pee-wee sandlot league sponsored by Mount Olive Church.

FUNKYGOOD

Boy sure was good. Could 'ave been a regular Jim Brown.

MAY

Could 'ave? Heard mothers who lost their sons say that time after time. Now I'm sayin' it.

LASHON

It's gonna be okay, Momma.

LASHON hugs her mother.

MAY

I know, baby. Your mother ain't gonna let nothin' happen to you or Rodney. Where is Rodney? Ain't seen him since . . .

FUNKYGOOD places the picture back down next to a candle.

FUNKYGOOD

Wasn't he up at the house with y'all?

MAY

Me and LaShon was talkin' to Reverend Miller about this Arlington stuff. Rodney came in, but then went out.

FUNKYGOOD

Arlington?

LASHON

The cemetery just outside Washington D.C. JFK is buried there. And so is our cousin Charlie Pickett. He fought in Vietnam like you done.

FUNKYGOOD

Oh yeah, I heard of that place. It's the Taj Mahal of Cemeteries for soldiers who died serving the U. S. of A.

MAY

Always wanted to be buried down south. That's where I was born. Got a nice little cemetery there in Exmore, Virginia. But I guess this Arlington place ain't so bad.

FUNKYGOOD

Better than Potters Field.

LASHON

What's that?

MAY

They bury you there when no one claims you or knows you.

LASHON

Sounds awful.

FUNKYGOOD

Like a jitterbug who ain't got no one to jitter with.

MAY

Well, Reverend Miller says at Arlington Cemetery Sonny T's gonna have a lot of soldiers and famous people around him.

LASHON

Why did he do it?

MAY

You know why Big Boy did it.

LASHON

No, why did Reverend Miller kill someone? He did a terrible thing.

FUNKYGOOD

The man he killed was an informant. Sent by the F.B.I. to get the goods on the Black Radical Society so we could be hauled off to jail.

LASHON

So Reverend Miller killed him?

FUNKYGOOD

Guess we all killed him with a dream for a better way of life for we people who are darker than blue.

LASHON

(*bitterly*) There's just too much killin'. I don't get it.

MAY

You ain't supposed to 'cause it ain't a good thing to get. Reverend Miller thought it was a good thing back then. But now he knows better.

FUNKYGOOD

Like marryin' an ugly woman. Over time, she just gets uglier and you's stuck with her.

CARLOS MENDEZ enters holding a LIT CANDLE encased in glass. All eyes watch him as he comes into the hall and places the candle down in front of Sonny T's photo. He crosses himself.

CARLOS

(*turning to onlookers*) I am truly sorry for what happened.

FUNKYGOOD

Ya shouldn't 'ave had that march. Tried to tell you and Rev but . . .

MAY

And you are?

CARLOS

Carlos Mendez. My brother, Hector, was shot a week ago, at the very store where . . . (*catches himself*) I spoke to Reverend Miller about it. I led the march last night.

MAY

You?

CARLOS

We had to march. We have faced much too much racial hatred over the last few months. And why? Because we have an accent, dark skin? Did not your people receive the same harsh treatment from whites throughout your history?

FUNKYGOOD

Still receivin' the same treatment if ya ask me.

MAY

Young ones, they feel trapped. No way out so they attack your kind. You're easy targets bein' new to the neighborhood and what not.

CARLOS

That is no excuse.

MAY

Ain't makin' excuses. Folks is gettin' shot. MY SON IS DEAD. I'm just tryin' to make some sense out of all this madness.

MAY, crying, sits in one of the remaining folding chairs.

People are hurtin' inside. They are angry, bitter, suffocating. There's a disease out here and there don't seem to be no cure. (*calms herself*) Marches . . . tired of marches, ain't you?

CARLOS

Si. (*beat*) And I am sorry about your son. He would 'ave loved the party, I am sure.

MAY

Made all his favorite food.

CARLOS

Again, I am truly sorry.

MAY

Sorry ain't never brought back no one.

CARLOS

I did not mean to offend you. I was just tryin' . . .

MAY

I know. (beat) Been a long night. I'm tired.

CARLOS

I should be going.

CARLOS begins to exit, then turns back.

CARLOS

(*to May*) I told Reverend Miller he looked brave. The man in the picture.

MAY

Why you call him brave? You didn't know him.

CARLOS

He is brave to put on a uniform and fight for a country that often considers him a second-class citizen. A country where security guards and cameras follow him around the fancy stores.

I know that same feelin'. (*beat*) A brave man who held his head up high no matter what obstacles got in his way. A man who was willing to fight for what is right.

MAY

And what is that?

CARLOS

Your son, the soldier, he tried to stop the other kids from yellin' racial slurs at my people. He put himself right in the middle of danger. But then . . .

MAY

He got shot.

CARLOS

(*in Spanish*) Si, he got shot.

REVEREND MILLER enters. LASHON quickly moves to confront him.

LASHON

(*to Reverend*) Didn't listen to you on radio this morning. Ain't listenin' to you ever again. You're just another murdering thug.

MAY

Child, don't talk to the Reverend that way.

REV MILLER

She got a right to say what she feels.

FUNKYGOOD

I listened.

CARLOS

Me too. I listened.

REV MILLER

I hope you all enjoyed it 'cause it was my last radio show.

MAY

Your last show?

REV MILLER

There's something I gotta do and I can't do it sittin' at no radio station.

MAY

What's so important that you gonna give up your show?

REV MILLER

If someone does wrong, they got to pay.

REVEREND MILLER starts to exit, but LASHON stops him.

LASHON

One day God's gonna forgive you for killin' that man. He's gonna forgive Big Boy, too.

REV MILLER

Good. (*beat*) And I pray that one day you'll . . . you'll do the same.

REVEREND MILLER turns and exits as MAY, CARLOS, FUNKYGOOD, and LASHON exchange concerned looks.

LIGHTS FADE.

ACT II
Scene III

The SAXOPHONE spits out quick, harsh notes in the darkness mixed in with the sound of rumbling humvees and tanks. The SAX and military sounds fade as the stage lights come up.

Late morning. RODNEY, with GUN IN HAND, ushers a disheveled BIG BOY into the main hall of the Harriet Tubman Center.

RODNEY looks back over his shoulder as he hurries BIG BOY inside past the smoldering candles, spilled letters from Sonny T, cards and flowers that still rest beneath Sonny T's photo.

BIG BOY's hands are TIED behind his back with the aid of a bandana. Blood TRICKLES down from a gash on BIG BOY's forehead. RODNEY forces BIG BOY to sit in one of the two standing metal folding chairs.

BIG BOY

YO, RD you'd better kill me 'cause when my ass gets free . . .

RODNEY

Don't worry, your <u>ass</u> is mine. Now you got anything to say before I smoke you?

BIG BOY

I was shootin' at them damn taco heads. Hell, your brother got in the way tryin' to be some super niggah.

RODNEY strikes BIG BOY across the face. He falls to the floor.

RODNEY

You should shut the fuck up!

BIG BOY

You trippin'! Untie me and I might not kill your dumb ass.

RODNEY

Talkin' a lot of shit for a fool who's about to die.

BIG BOY

You're sad, RD. You wanna be a player, a gangsta' but it ain't you. If you wasn't so scared to shoot I wouldn't 'ave had to.

RODNEY

Ain't afraid to shoot right now!

BIG BOY

I feel you dog. Go ahead. At least you'll finally be a man. Shit, when I shoot them rice and bean eaten mutherfuckas it makes my dick hard. Harder than when I look at LaShon.

RODNEY holds the gun up to BIG BOY's head.

RODNEY

Go ahead, say another fuckin' word about my sister.

BIG BOY

You know she's a hottie. Hell, every niggah out here wanna tap some of that ass.

RODNEY

Well, it ain't gonna be you.

BIG BOY

You can kill me but you ain't gonna protect her from all the dogs. Especially when your ass gets locked away. You ready for that? Huh, niggah?

RODNEY

Doin' time don't scare me. Nothin' scares me now. (*lowers gun*) Not even you.

RODNEY sits.

RODNEY

Hell, why did Sonny T have to come back home? If I get out of here I ain't never comin' back to this damn place.

BIG BOY

It's that soldier shit got him killed. Yes, sir! No, sir! Dyin' for his country attitude. Well, he's dead alright but it ain't my fault. Ain't yours either. Wanna shoot someone shoot that damn Reverend Miller. Where the fuck was he when this was all goin' down?

RODNEY

He tried to help my brother.

BIG BOY

Some help?

RODNEY

Got him out of here.

BIG BOY

He'd be alive if he went to prison with Jasper. Sonny T would be gettin' out right about now since he didn't kill nobody. He's lucky he didn't come home in a wheel chair and shit.

RODNEY

But he didn't. He was fine until . . .

BIG BOY

He was fuckin' lucky. Any dog who comes back with both his legs and arms is lucky. Lucky niggahs! Latinos! Lucky crazy white boys who wanna be Rambo! Reverend Miller played Sonny T.

RODNEY

And you played me!

BIG BOY

I'm tellin' you if you wanna smoke the person who killed Sonny T it's that bullshit talkin' reverend! He's one activist who ain't been active. Hell RD, when's the last time he threw a brick at someone or got his ass arrested? <u>When</u>?

RODNEY

I don't know.

BIG BOY

You don't know 'cause he ain't doin' shit. He's playin' with himself, with you, me, your moms . . .

RODNEY

That's enough.

RODNEY stands and aims the gun at BIG BOY.

BIG BOY

Kill me! I shot your brother. Didn't mean to but I did so shoot me right now!

REVEREND MILLER boldly strolls in, now in Black Panther attire.

REV MILLER

Indeed, kill him. Then yourself. White folks are sellin' you guns so you can all kill yourselves. And you're doing a pretty damn good job of it! (*beat*) Kill him 'cause if you don't I damn sure will.

BIG BOY is silent.

REV MILLER

What nothin' to say, Big Boy? Don't wanna die? Well, accordin' to the latest statistics you and RD, here, got a good chance of dyin' by a bullet. I am just trying to make sure the statistics come true. (*beat*) So go on and kill him, RD! I ain't gonna stop you.

BIG BOY

This is bullshit!

REV MILLER

(*punches Big Boy*) No, your little game of shootin' the Mexicans is bullshit and I'm tired of it. Everyone in this here community is tired of it! And Sonny T, who just come home from the war, who could have minded his own damn business also knew it was bullshit. He gave his life tryin' to stop your bullshit. (*beat*) So, kill him, RD! 'Cause I am really tired of all this bullshit!

RODNEY

You really want me to kill him?

REV MILLER

The way I see it is the man thinks your lives ain't worth a damn nickel. You add nothin' to our society so, he sells you guns and builds more prisons.

RODNEY

We ain't nothin'! We got movie stars, people in business, hell. We even got a Black president.

REV MILLER

But that ain't you. What have you two contributed? The only thing you have to contribute is your own demise. Help our society get rid of the vermin. Get rid of each other and we'll supply the weapons.

BIG BOY

Yeah, we ain't shit! And neither are you Reverend Miller. You think you're all high and mighty 'cause you make speeches, talk on the radio, show up and shake hands with the mayor twice a year? You ain't no real leader. You're a damn leech. You suck up the poor people's hope and dreams in a collection basket whenever you can. Sure, they let you have a community center. No big thing. As long as the

BIG BOY (CONT'D)

white man keeps his pockets filled with cash he don't give a fuck about you. And neither do I.

REVEREND MILLER lashes out at BIG BOY, hitting him harder.

REV MILLER

You're a damn sorry excuse for a person. But you, RD . . . you got somethin' inside you that wants justice, that wants a better way. Just like Sonny T wanted. He's gone now. But you can still finish what he wanted and what you truly want 'cause it ain't this.

REV MILLER (CONT'D)

So, give me the gun.

RODNEY

What?

REV MILLER

I said give me the gun and I'll do it.

RODNEY

I ain't gonna . . .

REV MILLER

Niggah . . . give me the gun 'fore I take it from you.

REVEREND MILLER stalks RODNEY. RODNEY backs away.

BIG BOY

Shoot this damn fool, RD. If you can't, untie me and I'll do it.

REV MILLER

Both of y'all don't know what being tough is. Don't know nothin' about sacrifice, or puttin' your blood, sweat, and soul into somethin' 'til your body cries out for death 'cause the pain is so unbearable.

BIG BOY

I said shoot him!

REV MILLER

He ain't gonna shoot me but I'm gonna shoot you. See, I'm just like Hurricane Sandy, boy. Nothin' you can do is gonna stop me. Just hope you's a niggah who knows how to swim. If not, you're about to die!

REVEREND MILLER fiercely walks towards RODNEY and snatches the gun from his hand. RODNEY is dumbfounded, speechless.

REV MILLER

(*to Rodney*) Go on, get out of here. Your momma needs you now more than ever. Time for you to be a man. Not some dumb ass thug who got nothin' better to do than hang out with a murderer.

RODNEY

I ain't dumb.

REV MILLER

You are if you tell anyone what I am about to do. (*beat*) NOW GO!

BIG BOY

You just gonna let him kill me?

RODNEY

Yeah . . . I am.

RODNEY exits. BIG BOY, now alone, is alarmed.

BIG BOY

This ain't right. You're a minister. You're supposed to help people.

REV MILLER

I'm gonna help you. Gonna help you pray.

REVEREND MILLER grabs BIG BOY and tries to force him to his knees. BIG BOY resists, then tumbles to the floor.

REV MILLER

Get on your knees, boy.

BIG BOY

The hell with you.

REV MILLER

Don't matter to me. I'll shoot you where you are. But I thought I'd give you a chance to confess, to ask God to forgive you for what you done.

BIG BOY

You can't do this! You'll go to jail. They'll give your ass life.

REV MILLER

I'll get what I deserve. And you will get what you deserve. (*beat*) Now get on your knees.

REVEREND MILLER drags BIG BOY into a kneeling position.

BIG BOY

When Jasper gets out of the joint, he's gonna come looking for you.

REV MILLER

Then you'd better pray for him, too!

BIG BOY

You know who really needs to be prayed for? A phony minister who got people to believe in his fairy tale. (*beat*) Yeah, you a trip Reverend Miller. You gotta kill me 'cause I got you figured out.

REV MILLER

You ain't prayin'!

BIG BOY

How long you been hidin' out.

REV MILLER

Who's hidin'? I'm right here!

BIG BOY

Rodney says you killed a man. Guess you ain't no better than me.

REV MILLER

Oh, I'm better. Much better.

BIG BOY

You think so? Least I took my battle to the street. Yeah, I shot that other boy three weeks back, then I shot that Hector kid. And if Sonny T didn't get in the damn way I would 'ave shot another one. (*beat*) What happened? After you killed you lost your nerve? What . . . you realized that for justice and equality you might have to shoot a lot of people. Not just one? Feelin' sorry for yourself, Reverend? Told Rodney to be a man but you ain't exactly one to be preachin'. But I guess 'cause you a minister you thought . . .

REV MILLER

Shut the hell up!

BIG BOY

Okay . . . guess I'm finish prayin'.

REV MILLER

Guess you are.

BIG BOY

Just tell me one thing before you put a cap in me.

REV MILLER

What?

BIG BOY

Was I right?

REV MILLER

You were right. (*beat*) Now tell me one thing.

BIG BOY

Whatever you want, playa'.

REV MILLER

You kill Sonny T by accident? Or was it something you were waiting to do.

BIG BOY

(*with a smile*) You already know the answer to that.

REV MILLER

Guess I do.

REVEREND MILLER raises the gun and takes aim.

QUICK TO BLACK as TWO GUNSHOTS are heard in darkness.

ACT II
Scene IV

Evening. Lights up at REVOLUTION RADIO. FUNKYGOOD is present. He is busy collecting books and papers that still clutter REVEREND MILLER's desk. He reads some of the book titles as he places them inside a brown cardboard box.

FUNKYGOOD

(*reading, to himself*) The Souls of Black Folks, Soul On Ice, The Autobiography of Malcolm X? Rev sure had a jones for the revolution.

FUNKYGOOD continues to place items inside the box. He picks up a letter, opens it and begins to read it.

FUNKYGOOD

(*reading letter*) Dear Reverend Miller . . . I don't like it over here. Maybe I should have gone to prison. Just jokin'! It ain't so bad. I could get shot at home so what's the big deal. At least over here folks expect you to carry a gun. Miss my mom's cookin', hope she's okay. Three years sounds like such a long time. Wonder what things gonna be like when I get home.

FUNKYGOOD places the letter inside the box.

FUNKYGOOD

Guess you found out, Sonny T.

LASHON enters as FUNKYGOOD continues to place things inside the box.

LASHON

Oh, sorry . . . I was just . . .

FUNKYGOOD

Reverend Miller ain't here.

LASHON

I know. Can't believe he ain't on the radio this morning. I know he said he was quittin' but . . .

FUNKYGOOD

Reverend Miller ain't comin' back for a long time. (*beat*) He's in jail.

LASHON

I heard. Guess Big Boy deserved what he got.

FUNKYGOOD

And Reverend Miller got his due.

LASHON

Tried to go see him at the police station but they wouldn't let me.

FUNKYGOOD

Maybe it's best. (*beat*) He's a tough old warrior. He'll be okay.

LASHON

What's gonna happen to the center?

FUNKYGOOD

Well, it could use a few coats of paint. And someone's got to fix them bullet holes
Rev put in the ceiling.

LASHON

Bullet holes?

FUNKYGOOD

Guess Reverend Miller gave Big Boy a good scare. Told me that he was gonna kill
him but changed his mind and brought him over to the police station.

LASHON

But if he just brought Big Boy to the station for what he done, why is Reverend
Miller in jail?

FUNKYGOOD

'Cause he finally told the truth. Rev killed a man so, he had to pay.

LASHON

But that was over thirty years ago.

FUNKYGOOD

Maybe to you. But to Rev it was just like yesterday.

FUNKYGOOD places the last book inside the cardboard box.

FUNKYGOOD

Now come on, let's get back to the center. Carlos Mendez is comin' by.

LASHON

That Mexican boy? What's he comin' over for?

FUNKYGOOD

Reverend Miller wants him to take over the food drive. Hurricane put a big hurtin' on a lot of folks.

LASHON

Really? But he's . . . I mean . . .

FUNKYGOOD

He's the right young man to lead the drive?

LASHON

Yeah . . . he's the right man.

FUNKYGOOD

You comin'? Army folks droppin' by . . . then your momma, RD and Mr. Mendez gonna take a car load of them groceries over to South Beach.

LASHON

Be over in a few minutes. Go on without me.

FUNKYGOOD

Don't get lost.

LASHON

I know where I'm goin'.

FUNKYGOOD

Yeah, I know you do.

FUNKYGOOD picks up the box and exits. A moment. LASHON sits in the REVEREND MILLER's seat. She solemnly looks around then begins to cry softly. Another moment, she wipes away her tears then leans forward whispering into the mic.

LASHON

(*finding strength*) This is LaShon Walker . . . (*beat*) . . . wake up . . . wake up and smell the revolution.

The stage lights fade to black. SPOTLIGHT UP on Sonny T's Photo.

The sound of a TWENTY-ONE GUN military salute is heard then SPOTLIGHT FADES TO BLACK. In the darkness "The Negro National Anthem" is played by the SAXOPHONE.

END OF PLAY

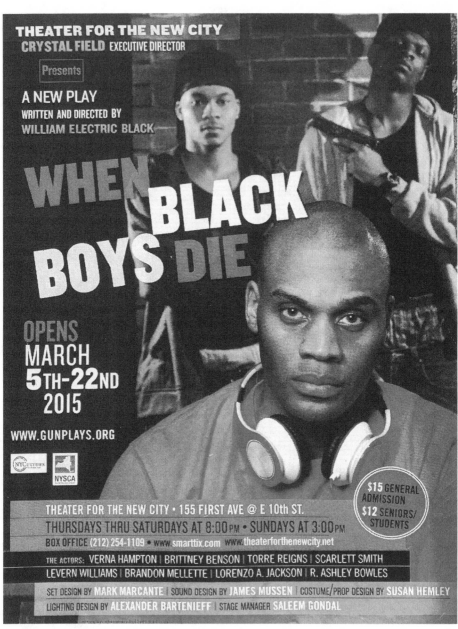

When Black Boys Die
Designer Sharon Jacobs, Urban Circle Design, NYC

When Black Boys Die

a play by

William Electric Black

CAST

DANIELLE (DANI) WEEKS: African American, 17-years-old, streetwise, athletic, she lives under the dark cloud of her brother's death a year ago.

RUBY WEEKS: African American, late 50s, single mother of Dani and Levon, bitter, frustrated, on a mission to keep her son's memory alive.

LEVON WEEKS: African American, 18-years-old, basketball player, wants more but is trapped by his surroundings, gunned down a year ago.

CECE TORRES: Hispanic, 17-years-old, sexy, flirtatious, has a 2-month-old baby boy, manipulative.

MR. JACKSON: African American, late 50s, teaches art at Booker High, cares about the neighborhood, tries to be a helping hand.

DRAYTON (DRAY): African American, 18-years-old, leader of the local Triple Z gang, violent, pushes drugs, he's all about money and power.

JB: African American, 18-years-old, Dray's loyal sidekick, a member of Triple Z, violent, a teen with no options.

SAY WHAT: African American, late 50s or early 60s, a ragtag fixture in the community, sells odds and ends, sort of a wise wordsmith of The Wood Haven Houses who has seen it all and lived it all.

SETTING

Act I, The Wood Haven Houses, Bronx, New York, July 4, 2014

Act II, The Wood Haven Houses, Bronx, New York, July 4, 2014

Act II, Scene III, The Wood Haven Houses, one year later

*(When RED WASH appears, we go to: July 4, 2013, a year earlier)

PLAYWRIGHT'S NOTES

THE RED WASH—(*used for flashbacks) represents the red blood spilled daily from inner city gun violence.

MYFOXNY.COM/AP—At least 21 people were shot across New York City over the weekend: Nine in Brooklyn, five in Manhattan, five in the Bronx, one in Queens, and one on Staten Island.

The July 4th weekend is always filled with the loud booms of fireworks. But in Chicago, residents are far more likely to hear the bangs of gunfire. More than 60 people were shot in the Windy City over the long holiday weekend, leaving at least nine people dead, ABC7 Chicago reported. The bloody weekend began around 2:30 a.m. Friday when a 34-year-old man was fatally shot in a drive-by. From there, the violence intensified. A teenager was shot in his car.

MINNEAPOLIS, MN—Community leaders gathered on a street corner pleading for change, holding signs and saying prayers, after a violent Fourth of July weekend in north Minneapolis.

"Families are not able to enjoy the Fourth of July festivities because of senseless murders around the city. Are you kidding me? This is a wake-up call," said Pastor Harding Smith of the Spiritual Church of God in Robbinsdale and of the Minnesota Acts Now. "We are tired. We are tired of the violence. We are tired of the killings! You kill a thousand dreams when you kill one person. It's a sad, sad situation." Police responded to three shooting incidents in north Minneapolis in the early morning hours of July 5. In the end, two adults died from gunshot wounds and at least three more were injured.

SILENCE (in the stage directions) is to be played whenever it appears. It represents a MAJOR BEAT, not to be overlooked. In the silence these characters seek and desire emotional peace. It is the silence that rarely happens in their neighborhood plagued by unending gun violence.

SCENE TRANSITIONS—Going from present day to flashbacks should happen without the stage going to black.

A LARGE SIGN, WELCOME TO THE WOOD HAVEN HOUSES, sits upstage right in plain sight. Slightly left of the sign, but still stage right is a partial facade of a faded brick building with a first-floor window visible to the audience. In the window we can clearly see a STEREO SPEAKER and an AMERICAN FLAG. The building is tagged **ZZZ** by the resident gang. A nearby garbage can is also tagged **ZZZ** with the same black spray paint. A worn, tan wooden bench sits DS of the building. A mix of pavement and grass is speckled about the sullen grounds. Stage left is the living room of the WEEKS FAMILY located on the 20th floor of The Wood Haven Houses. A torn couch, old chair, and stained coffee table are visible. Other rooms are OS. There is a slightly raised platform DSC, used primarily for *flashbacks (indicated by a RED WASH) and other scenes.

ACT I
Scene I

LIGHTS UP. We see that copies of a list of names on 8.5 by 11 sheets of paper have been taped to the "Welcome to The Wood Haven Houses" sign, the wooden bench, the garbage can, and to a section of fence. James Brown's "Super Bad" plays from a speaker in the first-floor window.

DANIELLE WEEKS (aka DANI), attractive, Black 17-years-old enters dressed in capris, sneakers, and a cute hoodie. Dani steps onto the platform dribbling a basketball.

DANI

(to audience) It's the 4th of July. Usually, a day to celebrate. It's mad hot and James Brown's "Super Bad" has been blasting from a nearby window all day long. Here in the Bronx folks be grilllin', chillin' and illin' from the heat and the gunshots. *(bounces basketball)* See at The Wood Haven Houses someone always dies on the 4th of July. Last year, a week after Mr. Jackson took us on a school trip to see some paintings, Levon Weeks got shot.

DANI exits into the darkness of her living room. A RED WASH FADES UP on MR. JACK-SON, a well-dressed high school teacher, late 50s, as he steps onto the raised platform. He looks out as if he is gazing at a painting.

MR. JACKSON

(to audience) Now class this painting, Man and Clarinet, is by Picasso. It may look odd because Pablo Picasso, an artist extraordinaire, used cubism as a new way to express his art.

The RED WASH FADES OUT on MR. JACKSON. Lights up in the living room as RUBY WEEKS, late 60s, towering Black woman heavy with pain, enters carrying groceries. DANI enters and takes the groceries from her.

RUBY

You put that boy's name on the list, yet?

DANI

I will!

RUBY

And then you gonna make copies of the list and put it around?

                              DANI

Yeah . . . I'm gonna. But I'll do it later when I get back.

                              RUBY

Where you think you going?

                              DANI

Just out for a little while.

                              RUBY

Out? After what happened in the courtyard almost two weeks ago?

                              DANI

It's July 4th, everyone's out.

                              RUBY

You ain't everyone. Now where is that list?

                              DANI

In your bedroom where you always keep it.

                              RUBY

Well, what are you waiting for . . . go on and get it.

DANI exits. Ruby sits, putting her feet up on the coffee table.

                              RUBY

Mrs. Lief kept me longer than I expected. Wanted me to help her with her dinner but I said I had to go. Don't like getting back here too late with them gangs running 'round like wild animals.

DANI returns with a list and hands it to RUBY.

                              RUBY

Heard we got more shootings here in the Bronx than they do in all of Manhattan.

                              DANI

More than Chicago or St. Louis?

                              RUBY

Do we live in Chicago or St. Louis? Don't give a damn about them places! We got enough to worry about right here. And you'd better watch yourself or you gonna end up like your friend, CeCe.

DANI

CeCe's mad cool. Don't matter that she got a baby.

RUBY

Don't matter? You better not be thinking about having one.

DANI

I'm not having a baby.

RUBY

(*adamant*) Just make sure you don't.

DANI

I'M NOT!

RUBY

(*gazing at the list*) A year ago, on this very day, we lost Levon, God rest his soul. Maybe I should have moved y'all to Long Island where they got trees and flowers.

DANI

And no red stains on the sidewalks.

LIGHTS FADE on RUBY and DANI. RED WASH UP on MR. JACKSON, now back on the platform with DRAY, a 17-year-old tall, lanky, cap wearing gang-banger, and JB, another teen gang member, heavyset, and into whatever mischief Dray sets in motion.

DANI crosses from RUBY and joins the flashback. The four now stand looking out towards the audience as if they are still gazing at the Picasso painting.

MR. JACKSON

Can you see the clarinet? Picasso wanted to represent what we see in a fragmented, revolutionary way. More two dimensional, so, we could see all sides of an object at once.

DRAY

YO, Mr. Jackson . . . I can't see no clarinet, but I can see the sign to the bathroom. Can I go?

MR. JACKSON

Please be quiet and take that cap off your head.

                    DRAY

But I gotta go, Mr. Jackson.

                     JB

Me too!

                    DANI

Why make us see something different?

                MR. JACKSON

He had the courage, the opportunity . . . so, he took it.

                     JB

Sort of like me and Dray. We want to get paid, so we take care of business.

                    DRAY

Can I please go to the bathroom so I can take care of some other business?

                MR. JACKSON

He didn't do it just to get paid. He did it to improve on what was done before him. (*beat*) And in doing so he became a great artist. And only now does his work sell for millions.

                    DANI

That painting's worth millions?

                    DRAY

I say why wait when you can get bank now.

                MR. JACKSON

But at what price? What happens when the money runs out?

The RED WASH CROSS FADES on DRAY, JB, DANI, and MR. JACKSON. LIGHTS UP on RUBY, still seated on the couch holding the list. DANI exits the platform and joins her, removing the list from her hands.

                    RUBY

This is the one-year anniversary of your brother's death and all you wanna do is go hang out?

                    DANI

And all you <u>want</u> me to do is write down names of people who get shot. (*beat*) Got 103 since last 4th of July. That's not enough?

RUBY

104 . . . you got to add that boy from two weeks ago.

DANI

The boy's name is Calvin Harris. Went to Booker High just like the rest of us. Shot to death at his own graduation party.

RUBY

At a party, on a stoop, on the sidewalk . . . bullets got a way of finding us, don't they.

DANI

Writing down names of dead kids is mad stupid.

RUBY

Them names is so we don't forget. So, no one ever forgets.

DANI

Forget? (*beat*) Momma, police vans are always parked across the street. And from my bedroom window I can see the white NYPD tower taking pictures of us 24/7 . . . tryin' to see who's dyin' next. (*beat*) Hell, I can't forget if I wanted to.

RUBY

You watch your mouth!

DANI

(*tosses list on table*) Omar Ford. Before him Parker Jones. Last month Jamaal Brooks. He got shot right in front of the corner store. (*beat*) I don't need your list or police cameras to tell me who's gettin' shot around here. I live it every day. And so do you!!

RUBY

You call this living?

DANI

Momma, they're laughing at your list. They say Ruby Weeks is one mad crazy Black woman!

RUBY

Maybe I am, but you still gonna put Calvin's name on my list.

DANI tries to exit but RUBY stands, blocking her path.

RUBY

Told myself I would not let my boy die for nothing. Someone's got to pay attention to the war going on 'round here!

DANI

War? (*beat*) No one's gonna knock on our door with a Purple Heart for Levon, Momma. No general's gonna give you a folded flag. America doesn't care about a war in The Wood Haven Houses 'cause it's just a war where Black boys kill other Black boys.

RUBY

Maybe you're right. Folks care more 'bout them Kardashians, iPhones, Jay Z, and global warming. Yeah . . . when Black boys die it don't matter much, only to us mothers who lose 'em, who grieve for them, who got to bury them. (*beat*) What about you, Danielle? You grieve for your brother?

DANI

Got my own life to deal with. Or maybe you forgot about that?

RUBY

Yeah . . . you still got your life. Ain't you lucky?

DANI tries to move around RUBY. RUBY grabs DANI and slaps her across the face. DANI backs away rubbing her cheek.

RUBY

I got no Purple Heart but I still got my own heart. And as long as it pumps blood there will be a list. (*beat*) Now you want some more of what I just gave you?

RUBY raises her hand, ready to strike, but DANI holds her ground.

DANI

Didn't keep Levon alive. You used to hit him, too.

RUBY

Write down that boy's name.

A moment, then RUBY lowers her hand. DANI finds a pen and picks up the list from the table.

DANI

(*says name as she writes*) Calvin Harris, killed June 20th, 2014. You happy? I wrote it down.

RUBY

Now read the first name like we always do.

DANI

Levon Weeks, killed July 4th, 2013.

RUBY takes the list, ponders over it, as the lights CROSS FADE and a RED WASH FADES UP in the courtyard on LEVON, a solidly built, broad shouldered, streetwise 18-year-old. He enters dribbling a basketball.

In the flashback, LEVON wears long jean shorts, a T-SHIRT that says Syracuse, matching baseball cap, and red Beats headphones. DANI crosses to him as he continues to dribble the basketball.

LEVON

LeBron, who? Can't touch this!

DANI

You headed to Willis Park?

LEVON

Where else?

DANI

You get any firecrackers?

LEVON

Yeah, I got me some from Say What. Cherry bombs, M-80s . . . (*beat*) Let me see your crossover.

LEVON tosses DANI the ball. She demonstrates her crossover.

LEVON

Not bad.

DANI

Come on, Levon. Let me go play some ball with you.

LEVON

You just wanna go hang out.

DANI

Can't see no rooftop fireworks from over here. Buildings are too tall. Besides, everyone just sits outside cooking, playing cards, and being loud.

LEVON

Hell . . . you know how to be loud. Shouldn't be a problem for you.

DANI

You're not funny.

LEVON

You want some firecrackers so you and CeCe can blow up some shit?

LEVON takes his ball back, digs into his pocket then hands DANI a fistful of firecrackers.

LEVON

Don't hurt yourself. Momma will kick my ass if you do.

DANI

Why you let her treat you like she does?

LEVON

What are you talking about?

DANI

She always be hittin' you. Why you let her do it?

LEVON

She's scared. She only hits me 'cause she don't want nothin' to go wrong. Don't wanna see me get into any trouble, that's all.

DANI

Like Daddy?

LEVON

Yeah . . . like Daddy.

DANI

Maybe when she's hittin' you, she's really hittin' him.

LEVON

Don't matter . . . I'm off to Syracuse in August. Play me some ball, get drafted by the NBA, then buy us a big house so we can get the hell out of here!

DANI

What . . . you don't like the three R's? (*beat*) Rats, roaches, and raccoons?

CECE (same age as DANI in the flashback) enters in tight shorts, halter top. She's fast for her age.

CECE

Hey, y'all . . . (*sings*) It's gettin' hot out here, so take off all your clothes. (*beat*) We going over to Willis Park?

LEVON

I'm going . . . not you two.

DANI

Come on, Levon.

LEVON

They be actin' mad crazy over there.

CECE

They be actin' mad crazy over here.

LEVON

Three people got shot last 4th of July in the park. Remember?

DANI

Maybe you shouldn't be goin'.

CECE

Unless you got a gun. You got a gun, Levon?

LEVON

You crazy?

CECE

You want to borrow mine?

LEVON

You gotta gun?

CECE

Maybe I do and maybe I don't.

LEVON

Girl, you ain't got no gun. Go home and play with your Barbies!

CECE

I'd rather play with you.

LEVON

YO, your girlfriend is trippin'!

DANI

For real.

CECE

I'm only two years younger than you. (*beat*) What . . . you don't date sophomores?

LEVON

No . . . I don't!

CECE moves closer to LEVON. Their eyes lock for a moment.

CECE

Not yet.

DANI

This heat must be giving you a sun stroke.

LEVON

For real.

DANI pulls CECE away from LEVON.

CECE

A Levon stroke! Right, Levon?

LEVON

YO, I gotta step. Don't get into any trouble.

LEVON exits the platform, dribbling, into the darkness.

DANI

(*to CeCe*) A Levon stroke?

CECE

(*jokingly*) Chill, Dani . . . I was just playing. Your brother is fine. Every girl out here be sexting him. Sending him naked pictures and what not.

DANI

He's still my brother.

CECE

Sorry. (*beat*) We cool?

DANI

Yeah, we cool. (*beat*) Levon gave me some firecrackers.

CECE

Tight! We can blow up some old ladies. (*beat*) But first let's go to the corner store and get us some Old English.

DANI

For what?

CECE

For what? If we gotta stick around here we might as well get nice.

SILENCE.

CECE

What, can't have no fun? Afraid of your momma?

DANI

Can't get no beer without ID.

CECE

You kiddin'? In this outfit I can get Two Chains to give me one chain!

DANI

You are trippin'!

CECE

You know what happens when we shake it.

CECE starts shaking her booty. DANI joins her. They sing . . .

CECE/DANI

It's gettin' hot in here, so take off all your clothes. I am gettin' so hot I'm gonna take my clothes off.

The girls laugh.

DANI

You really got a gun?

CECE

No . . . but I bet your brother got one.

DANI

My mother would kill him.

CECE

Probably got it hidden.

DANI

Girl, you mad crazy!

CECE

Ten dollars says he does.

RED WASH CROSS FADES from the platform to RUBY in her living room.

She removes a dollar bill from her purse.

RUBY

Here's some money for you to make copies of the list.

DANI returns to the living room and takes the dollar.

DANI

Man, I'm sick and tired of makin' copies then hangin' them up.

RUBY

Not too tired to hang out last 4th of July.

DANI

Don't . . .

RUBY

Don't what? Don't remind you that when Levon went to look for you that's when he got shot?

DANI

I came home.

RUBY

It was too late. I had already sent him after you.

DANI

It wasn't my fault.

RUBY

Beer on your breath. Drinkin' with that no good, CeCe. Was it worth it?

SILENCE.

RUBY

As long as you live under this roof you will always remember what happened a year ago, July 4th. And so help me God, you will keep puttin' names on this list 'til I'm dead or the boy who killed Levon is dead.

DANI

You really want that?

RUBY

Yes, I do.

DANI

You ever think that the person who killed him might already be on this list?

RUBY

Detective Sullivan, the one working his case, said he's looked at every person on this here list to see if a bullet found in them matches the one they pulled out of Levon.

DANI

He find anything?

RUBY

Yes . . . he did. Ten boys on this list been killed by the same gun that took your brother's life. That includes the Harris boy who just got killed almost two weeks ago. So, don't tell me the boy who shot Levon is on this here list.

THE SOUND OF GUNSHOTS. RUBY and DANI turn towards the shots.

RUBY

You hear that?

DANI

Didn't sound like no fireworks.

RUBY

Lord . . . give me a sign. Find my son's murderer.

DANI

You don't really care about anyone on this list, do you?

RUBY

They're dead. They ain't comin' back. Ain't nothin' I can do for them now.

DANI

You are crazy. Just like everyone says.

DANI starts to exit with the list.

RUBY

Might be . . . but you still gonna make copies of the list, then put 'em around.

DANI

Levon was wrong.

RUBY

Wrong? About what?

DANI

You're not scared.

RUBY

Scared?

ANOTHER GUNSHOT. RUBY turns . . . listening for another.

DANI

You need feelings to be scared. And you have none.

LIGHTS FADE.

ACT I
Scene II

Lights up. SAY WHAT, a rag-tag, unkempt, 60-year-old Black street vendor enters the court-yard. He wears old sneakers, shades, an American Flag bandana, and hand-me-down overalls while wheeling a cart filled with red, white, and blue Uncle Sam type hats, flags, boxes of July 4th sparklers, glow sticks, and American Flag bandanas. A boom box blasting old school rap by "Kool Moe Dee" is tied to his cart.

SAY WHAT

(*to audience*) Alright you cheap Negroes, colored folk, afro cloaked, slave revolt, doo-rag wearin', black power carin' African-Americans . . . (*loudly*) GET ON OVER HERE AND BUY SOMETHING FROM OLD SAY WHAT! Say, what? Credit? Credit my ass! Do I look like Visa, mutherfuka? (*beat*) Got your glow sticks, your sparklers, red, white and blue hats, got T-shirts, and flags, too! Sunglasses, sunscreen, a few copies of Native Son, Raisin In The Sun, and Nina Simone's "Here Comes The Sun." (*Puts glow stick on*) Say, what? How long Say What been doing this street corner gig? Since this place was a palace. NO GRAFFITI, NO BULLET HOLES, NO CHIPPED PAINT, NO SEE SOMETHIN' DO NOTHIN', NO BROKEN ELEVATORS, NO . . . NO . . . know what I mean?

SAY WHAT clicks off his boom box.

SAY WHAT (CONT'D)

(*to audience*) Was a time when I knew you and you knew me. Spot you a ten? No problem my brother. Tell your boy to act right and he'd listen with no lip. Play the number and give you a taste if I hit. Get me some bread, eggs, milk, and butter from the neighborhood store Monday, pay for it on Friday. And from the Baptist church I could always get me a used coat and a familiar prayer. AMEN! (*loudly*) ALRIGHT, YOU DASHIKI WEARING, BEYONCÉ STARING, EBONY READING, BEAN PIE EATIN', CORN-ROE WEAVING, MALCOLM X BELIEVING, KINGS AND QUEENS WHO RIDE THE A TRAIN! Come and get it! Ain't got all day to be standin' out here sellin' my fine goods to your lazy behinds!

SAY WHAT (CONT'D)

(*stands*) Say What got things to do, places to go, people to see . . . Yeah, that's right! Folks know I know things, be askin' me for advice like I was Dr. Oz or some shit. Who told Huey to put Black in front of Panthers, that's right . . . shut your revolution will not be televised mouth! And who told Diana to forget them other Supremes! That's right, show ME some BABY LOVE. And who said, NO, NO, NO, not 11 years. Make it 12 years a slave! BOOM! HOMERUN! FIREWORKS! IT'S INDEPENDENCE DAY, NIGGAHS! (*beat*) Say What got what you need!

DRAY and JB, dressed in black baseball caps and hoodies, enter as SAY WHAT removes a cassette tape from his boom box and inserts another. The teens stop to see what SAY WHAT's selling. They know him from the neighborhood.

JB

My niggah, Say What!

SAY WHAT

Ain't nobody's nigger, ya hear?

DRAY

Bet you can hear cash money?

DRAY waves a stack of bills in SAY WHAT's face.

SAY WHAT

That your money?

DRAY

What you think, we stole it?

SAY WHAT

Stole it from the Black faces you sellin' your drugs to. Stole their money, their dreams, their hopes. Ain't no thing but a chicken wing to you so, pass the damn hot sauce 'cause you gang-bangers ain't nothin' but lost!

JB

YO, this fool is mad crazy, Dray.

SAY WHAT

Yeah, I'm crazy alright. A crazy, angry, pissed off, belligerent, beautiful Black man! (*beat*) Who are you? Some fools with guns trying to shoot other fools with guns, but you ain't foolin' no one 'cept your own foolish selves.

DRAY

Do what we gotta do to survive.

SAY WHAT

If everyone's dead, who survives?

JB

Man, you buggin'! Got any sparklers and shit?

SAY WHAT

Sparklers, yes . . . shit, no! Ain't no one buying shit . . . unless it's good shit.

DRAY

YO, we'll take some sparklers, two hats, and some cherry bombs.

SAY WHAT hands them two hats, a box of sparklers, and a dozen cherry bombs.

SAY WHAT

That's twenty dollars.

DRAY

Said we'll take 'em not pay for 'em.

DRAY and JB start to head off, but SAY WHAT blocks their path.

SAY WHAT

Where's my money you uneducated, undesirable, ungrateful, uncool, unruly, unimportant, unemployed, meet me under the highway jackasses so I can kick your Black behinds.

CECE enters pushing a stroller. She tries to turn away but . . .

DRAY

Damn girl . . . where you going? You lookin' fine. Hell, might have to give you another kid.

CECE

And I might have to give ya an STD.

DRAY

That ain't funny.

SAY WHAT

Said give me my money or someone might get hurt.

DRAY

JB, pop this fool.

JB

Ain't got my piece. Ain't seen it in nearly two weeks. You have it?

DRAY

Hell no . . . got my own.

DRAY takes out his gun while grabbing hold of SAY WHAT.

DRAY

Now what did you say?

SAY WHAT

My money or someone's gonna get hurt.

DRAY shoves SAY WHAT to the ground then aims his gun at him.

DRAY

You're about to get hurt.

CECE

Leave him alone.

CECE steps in between DRAY and SAY WHAT. DRAY moves towards CECE and gently strokes his gun across her cheek.

DRAY

(*to CeCe*) You remember what happened last 4th of July when you tried to be a player?

CECE

Wish I could forget.

DRAY

But you can't! (*beat*) Give this to Tyson when he wakes up.

DRAY places one of the red, white, and blue hats on CECE's head.

DRAY

I'll be by your crib later.

DRAY kisses her hard then he and JB exit. SAY WHAT staggers to his feet. CECE helps him.

SAY WHAT

Them boys is poison. The kind you can't suck out of the wound. The kind that runs through your veins faster than the River Niger. Til you turn blue, Miles Davis Kind of Blue . . . then Blue Magic, PUFF . . . YOU IS GONE.

CECE hands the hat back to SAY WHAT but he refuses to take it.

SAY WHAT

Keep it! Give it to your little one.

CECE

He's only two months old. No way it's gonna fit.

SAY WHAT

He'll wear it when he gets older.

CECE

Older? Way things be goin' on around here I'm gonna have to get Tyson some damn bullet proof diapers.

SAY WHAT

Might come a time when ya gotta bite the snake 'fore it bites you. You hear me? (*beat*) Now I'm gonna go find them punks and get my money.

CECE

I'll pay for what they took.

CECE reaches into her pocket and pulls out a twenty-dollar bill.

SAY WHAT

That's your money. I want my damn money. And I ain't afraid to bite no snake to get it.

CECE

Dray and JB aren't playin'. They belong to Triple Z.

SAY WHAT

They's triple punks! Hoodlums, thugs, and wanna be startin' somethin' niggahs.

CECE

Triple Z runs Wood Haven. Mess with them and you die.

SAY WHAT

Gang members is punks! Your boy is gonna be somebody, someday. Not no punk.
(*beat*) Don't believe me? Ask Tyler Perry. Told him if he wanted to make it big . . .
PUT ON A DRESS! OH, YEAH . . . WHO'S YOUR MADEA NOW!

CECE chuckles as SAY WHAT hands her a flag.

SAY WHAT

Alright you cheap Negroes, colored folk, afro cloaked, slave revolt, doo-rag
wearing, black power caring African-Americans . . . I got the goods so come on
with the come on!

*SAY WHAT clicks on his boom box blasting Melly Mel. He exits as DANI enters. She removes
an old list of names then tapes a new list onto the "WELCOME TO THE WOOD HAVEN
HOUSES" sign. She heads over to the bench and replaces an old list with a new one.*

CECE

(*calls to Dani*) Hey, girl! Is that the new list?

DANI

Yeah . . .

CECE

How many died since the last 4th?

DANI

One-hundred-four!

CECE

Damn, don't Ruby get tired?

DANI

She don't, but I do.

CECE

How long is she gonna keep this up?

DANI

Until she finds out who killed Levon. That's the only way she'll stop.

CECE

But the police don't even know. They interviewed everyone livin' here. Even had to tell 'em 'bout me and Dray.

DANI

What about you and Dray?

CECE

It was after you went home, after your mother called you.

RED WASH FADES UP on RUBY. She is pacing in the living room with a cell phone in hand. RED WASH FADES UP on DANI as she takes out her cell phone and enters onto the platform.

DANI ON CELL

Momma?

RUBY ON CELL

Girl, where you at? It's after 11pm and the elevators is out.

DANI ON CELLPHONE

I'll be right home.

RUBY ON CELLPHONE

Been calling you!

DANI ON CELLPHONE

Had my phone on silent.

RUBY ON CELLPHONE

Silent! I been worried sick. Just sent Levon to look for you.

DANI ON CELLPHONE

Said I'll be right there.

CECE steps into DANI's RED WASH sipping on a bottle of Old English. DANI hangs up and turns towards her.

CECE

Told you to leave your phone off.

                                    DANI

Man . . . I gotta go.

                                    CECE

Want some more?

                                    DANI

Are you mad crazy? I can't go home smelling like beer.

CECE sniffs DANI, then laughs.

                                    CECE

You already do!

CECE tumbles to the ground.

                                    DANI

Girl, get up.

                                    CECE

I like it down here.

                                    DANI

Get up! You're wasted.

                                    CECE

Help me.

                                    DANI

I have to go.

                                    CECE

You gonna leave me?

                                    DANI

No, but . . .

DANI tries to help CECE. CECE pulls her down, spilling beer on her.

                                    DANI

Oh, damn!

CECE

Now you really do smell like beer. Might as well have some more.

DANI

My ass is in so much trouble.

CECE

'Cause you always shakin' it!

DANI finally helps CECE get to her feet. CECE starts to shake her butt.

CECE

(*sings*) It's gettin' hot . . . so take . . . take off all your clothes.

RED WASH FADES on CECE and DANI as they exit the platform. A FLASHLIGHT is seen in the darkness, then a FAINT RED WASH comes back up on the platform (now representing a stairwell). LEVON enters wearing his red Beats headphones as the flashlight shines in his face.

LEVON

What the hell . . .

MR. JACKSON

It's me . . . Mr. Jackson. Elevators are down. Hallway lights are broken. With no security cameras working I'm just making sure folks are safe.

LEVON

I'm looking for my sister. She's hangin' out somewhere. You seen her?

MR. JACKSON

Haven't see her on the stairs. She's probably in the courtyard doing what teenagers do.

LEVON

Well, I gotta find her 'fore she does somethin' she's not supposed to do.

MR. JACKSON

Heard you're headed to Syracuse to play some ball.

LEVON

Can't wait to get out of here.

MR. JACKSON

You got a major?

LEVON

A major?

MR. JACKSON

Something you like. Something you want to study. (*beat*) Me . . . I was always fascinated by colors. Steel blue, burnt orange, aqua green . . . You got a favorite color?

LEVON

Only colors I know are gang colors.

MR. JACKSON

I'm not talking about gang colors. What color do YOU like?

LEVON

Gold, I guess.

MR. JACKSON

The color of royalty, of emperors . . . from Timbuktu to Watts.

LEVON

YO, Mr. Jackson, I gotta find my sister.

MR. JACKSON

Sorry . . . didn't mean to hold you up.

LEVON takes a few steps then suddenly turns back around.

LEVON

Why do you do it?

MR. JACKSON

Well, anything can happen on these stairs when the elevators are out. So, I'm here to . . .

LEVON

No, I mean why do you stick around here? You teach art at Booker High. You gotta good job, good clothes . . . you could be livin' anywhere.

MR. JACKSON

I was born here at The Wood Haven Houses. My parents worked hard so I could make something out of my life. Took care of them until they died. Now I take care of other folks, their friends, neighbors . . . young men like you.

LEVON

What do you mean?

MR. JACKSON

I try to be an example. Be there for those who might need someone.

LEVON

Like a father? Don't need another damn father. The one I had was one too many. You feel me?

MR. JACKSON

Yes, I feel you. (*beat*) No harm meant.

LEVON

Yeah . . . whatever.

MR. JACKSON

Well, good luck with basketball. Some talented players have come out of Syracuse University.

LEVON

I plan to be another one.

MR. JACKSON

And if it doesn't work out, well, we can always use another Thurgood Marshall, Dr. Charles Drew, or James Baldwin. (*beat*) Ever read anything by James Baldwin?

LEVON

Notes of A Native Son? Made me think.

MR. JACKSON

Yes, me too.

SOUND OF the elevator is heard, the FAINT RED WASH flickers.

MR. JACKSON

Guess the elevators are working again. Power must be back on.

LEVON

For now . . .

MR. JACKSON

Yes, for now. (*beat*) Say, I have a print by Romare Bearden you might like for your dorm room. He's a talented Black artist. Bet you'll like his work. (*beat*) I'll bring it by before you go.

The FAINT RED WASH cross fades to a FULL RED WASH on CECE, sprawled out on the bench holding the beer bottle.

CECE

(*mumbles to herself*) So take off all your . . .

DRAY and JB stroll up and notice CECE on the bench.

JB

Dray . . . look at the hottie. She mad drunk and shit.

DRAY

YO . . . CeCe, what's up girl?

CECE

Where's Dani?

DRAY

She ain't here.

CECE

Oh right, she had to run home to her momma!

CECE sips on the last of her beer.

CECE

Damn . . . it's empty.

DRAY

Don't worry . . . I got some good shit. (*looks around*) Here, take this.

DRAY reveals a small bag of heroine. He offers CECE some to snort. CECE eagerly takes it then wipes her nose.

DRAY

YO, JB . . . keep a look out.

JB

Huh?

DRAY

Niggah stand over there and make sure no one's comin'!

JB

You gonna tap that ass right here?

DRAY

Hell, yeah! Now go keep watch.

JB moves away as DRAY pulls CECE up from the bench.

DRAY

Damn girl, you lookin' good.

CECE

I don't feel so good. I . . . . I gotta get home.

DRAY

Chill . . . your moms ain't worried. I'll bring you home later. Now we got business to take care of.

DRAY kisses her, roughly.

DRAY

You like that?

CECE

I . . . I gotta go clean up her bottles. Her dishes . . .

DRAY

You ain't goin' nowhere 'til I say so.

CECE

I'm going home.

DRAY starts to undo CECE's belt.

                              DRAY

Said you ain't leavin', bitch!

DRAY grabs CECE and drags her behind the bench.

                              CECE

What are you doing?

CECE struggles to get free, but DRAY is too strong. He pushes her to the ground and starts tugging at her clothes.

                              CECE

WAIT . . . STOP! NO!!!

                              DRAY

Gonna do you real good.

                              CECE

NO!!! DON'T!

                              DRAY

You got no choice.

                              CECE

HELP ME! SOMEONE . . .

                              JB

(from off) YO, keep the bitch quiet!

                              DRAY

(to CeCe) Shut the fuck up!

DRAY grabs CECE's neck, choking her.

                              DRAY

Oh, yeah . . . I'm ah bust this shit.

                              CECE

(gasping for air) NO, PLE . . . PLEASE! STOP!!!

LEVON enters the courtyard. JB blocks his path.

JB

YO, hold up, dog!

LEVON

Get the fuck out my way!

JB

Dray is taking care of business so step the fuck off.

CECE

(*from behind bench*) Help me!

LEVON

(*calls out*) CECE!!!

LEVON pushes JB aside then races behind the bench to grab DRAY.

LEVON

Get off her!

DRAY

Niggah, you about to get . . .

DRAY starts to reach for his piece when LEVON suddenly reveals a gun. He aims it at DRAY's head.

LEVON

About to get what, fool?

DRAY

Oh, so you wanna be a hero?

LEVON

What do you wanna be?

CECE stands, straightens her clothes, then approaches DRAY and spits on him.

CECE

(*to Dray*) Go to hell!

JB tries to reach for his piece, but LEVON quickly aims his gun at him, ready to fire if he has to.

LEVON

Ain't gonna happen, JB. (*beat*) So, you and Dray better take your tired asses on out of here.

DRAY

You know this ain't over. Got no place to hide, no hole to crawl into.

LEVON

Goes for you, too!

DRAY

Okay, I feel you, player. Got them serious red Beats and shit.

JB

Dray, you gonna let him disrespect Triple Z like that?

LEVON

He don't got a choice.

CECE

Kill him! You seen what he did to me!

DRAY

Momma's boy ain't down with that.

JB

Yeah . . . he's too soft. He should be more like his momma. Now that bitch is . . .

LEVON whacks JB across the face with his gun. JB drops, in pain.

LEVON

Who's the bitch now?

CECE

Shoot both of 'em!

DRAY

Yeah, while you got the chance 'cause when it's my turn . . . (*beat*) POW! POW! You dead, niggah.

JB

Like Tupac, like Biggie . . . for real dead.

SILENCE.

DRAY
Let's step, JB. (*beat*) We gonna catch up to Levon a little later. Hell . . . it's still the 4th of July. Let's go light some more fireworks and shit.

JB
Yeah . . . fuck this niggah.

DRAY and JB start to exit but DRAY turns back.

DRAY
And CeCe, you and me still got some business to finish. (*smells his fingers*) We was just gettin' started.

DRAY and JB exit. CECE races towards LEVON trying to wrestle his gun away.

CECE
Kill him! Kill him! HE RAPED ME!

The RED WASH CROSS FADES, present day lighting returns.

DANI
So . . . so Dray caught back up to my brother and shot him?

CECE
I went home. Levon said he was going home, too. But . . .

DANI
Why didn't you say anything to the police?

CECE
I told them I saw Levon, but . . . but not the other stuff. (*beat*) What Dray did to me.

DANI
What he did to you? What about what he did to my brother?

CECE
I was gonna tell you, but . . .

DANI
But nothing. His ass is next on this list.

CECE

What are you saying?

DANI

What am I saying? (*beat*) Soon as I find my brother's piece Dray is fuckin' dead!

CECE

Dani . . .

DANI

Gonna do what Levon should have done.

CECE

I tried to . . .

DANI

You didn't try hard enough. And now you be strolling around with Dray's baby? How messed up is that!

CECE

You don't understand.

DANI

Oh, I understand. (*beat*) You've been frontin' for Dray the whole time. Protectin' him and shit.

CECE

I hate Dray. I can't stand the sight of him. You know that.

DANI

My mother was right. You're nothin' but bad news. Dray's piece of ass. You been keepin' his secret just so Tyson can have a gang-banger for a daddy!

CECE

That's what you think?

DANI

Well, he's gonna be sayin' goodbye to his daddy. And if you get in my way . . . he's gonna be sayin' goodbye to you, too.

DANI storms off.

CECE

(*calling after*) YOU DON'T UNDERSTAND!

LIGHTS CROSS FADE BACK to THE RED WASH. LEVON and CECE continue to wrestle over the gun.

LEVON

They're gone. Let go of the gun.

CECE lets it go.

CECE

Me and Dani was drinkin' . . .

LEVON

Where is Dani? Did they . . .

CECE

No! She . . . she went home before they came.

LEVON

Damn! Must have just missed her.

ANOTHER RED WASH comes up in the living room (still flashback).

RUBY

(*anxious*) You seen Levon? He just run down the steps looking for you 'cause the elevators was out again.

DANI

They're working now. Just come up in one!

LEVON and CECE, still in their RED WASH, continue talking as the RED WASH REMAINS on DANI and RUBY.

NOTE: Dialogue in the two flashback scenes happens at the same time.

LEVON

You should go to the hospital. (*beat*) I'll take you.

RUBY

Lord . . . where is that boy?

CECE

Hospital?

LEVON

'Cause of what Dray did.

CECE

Dray?

LEVON

He raped you. You have to go to the hospital. They'll report it to the police and . . .

DANI

Maybe he's walking up the stairs 'cause he thinks the elevators might stop working again.

CECE

He didn't do anything.

LEVON

But I saw him. You were down on the ground and . . .

CECE

He didn't rape me. He was about to but then you came along.

LEVON

But you said . . . (*alarmed*) Damn, I almost shot him.

CECE

You should have.

LEVON

Then what? Go to jail! (*beat*) What the hell were you thinking?

RUBY

Elevators ain't no place to be stuck. Mrs. Walker got stuck in one and was robbed.

RED WASH FADES on RUBY and DANI but remains on CECE and LEVON.

CECE

Dray needs to be shot. If you don't do it somebody else will.

                              LEVON

Then let them do it. (*beat*) Come on . . . I'll walk you home.

                              CECE

I don't feel so good.

CECE sits on the bench. LEVON puts his arm around her shoulder.

                              LEVON

How much did you and Dani drink?

                              CECE

Me and Dani drank one bottle. Then I drank one by myself. (*beat*) Stupid, huh?

                              LEVON

Yeah . . . (*beat*) Look, about my gun . . .

CECE suddenly kisses LEVON.

                              CECE

I'm not gonna tell Dani if you don't want me to.

                              LEVON

Don't do that again.

CECE kisses LEVON, deeper.

                              LEVON

I said stop.

                              CECE

Why? You gotta a girlfriend?

                              LEVON

You're like my little sister.

                              CECE

But I'm not.

                              LEVON

Let's go!

RED WASH FADES BACK UP in the living room.

RUBY

Got beer on your breath. You was drinkin'?

DANI

I had a sip. No big deal.

RUBY

Drinkin' was no big deal to your father, 'til he'd start hittin' me.

RED WASH FADES on RUBY and DANI. RED LIGHTS UP on CECE and LEVON.

CECE

Don't you like me?

LEVON

Yes . . . but not the way . . .

CECE takes LEVON's gun from his waist, stands and aims it at him.

LEVON

That gun is loaded.

CECE

I want you.

LEVON

You're high.

CECE

Maybe I'll tell Dani you got a gun. Or Ruby!

LEVON

Give me the gun before someone sees you.

CECE

You want it?

LEVON

Yeah . . . now stop playin' 'fore that thing goes off.

CECE

Okay . . .

CECE lowers the gun.

LEVON

I said give it to me.

CECE quickly puts the gun down her shorts.

CECE

Oops! I think it slipped down my shorts.

LEVON

Girl, now you're being a pain in my ass.

CECE sits down next to LEVON.

CECE

If you want it . . . TAKE IT.

LEVON

Ain't got time for this.

LEVON stands and starts to walk away.

CECE

You don't want your gun? You heard what Dray said. He's comin' back lookin' for you.

180. LEVON turns back.

LEVON

Hell . . .

LEVON goes to CECE who abruptly pulls him down on top of her.

CECE

You want the gun?

LEVON

Yes, I want it.

CECE

Then reach inside my shorts and get it.

> LEVON

Give me the damn gun!

> CECE

You afraid?

CECE kisses him, again.

> LEVON

Of you?

> CECE

I'm too much woman for you.

> LEVON

You're a mad crazy, over-sexed, little girl.

> CECE

When my mother's on her back I know the men she's screwin' don't care nothin' about her. They see her as nothin' so they don't care nothin' 'bout her. *(beat)* But you . . . you're different, I . . . I can tell. You care about me. You're sweet, kind. Saved me from Dray. From myself.

> LEVON

You sure I'm different? *(beat)* I gotta gun. Maybe I'm just like the other dogs.

> CECE

If you were . . . Dray would be dead. *(beat)* Now do you want your piece or not?

> LEVON

Yeah . . . I want it.

CECE grabs his hands and places them between her legs.

> CECE

Then take it.

SOUND OF CELL PHONE buzzing. LEVON tries to move his hand to get to his phone but CECE stops him, then kisses him.

RED WASH FADES on CECE and LEVON. RED WASH UP on RUBY and DANI.

RUBY

(*concerned*) Did you text him, Danielle? Is he textin' you back? Where is he?

DANI

He didn't answer.

RUBY

Well, try again. And if he don't answer . . . TRY AGAIN!

RED WASH CROSS FADES to CECE, back to present day lighting. She stands near her stroller looking off in the direction where DANI left.

CECE

(*to herself*) You don't understand that if you kill Dray . . . I'll be free.

Sound of TYSON faintly crying from his stroller. CECE approaches the stroller and gently moves it back and forth.

CECE

Don't cry, everything's gonna be okay. (*softly, to Tyson*) Gettin' hot in here so take off all your clothes. Gettin' so hot I'm gonna take my . . . (*to Tyson*) We'll both be free.

FADE TO BLACK.

End of ACT I

Say What—role played by R. Ashley Bowles.
Photo by Jonathan Slaff

Say What gives Dani advice.
Photo by Jonathan Slaff

CeCe stops Dray from shooting Say What.
Photo by Jonathan Slaff

ACT II

Scene I

A short time later. LIGHTS UP in the living room. DANI enters holding LEVON's old gym bag. She begins to rummage through the contents revealing a pair of shorts, a sweatshirt, assorted socks, sneakers, and his basketball. Frustrated, she stuffs everything back inside the bag and tosses it to the floor.

DANI

Damn, it's not here. (*to audience*) Told you someone's gonna die today. But now I know his name and I already put it on the list . . . right here.

DANI takes out a crumpled list from her back pocket.

DANI

(*reads name, then to audience*) Dray Oliver. Drayton, back in the day when he wore faded, torn pants that were too big for him, he used to get his brother Odell's old clothes. Odell ran Triple Z 'fore he got shot right in front of Red's Barbershop. Folks said Odell always wanted to look good 'cause he knew that somebody, someday was gonna put his name on their list. A list started by a gang member from another project. Gangs, guns, ganja . . . the A-B-Cs of the hood. At Wood Haven you learn these before you learn to walk.

(*beat*) My brother wasn't a gang-banger but I guess he figured that one day there might be a bullet with his name on it and he had to be ready. But it didn't help, did it? Guess a gun's better at killing people . . . than saving them.

DANI puts the list away as RUBY, now dressed in a jumper, enters the living room holding a plate of food. Her hair is now tied up with a scarf.

RUBY

What's that on the floor?

DANI

Nothing.

RUBY

Nothing?

RUBY puts the plate down and crosses to DANI.

                    DANI

It's only Levon's bag. I was just looking for his old ball.

                    RUBY

Don't you got your own?

                    DANI

It's just that today, being the 4th and all, made me think 'bout him playing over in the park. Thought I might use it one day.

RUBY picks up the bag and looks through it.

                    RUBY

Yeah, he did love playing in that park. Took him there at least 10 times a day when he was just a little thing.

RUBY takes out the basketball.

                    RUBY

(*puzzled*) You ain't taking his ball?

                    DANI

Think it needs some air.

RUBY places the ball back inside the bag then hands it to DANI.

                    RUBY

You put up the new list?

                    DANI

Yeah . . . (*beat*) But after today . . .

                    RUBY

After today, what?

                    DANI

Nothing. (*beat*) Better put his bag back.

DANI exits into the darkness with the bag as RUBY takes a bite from a piece of chicken on her plate.

RUBY

(*calling*) What happened to hangin' out with CeCe?

DANI returns.

DANI

She has Tyson to look after.

RUBY

Yeah, well . . . things change.

DANI

What's that supposed to mean?

SILENCE.

DANI

Hello? I asked you a question.

RUBY puts down her plate down and gazes long and hard at DANI.

RUBY

Look, I know you think I'm just another bitter Black woman who don't give a damn about no one, except her son and gettin' him justice.

DANI

Yeah . . . that's you alright.

RUBY

Well, it ain't all I'm about. I do have feelings . . . especially for that child being wheeled around this here place by a teenager who ain't much older than he is.

DANI

CeCe's a good mother. She's gonna do okay no matter what you think.

RUBY

In that apartment? With her mother carrying on and what not, all hours of the night with strange men? Ain't no place to raise a child.

DANI

Sometimes you gotta deal with what's handed to you.

RUBY

And sometimes not!

DANI

What, you Donald Trump now? You gonna get CeCe and Tyson out of here. Put her up in midtown with a doorman and a big bank account? Like Mrs. Lief, the woman you cook and clean for?

RUBY

Ain't no Donald Trump here. Just Ruby Weeks who watches the kids of a well-off family in Manhattan five days a week. Does what she can and wishes she could do more.

DANI

I have to go. There's something I gotta do.

DANI *turns away and starts to exit.*

RUBY

I spoke to Yvonne, CeCe's mother. We both come to an agreement.

DANI

(*turning back*) An agreement? About what?

RUBY

Doing what's best for the baby . . . and for CeCe.

DANI

What are you talkin' about?

RUBY

Told Yvonne the way she be living ain't the best environment to raise no baby. Told her so and she agreed.

DANI

Does CeCe know you've been talkin' to her mother?

RUBY

Not yet. But tonight, after the ACS done come and gone she'll understand what's what.

DANI

The ACS? What did you do?

RUBY

Told Administrative Child Services about that household. They comin' by to set things straight.

DANI

What are they going to do?

RUBY

Whatever they feel is the right thing to do.

DANI

CeCe's his mother! They have no right to . . .

RUBY

They been by once, already. Come by the other day and seen what a mess things is over there. Told Yvonne to make sure CeCe wasn't there. Now they's coming back to see if . . .

DANI

Didn't realize how dangerous you really are until now.

RUBY

I'm doing this for Tyson and for CeCe. What kind of life does you think she's gonna have with that kid around? She already missed a half a year of school. Be lucky if she even graduates.

DANI

She's coming back to Booker in September. Told me she wants to go to community college.

RUBY

And now she might get the chance!

DANI

She's not going to hand her baby over to child services.

RUBY

She might not have no choice. They already seen the bottles, the crack pipes, the filth, the dirty dishes . . .

DANI

CeCe is doing the best she can. They have no right to take her baby away. What if someone had come to take us away after Daddy beat on you? Would you have just let them? Huh?

RUBY

Every day I was praying for ACS to come. Praying for them to get you and Levon out of this hell hole.

Sits, lost in memories.

RUBY

Guess I didn't pray hard enough. If I did maybe Levon would still be alive.

DANI

You didn't want us? Is that why you hit Levon? Hit me?

SILENCE.

DANI (CONT'D)

All this time I thought Daddy was the monster. And you . . . you were the victim. I felt sorry for you. You had no choice, no opportunity.

RUBY

Sorry for me? (*beat*) Don't make me laugh.

DANI

Yeah . . . sorry for a poor, tragic, Black woman swallowed up by the rage of her husband who could get one foot in prison easier than he could in any other door. (*beat*) Daddy should have hit you harder. Maybe he would have knocked some damn sense into your head.

RUBY

He would have, but he loved his pint of Johnnie Walker more than he loved smackin' me around.

DANI

I'm gonna tell CeCe what you've been up to.

RUBY

Ain't nothing she can do. Nothing you can do either. So, you best let things be.

DANI

I can't do that.

RUBY

She's gonna hate you . . . me . . . her mother! You might think you're doin' the
right thing by telling her, but you ain't. So let it be.

DANI

Dray is Tyson's father. Did you know that?

RUBY

Don't matter.

DANI

Don't matter? (*beat*) When Dray finds out you spoke with the ACS he's gonna send
JB after you.

RUBY stands and crosses to DANI.

RUBY

I died a year ago when your brother got murdered. Ain't nothin' no gang member
can do to me that hasn't already been done.

*DANI reaches into her pocket and pulls out a list. She scribbles a name onto the list then hands
the list to RUBY.*

RUBY

(*reading name on list*) Ruby Weeks? (*beat*) You put my name on the list?

DANI

You said you were dead. I just never realized it until now.

A KNOCK is heard at the door.

RUBY

You expecting someone?

MR. JACKSON

(*off stage*) RUBY! YOU HOME? IT'S ME, MR. JACKSON!

RUBY

Get the door. Go on, now.

DANI exits to answer the door. RUBY tries to quickly tidy up. A moment, then DANI returns followed by MR. JACKSON who enters holding a wrapped, framed Romare Bearden print.

MR. JACKSON
Evening, Ruby . . . Danielle. Hope I'm not disturbing you.

DANI
I was just going.

MR. JACKSON
I'll only be a few minutes.

RUBY
Mr. Jackson, would you like some water or juice? We even got some of that green tea.

MR. JACKSON
Water is fine.

RUBY
Danielle, please get Mr. Jackson some water.

DANI hesitates.

RUBY
Danielle? You hear me?

DANI exits off.

RUBY
Please, have a seat. Got home not too long ago so the place is not what it should be.

MR. JACKSON
Place looks fine. Just fine. You heading over to Willis to see 'em shoot fireworks from the rooftops?

RUBY
That's for the young folks. Let them hang out and carry on. I'll be just fine sitting on my couch and watching the fireworks on television.

MR. JACKSON

You're still young.

RUBY

Tell that to my aching feet. Lord, that white woman I work for had me washing, scrubbing, mopping, cleaning . . .

MR. JACKSON

Well, you still look young to me.

DANI enters with a glass of water and hands it to MR. JACKSON.

MR. JACKSON

Thank you, Danielle. (*beat*) Bet you're heading out. Got some plans for the 4th, have you?

DANI

Going to see my friend, CeCe. Have something to tell her.

RUBY

Her and CeCe always hang out. Hung out last 4th of July. Sent Levon out to look for her but he never come back.

MR. JACKSON

Yes, that was a real tragedy.

RUBY

Yes . . . it was.

MR. JACKSON

I spoke to Levon that night. Saw him on the stairwell. He was really looking forward to playing basketball at Syracuse. Asked him if he picked a major.

DANI

Did he?

MR. JACKSON

No . . . but I tried to get him to think about one just in case basketball didn't work out.

RUBY

That was very thoughtful of you, Mr. Jackson.

MR. JACKSON

Told him I had a print by Romare Bearden for his dorm room. I was going to give this to him before he left for school.

RUBY

What made you bring it by now?

MR. JACKSON

Well, it's been sitting in my apartment for a whole year now. And every day I'd say to myself, I'm gonna bring it over to Ruby's.

DANI

Guess today is the day.

MR. JACKSON

Well . . . it being a year since he passed. I just thought . . .

RUBY

It was nice of you to remember him. Some folks would rather forget. Got their own lives.

Awkward SILENCE as DANI and RUBY exchange hard looks.

MR. JACKSON

Was a real loss to the community when he got killed.

RUBY

Not as real as it was and still is, to me.

DANI

That's why she makes the list, Mr. Jackson. You know about my mother's list?

MR. JACKSON

(*to Dani*) Anyone living here at Wood Haven knows about Ruby's list.

SILENCE.

DANI

She's making a new list. A list of people she's gonna help leave The Wood Haven Houses.

MR. JACKSON

A new list?

RUBY

Gotta be another way for folks to get out of here instead of being carried off in a coffin.

MR. JACKSON

Amen to that!

RUBY

Did you know there's been 104 folks killed here in the Bronx since the last 4th of July?

MR. JACKSON

Yes, I saw the new list on the way over here.

DANI

Levon's killer is gonna get shot tonight. Then they'll be no more lists. That's what my mother said.

RUBY

Why you talking such foolishness?

MR. JACKSON

I'm sure that today, the anniversary of her brother's death, has got her feeling and saying a lot of things. You too, Ruby. If it was my son, well, I'd want to see some justice for his senseless demise. But spilling blood? Will it really make a difference? Will it bring back anyone on that list? Will Levon walk through that door if the boy who shot him is killed?

RUBY

No . . . it won't.

DANI says nothing, still determined to make things right.

MR. JACKSON

I think you should have this, Danielle.

DANI

Wasn't it supposed to be for Levon?

MR. JACKSON

You seemed to enjoy my art elective last year. Thought when you go off to college one day you could hang it on your dorm room wall.

DANI

Thanks, but . . .

MR. JACKSON

I'm sure your brother would like you to have it.

Mr. Jackson hands Danielle the wrapped print. She stares at it, not sure what to do or say.

MR. JACKSON

Go ahead, unwrap it.

RUBY

Lord, I remember how excited he was when we gave him his graduation gift. (*beat*) Remember, Danielle?

DANI

Yeah . . .

LIGHTS FADE in the living room. A RED WASH FADES UP on RUBY as she enters onto the platform. She holds a small wrapped gift and hands it to LEVON, as he enters onto the platform wearing a cap and gown.

RUBY

Go ahead. It ain't gonna unwrap by itself.

DANI

Yeah . . . what you waiting for?

LEVON

Didn't have to get me anything.

RUBY

You graduated today. And I am so . . . so proud of you.

DANI

Me too.

RUBY hugs LEVON, then he hastily opens his gift to reveal a pair of red Beats headphones.

RUBY

Danielle picked 'em out.

DANI

They're Beats!

LEVON

YO, these headphones are mad hot! (*beat*) Thanks . . .

DANI

Everyone squeeze together. (*takes out cell phone*) I got this.

They huddle together as DANI takes a selfie of the three of them. RED WASH FADES OUT as DANI and RUBY return to the living room. LIGHTS UP in the living room.

DANI

(*to Ruby*) You seen his headphones?

RUBY

Headphones? What on earth you talking about?

DANI

The red ones he always wore after he graduated. The present we got him.

RUBY

Maybe they's in his gym bag.

DANI

You just looked in the bag. Did you see them?

RUBY

They could be anywhere. What are you fussing so much about?

DANI abruptly hands MR. JACKSON the wrapped print.

DANI

Sorry, Mr. Jackson. I have to go.

MR. JACKSON

Not a problem. I'll leave the print with your mother. How's that?

DANI exits in a hurry.

MR. JACKSON

Is something wrong? She seems very upset about those headphones.

RUBY

Around here there's always something to be upset about.

MR. JACKSON

Guess you're right about that. Well, I should be going, too.

MR. JACKSON stands. He hands RUBY the wrapped print.

MR. JACKSON

His favorite color was gold.

RUBY

Whose?

MR. JACKSON

Levon's.

RUBY

He told you that?

MR. JACKSON

On his way to find Danielle.

A moment, then RUBY slowly begins to unwrap the print.

RUBY

Year ago, when he got shot, we marched.

MR. JACKSON

Yes, I was there.

RUBY

We chanted "Enough, no more violence!" The news reporters come, the ministers, the mayor, now they's all gone. They leave but my tears, they will always be here. They will fall from this old, wrinkled face day after day, night after night, until I die, I suppose.

RUBY admires the print, now unwrapped.

RUBY

This here art sure is beautiful . . .

MR. JACKSON

It's called "Jammin' At The Savoy."

RUBY

. . . But this place, where we live, where my boy died? (*beat*) Ain't no beauty here.

She hands the unwrapped print back to MR. JACKSON.

RUBY

None at all.

A TELEPHONE is heard ringing.
LIGHTS FADE.

ACT II
Scene II

SAY WHAT enters the courtyard. He holds a bloody American Flag bandana up against a gash on his forehead as he wheels his cart. It is apparent that his cart has been rifled through. His boom box is gone, and so are most of his supplies.

SAY WHAT

Them Triple Z boys wanna play rough, huh? Give old Say What a beat down. Whupped me upside the head, then left me for dead. Hell, I ain't dead! Fred is dead but Say What is still here. Living large and in charge! (*starts to shadow box*) I'll bite your ear like Mike, rope ah dope you like Ali, or make your ass pay with a flurry like Sugar Ray. Yeah, I'm gonna get you sucker! The Mothership is gonna put an atomic dog on your ass. Bow-wow-wow, yippee-ay, yippee-yay, bow-wow, yippee-ay, yippee-yay! (*beat*) Gonna get me a lickin' stick and give that Dray and JB somethin' their mommas should have givin' them from jump street. Yeah, I's a mean street niggah when I's gotta be. Ask Willie Joe Williams. He tried to cheat me at craps. Cut the niggah so deep he saw Jesus, he did. WHO'S BAD? Say What is bad, and you Z boys is gonna find out HOW BAD! Yeah, I'm bad news, bad luck, bad for your goddamned health, you hear? I'm high cholesterol and you's about to have a damn heart attack! (*shouts*) Oh yeah, I'm the Lion King and you gonna wish you never come into my jungle. Gonna Mustafa your Black butt right to Never Never Land. And when you get there tell Willie Joe Williams I says "hello"!

DANI enters on her way to find CECE. She notices SAY WHAT holding his bloody head.

DANI

YO, Say What . . . what happened to your head?

SAY WHAT

Got struck by enlightenment. Ran head first into it.

DANI

Huh?

SAY WHAT

Come out of the sky like a lightning bolt. Zapped me, it did. Said there's something you gotta do.

DANI

Like what?

SAY WHAT

It's all about truth! Truth, justice, and the big pay back.

DANI

Yeah, I feel that.

DANI starts to head off.

SAY WHAT

(*calling after her*) It don't come easy. There's usually a big price to pay.

DANI turns back.

DANI

What doesn't come easy?

SAY WHAT

Enlightenment! Makes you bleed. See my head?

DANI

Maybe you'd better get your head looked at.

SAY WHAT

Don't hurt. That's the beauty of enlightenment. Just makes you see things much clearer. But once ya does, ain't no turning back. No do overs, no get out of jail cards, no sorrys 'cause sorry is a sorry ass word.

DANI

I'll remember that.

DANI starts to leave.

SAY WHAT

Say, ain't you the girl whose momma makes that dyin' list? And once you get on, you ain't gettin' off?

DANI

There's no more list.

SAY WHAT

No more folks dyin'?

DANI

They're dyin' whether there's a list or not. So, what's the point of a mad stupid list?

SAY WHAT

Got to be a point.

DANI

Haven't found it yet.

SAY WHAT

Ain't about you finding it. It's about your momma. She's looking, but she ain't seein'. Seems like most folks around here ain't seein'. But we gotta keep on lookin'! 'Cause ain't no mountain high enough, ain't no valley low enough, ain't no river wide enough . . . (*shouts*) . . . to keep me from goin' back to Willis Park and enlighten them boys right upside their heads!

SAY WHAT starts to exit.

SAY WHAT

(*shouts*) Yeah . . . I'm bad news, bad luck, bad for your goddamned health, you hear?

SAY WHAT exits pushing his disheveled cart. A moment, then CECE enters the courtyard wearing a shoulder bag. DANI stares at her.

DANI

I was looking for you.

CECE

Yeah? I was looking for you, too.

DANI

Where's Tyson?

CECE

My mom's watching him.

DANI

You think that's a good idea?

CECE

Said she wanted to. Wanted me to go out and have some fun.

DANI

With Dray?

CECE

Not with Dray. With you.

DANI

Maybe you'd better go home.

DANI sits. CECE sits next to her.

CECE

She's not havin' any men comin' over tonight. She promised me.

DANI

And you believed her?

SOUND OF FIREWORKS EXPLODING.

CECE

Hear that? They started shooting fireworks off the rooftops. Can't see them from here. Let's go to the park.

DANI

I said go home.

CECE

I watch Tyson 24/7. I need a few hours to myself. If my mom wants to look after him, well . . . fine.

DANI

So . . . so you really don't care about him?

CECE

Are you for real? Tyson's my child . . . he came from me. I'd do anything for him. Anything!

DANI

Even leave?

CECE

What do you mean?

DANI

I mean take him and get the hell out of here.

SOUND OF MORE FIREWORKS.

CECE

And go where? With what money?

DANI

I could help you.

CECE

You wanna help me?

CECE reaches into her shoulder bag and reveals a gun.

CECE

Then kill Dray! (*beat*) Here . . .

DANI

What are you doing with that?

CECE

It's not mine.

DANI

Where did you get it?

CECE

Took it from JB.

DANI

JB? You crazy?

CECE

Heard him say it once belonged to Levon. But now it's his.

DANI

My brother's gun? How did JB get his hands on it?

CECE

How do you think? Dray must have given it to him after he killed your brother.

DANI

So, you stole it from JB?

CECE

Nearly two weeks ago, after he shot Calvin Harris.

DANI

You were there?

CECE

No, but I'm Dray's whore, remember? (*beat*) I see and know everything Triple Z does. Even know where they hide their guns. I was thinkin' about shootin' Dray, but after you said . . .

DANI stands, confused. She starts to pace back and forth. Her mind is spinning.

DANI

Man . . . I hate this place.

CECE

Me too.

CECE stands, stopping DANI in her tracks. CECE places the gun in DANI's hands. A beat, then DANI tucks it inside her shorts.

CECE

After tonight we'll all go away. Me, you, Tyson . . . (*beat*) Just like you said!

DANI

Okay . . . (*beat*) Now go home. I'll meet you later.

CECE

But I told you my mom's watchin' Tyson.

DANI

So, you can hang out? When has she ever done that?

CECE

She just wants me to have fun. Come on . . . let's have some fun!

CECE starts dancing as she sings.

CECE

(*sings*) It's gettin' hot, so take . . .

DANI

Haven't you takin' them off enough?

CECE

You think you're better than me just because I got a kid?

DANI

Go home and take care of your kid.

CECE

Guess what Ruby thinks about me is rubbin' off on you.

DANI

I'm sorry. I didn't mean anything. It's just that I think you should go home, now.

CECE

Why?

DANI

Because your mother and my mother have been . . .

MR. JACKSON and RUBY enter.

MR. JACKSON

Anyone headed to the park? Got a beautiful night for some rooftop fireworks.

CECE

Hey, Mr. Jackson . . . Mrs. Weeks. Going to see the fireworks?

RUBY

Don't know about all that. Just thought I'd like to go for a walk.

MR. JACKSON

Nice night for a walk.

RUBY

Nice? It's hotter than a hot comb cuttin' through some nappy hair.

DANI

(*to Ruby*) Don't you wanna know about Tyson?

RUBY

I do. (*pause*) How is Tyson?

CECE

He's fine, thanks.

MR. JACKSON

How old is he, now?

CECE

Just a few months. I was out spring semester so I couldn't take your art class. But I want to take it in the fall.

MR. JACKSON

I hope you do. (*beat*) Danielle took it last year.

RUBY

How's Yvonne, CeCe?

CECE

Ah, good . . . you know. She does her thing. And I do mine.

RUBY

Must be tough.

CECE

What do you mean?

DANI

You know what she means. You said you know what Ruby thinks.

CECE

You mean having a baby when I'm only seventeen?

DANI

Yeah . . . that's what she means.

RUBY

How you planning to go back to school with a child? Who's gonna watch him?

CECE

Guess I'll have to figure that out. Same way you figured it out when your husband went to prison. Same way my mother figured it out after my father left.

SOUND OF MORE FIREWORKS.

MR. JACKSON

We're gonna miss those fireworks.

DANI

CeCe's headed home, but first I think my mother's got something to say to her.

CECE

She does?

DANI

Yeah . . . (*looks at Ruby*) She does.

CECE

Good, 'cause I have something I wanna tell her.

MR. JACKSON

(*to Danielle*) Guess it's you and me, Danielle.

DANI

Guess so.

DANI and MR. JACKSON exit. RUBY sits down on the bench.

CECE

I miss Levon.

RUBY

You do?

CECE

I liked him a lot.

RUBY

Is that what you wanted to tell me?

CECE

No, there's more. But I'm not sure how to say it. (*beat*) What did you want to talk to me about?

RUBY

I dropped by to see your mother.

CECE

Really? Thought you hated her. Most people around here do, except the men who sleep with her.

RUBY

Never hated her.

CECE

You don't have to lie. Dani told me how you really feel. But I don't care. This isn't about me. It's about Tyson.

RUBY

Yeah, I'm glad you see that.

CECE

It's always been about him.

RUBY

Yvonne and me, well, that's what our talk was about.

CECE

About Tyson?

RUBY

She cares about him. Maybe you don't think so but . . .

CECE

About Tyson? (*beat*) Don't let my mother fool you. She only cares about feeding her habit. And she has lots of sex to pay for that.

RUBY

Ain't no place to raise a child, is it?

CECE

No, I was thinking the same thing. That's what I wanted to tell you.

> RUBY

So, you understand?

> CECE

I do, but I hope you do. See that night when Levon came to look for Dani, well, I saw him.

> RUBY

I know. It was in the police report. You was one of the last people to see him alive. Then you went home and . . . and, Lord only knows what happened to my boy after that. That's why . . . there's got to be something better for your boy.

> CECE

Yes, I know. You see, I did see Levon that night . . . and . . . we got close. We . . .

> RUBY

Me and Yvonne, we been talkin'. See, we figured with all of her drinkin' and what not . . .

CECE crosses towards the raised platform as the lights FADE ON RUBY. The RED WASH FADES UP on the platform as LEVON enters, his shirt is off. He puts his arms around CECE and kisses her.

> CECE

Always thought making love to you would be magical.

> LEVON

Was it?

> CECE

Right out some fairy tale. A love story just waiting to be told.

> LEVON

Love story?

> CECE

You do love me, don't you?

> LEVON

I care about you.

CECE

Care?

LEVON

CeCe, you're still in high school. I'm heading off to college.

CECE

So . . . you'll be back. Or maybe I can come visit.

LEVON

I'm gonna be busy. I mean with basketball and a major . . .

CECE removes LEVON's gun from his waist, then pushes him away. She aims the gun at Levon.

CECE

So, forget the sex crazed teenager, right? Trash just like her mother.

LEVON

I didn't say that.

CECE

You didn't have to. I fuckin' get it.

CECE turns her back to LEVON as his cell phone beeps. He looks at the number then puts it away.

LEVON

Look, give me the gun. That was Dani textin' me.

He spins her around and the two teens wrestle over the gun.

RED WASH CROSS FADES back to the present. DANI enters the courtyard, she drops the gun to the ground.

DANI

It's over.

RUBY

What's over? And where did you get that gun?

DANI

Does it matter?

CECE

Is Dray . . .

DANI

Dray and JB are both dead.

RUBY

Drayton Parks dead? Dear Lord, give us all strength.

RUBY, lost for words, sits. MR. JACKSON enters, dazed.

MR. JACKSON

Danielle, the police want to have a word with you.

RUBY

Police?

CECE

Dani, I'm . . . I'm so sorry.

RUBY

Sorry?

RUBY (CONT'D)

Danielle, what's going on? What did you do?

DANI

I went to look for Dray. To kill him!

CECE

I was afraid of him. I needed Dani's help. I needed him out of my life. Tyson's life.

SOUND OF POLICE SIRENS in the distance.

DANI

What about Levon? He needed your help that night. Where were you?

DANI picks up the gun and points it at CECE.

SFX: SIRENS GETTING CLOSER

RED WASH FLOODS the stage as LEVON appears. CECE and LEVON go back to wrestling over the gun. Dray appears and aims his gun at CECE and LEVON.

LEVON

Damn it! I do love you . . . now just give me the . . .

SUDDENLY THE GUN FIRES. LEVON clutches his stomach and starts to fall. CECE drops the gun and tries to hold him up, but he's too heavy.

CECE

Levon, no! NO!

DRAY

(*calls off*) YO, JB! The bitch just popped Levon. Saved my ass the trouble.

LEVON falls to the floor as JB rushes in.

CECE

No . . . please, God. No. I didn't mean to . . .

DRAY and JB approach.

DRAY

Niggah got what he deserved.

CECE lunges towards DRAY.

CECE

I hate you!

DRAY grabs her.

DRAY

Now you listen up? Me and JB gonna fix this shit. (*beat*) JB, take his piece.

JB

What about them headphones and his cell?

DRAY

Leave the phone! Just grab the gun and let's bounce this niggah to Willis Park.

JB

But them headphones is nice.

DRAY

And when the police find you wearin' them it won't be nice! (*beat*) Let her take the damn headphones.

JB grabs the gun from the ground. He removes LEVON's headphones and hands them to CECE.

CECE

Just gonna dump him in the park? That ain't right.

DRAY

You shot him. You wanna go to jail, bitch? (*beat*) I asked you a fuckin' question!

He shakes CECE violently.

CECE

(*crying*) No, NOOO!

DRAY

You're mine, now. Got that? You wanna stay out of jail keep your mouth shut and your legs open. Or else I will tell the fuckin' cops who shot Levon.

DRAY shoves CECE aside then he and JB start to lift LEVON's body as the RED WASH FADES OUT. Lights back up on RUBY, DANI, and CECE. DANI, still aiming the gun at CECE, lowers it.

DANI

You saying what I think you're saying?

CECE

It was an accident. I swear! I had that gun, the one you're holding, and when I turned . . .

DANI

You played me? Set me up to kill Dray?

CECE

I'm sorry. I'm so sorry.

RUBY

All this time, all this pain and you just strollin' up and down with that damn baby thinkin' you're so cute. Probably knocked up right now. Well at least you ain't gonna do no more harm to the first one.

CECE

I loved Levon and he loved me.

RUBY

Love? You just as crazy as that mother of yours! You think my boy could love you? Look at you? What ya got to offer? Where you think you're going in life?

CECE

Nowhere . . . just like you!

RUBY

Just like me? Girl, you should be thanking me for taking that child of yours.

CECE

You'll take him? And I was afraid that . . .

RUBY

Take him? What do I want with him?

CECE

But you just said . . .

RUBY

Only people taking him is child services.

CECE

What?

RUBY

Your mother called me right 'fore me and Mr. Jackson come outside. Right after Danielle left.

RUBY

ACS took your boy about fifteen minutes ago and I'm glad they did.

CECE

Dani, did you know about this?

                          DANI

I told you to go home.

                          RUBY

See, you took Levon's life so it's only fair that . . .

                          CECE

Stupid bitch! I was gonna let Tyson live with you. I turned myself in to the police
today so I thought that you, being his grandmother, would . . .

                          RUBY

His grandmother?

                          CECE

Levon's the father. Don't you get it?

                          DANI

You're lyin'!

                          CECE

Been lyin' to you, to myself but not anymore. I swear I'm tellin' the truth.

                          DANI

Truth? Dray is dead! The father of your baby is dead! What truth are you talking
about?

                          CECE

I had Tyson's blood tested. (*beat*) Dray's not his father, Levon is! Got his DNA
from the hair he left on his headphones.

                          DANI

What headphones?

CECE reveals the red Beats headphones from her bag.

                          CECE

Took these from him a year ago. The night he died.

                          RUBY

I ain't fit for livin'. Done give away my own grandson.

MR. JACKSON

You didn't know.

MR. JACKSON puts his arm around RUBY's shoulder to comfort her.

RUBY

But now I do. Now . . . I do. And it hurts, Lord, does it hurt.

DANI

(*to CeCe*) Give me one reason why you shouldn't be dead, too.

CECE

Tyson's gone . . . so I ain't got one.

The SOUND OF POLICE SIRENS floods the stage.

LIGHTS FADE.

ACT II
Scene III

A year later, 4th of July. MR. JACKSON, in casual attire, enters the courtyard pulling a red wagon filled with colorful wildflowers (SUNFLOWERS, RED POPPIES, CORN FLOW-ERS, GOLDEN TICKSEED, and PURPLE ORACHES). RUBY follows him sporting cover-alls and a straw hat. The music of JAMES BROWN blast from the open window, then fades.

MR. JACKSON

You're right, Ruby. This is truly the perfect way to celebrate the two-year anniversary of Levon's passing.

RUBY

And you're right about these here colors. Never knew flowers could bring so much beauty to a place as dark as The Wood Haven Houses.

MR. JACKSON

I think that's why I became an art teacher. It's all about the colors and what you can do with them.

RUBY picks up some red poppies.

RUBY

What God can do with them.

MR. JACKSON

Amen to that! Where do you want these?

RUBY

Let's plant some near the bench so when folks sit down they'll see 'em.

MR. JACKSON wheels the flowers over to the bench. RUBY grabs a trowel from the wagon and begins to dig in the courtyard grass.

MR. JACKSON

Guess the teenagers will have to find another park for tonight.

RUBY

Can't blame the police for closin' Willis Park to all 4th of July activities after Drayton's death.

MR. JACKSON

I'm not one to condone violence, but the drugs, the guns, the harassment of the good people who live here . . . that boy was bound to get his sooner or later.

LIGHTS FADE on RUBY and MR. JACKSON as the RED WASH FADES UP on the platform area. DRAY, sucking down a bottle of beer, sports one of the July 4th hats he stole from SAY WHAT. He notices DANI as she approaches.

DRAY

You seen CeCe? Been looking for her.

DANI

She's not comin'. I came instead.

DRAY

Oh, Miss Stuck-Up Bitch finally wants some of me. Shit . . . I got enough for all you honeys.

DANI

Yeah . . . I want some.

DRAY

Well bring that ass over here!

DANI

How 'bout this instead.

DANI reveals a gun and points it at DRAY.

DRAY

What, you gonna shoot me in front of everyone out here in the park? You just like your dumb ass brother. Weak and shit!

DANI

Is that why you killed him? He was weak.

DRAY

Bitch, you trippin'. Get that piece out of my face 'fore I kill you and your crazy list writin' momma.

SAY WHAT enters the platform.

SAY WHAT

Better listen to him, girl.

DRAY

Guess I did knock some sense into your foolish head.

SAY WHAT

Yeah, you did, Mr. Big Stuff, who do you think you is? But I know, who you is. You's the air sucker! Like one of them vampires suckin' and suckin' 'til there ain't no air! Nothin' to breathe! A NOOSE AROUND MY NECK, HER NECK, THE WHOLE DAMN NEIGHBORHOOD! BUT I GOTTA NOOSE FOR YOU.

DRAY

Go on, fool, 'fore I tell JB to hit you upside your head, again.

SAY WHAT

You can tell him . . .

SAY WHAT suddenly plunges a knife into DRAY's chest. DRAY falls to the ground as DANI looks on.

SAY WHAT

But he's dead, just like you! (*beat*) You ain't so big now.

RED WASH CROSS FADES back to present day lighting. RUBY and MR. JACKSON continue to plant flowers in the courtyard.

RUBY

Drayton was always messin' with Say What.

MR. JACKSON

He was messin' with a lot of folks around these houses, if you ask me.

RUBY

Think I'll put some of these red poppies right by this here sign.

DANI enters pushing TYSON, now in a little larger stroller.

DANI

Tyson's asleep so I thought I'd come down and help. (*beat*) Flowers look much better than that list of yours.

RUBY

Hush!

MR. JACKSON walks over and glances at a sleeping TYSON.

MR. JACKSON

Looks just like Levon.

RUBY stands and crosses to the stroller.

RUBY

Yeah, he's a handsome boy. Took some paperwork, and a fancy lawyer Mrs. Lief knows, to get him back from the ACS.

DANI

But we got him.

MR. JACKSON

How's CeCe doing? Must be real hard on her in that correctional facility.

RUBY makes her way to the sign and starts to dig.

RUBY

She's good. Me and Dani done went up to Bedford to see her last week. Even took little Tyson along. (*beat*) She'll be out soon enough. God willing.

MR. JACKSON

Glad to hear it.

RUBY

Decided we all gonna raise him, watch over him.

MR. JACKSON

If there's anything I can do, well . . .

RUBY

You can help me plant these here flowers. Got to get this place looking like life belongs here, not death. (*beat*) You too, Dani. This here ain't no funeral. This is a celebration for Levon and for them other names that was on my list.

DANI goes to the wagon and grabs some sunflowers.

> DANI

Funny.

> RUBY

Sunflowers is funny?

> DANI

No, it's funny 'cause it's so quiet.

> RUBY

With music blasting now and then from every window you think it's quiet?

> DANI

Don't hear any gunshots. Do you?

SILENCE.

RUBY looks up. She listens. MR. JACKSON does the same.

> MR. JACKSON

Why, she's right. Quiet as a church mouse out here.

> RUBY

No gunshots . . . no heartaches . . . no sirens, no soft words. No mothers weeping for their sons.

> DANI

Just silence.

> RUBY

Well . . . (*beat*) In this moment of silence, we gonna plant these here flowers. Plantin' them for little Tyson. For his future and the future of them other Black boys who's about to be born. See, I'm tired of thinkin' 'bout Black boys dyin'. Time to think about them livin'. (*beat*) Ain't that right, Danielle?

RUBY crosses to DANI and puts her arms around her.

> DANI

That's right, Momma.

> RUBY

Ain't that right, Mr. Jackson?

MR. JACKSON

Right as rain. Rain that will make these flowers even more beautiful.

MR. JACKSON begins to plant some flowers near the bench.

RUBY

Time to think about Black boys livin'. Not dyin'.

MR. JACKSON

Sounds good.

RUBY

Not as good as the sound of silence! (*beat*) Can you hear it?

They all pause to listen.

SILENCE AND MORE SILENCE AND MORE.

LIGHTS FADE TO BLACK.

THE END

The Death of a Black Man (A Walk By).
Erikka James

The Death of a Black Man (A Walk By)

a play by

William Electric Black

PROLOGUE

THERE ARE NO SEATS—THE PERFORMANCE IS IMMERSIVE.

THE AUDIENCE ENTERS—IT'S DARK. ASSORTED CAST MEMBERS, IN STREET CLOTHES, ENTER SAYING, "Book, Backpack, Gun." THERE IS A WOODEN RAISED PLATFORM AT CENTER THE AUDIENCE HAS GATHERED AROUND.

SWEETS WALKER, high school teen, enters and strolls up onto the platform. On the platform sits a locker and a water fountain. He opens the locker and TAKES OUT A GUN. He holds it high!

SWEETS

They was playin' me
YO, you heard what dem bitches was sayin' bout me
I'll shoot a niggah dead, word that's my philosophy
Don't care who he be, ain't feelin I love you
Or you love me
Niggah find his OB in the Huffington Post
On Page Three
Yeah, I'm mad crazy B, like after Hamlet seen a Ghost
And rocked a fuckin tragedy
Ain't gonna be happy
Cause a gun up in da hood brings nothing but calamity

The ENSEMBLE continues to chant.

ENSEMBLE

They was playin' me
YO, you heard what dem bitches was sayin' bout me
I'll shoot a niggah dead, word that's my philosophy
Don't care who he be, ain't feelin I love you
Or you love me
Niggah find his OB in the Huffington Post
On Page Three
Yeah, I'm mad crazy B like after Hamlet seen a Ghost
And rocked a fuckin tragedy
Y'all ain't gonna be happy

ENSEMBLE (CONT'D)

Cause a gun up in da hood brings nothing but calamity
Cause a gun up in da hood brings nothing but calamity
Cause a gun up in da hood brings nothing but calamity

The CHANT continues as PRINCIPAL SMALLS and ASSISTANT PRINCIPAL WELLS enter the platform.

PRINCIPAL

All right people, let's get to class!

ASSISTANT

Let's get to class . . .

PRINCIPAL

CLEAR THE HALLS. LET'S GO!

VOICE 1

Who needs chemistry!

VOICE 2

You going out to lunch?

VOICE 3

Why you taking Spanish if you Spanish?

VOICE 4

I'm Mexican!

VOICE 5

I'm gay!

VOICE 6

I'm gay and Mexican!

VOICE 7

You got a pencil?

VOICE 8

I got History next period?

VOICE 9

My locker's stuck!

VOICE 10

Where's the nurse's office?

VOICE 11

I pulled the fire alarm once!

VOICE 12

I pulled it twice!

VOICE 13

You a freshman?

VOICE 7

Got a pencil?

VOICE 4

I ain't going to gym!

ENSEMBLE

You got the homework? Got the homework? You got the homework? Got the homework . . .

PRINCIPAL

Let's go! Get out of the hallway!

ASSISTANT

Or late slips **will** be handed out.

PRINCIPAL

MOVE IT, PEOPLE! MOVE IT!

SOME of the ENSEMBLE members transform into POLICE OFFICERS.

POLICE/ALL

Move back! This is a crime scene! MOVE BACK NOW! CLEAR THE AREA!

They move the audience back as they fence off a crime scene area around the platform.

1. GOT A GUN

PROJECTED ON A LARGE SCREEN—POLICE CARS, OFFICERS . . .

THE INNER CIRCLE AROUND THE PLATFORM IS DEFINED BY POLICE TAPE AND CONES, AND ACTORS AS POLICE. A SEARCH LIGHT CRISS CROSSES THE CIRCLE.

KID BANG, A STREET DRUMMER, BEATS ON A BUCKET AT THE EDGE OF THE INNER CIRCLE.

THE AUDIENCE SURROUNDS THE INNER CIRCLE DEFINED BY ACTORS IN POLICE UNIFORMS. IN THE MIDDLE OF THE CIRCLE ARE YELLOW MARKERS WHERE SHELL CASINGS ARE SEEN. OTHER OFFICERS STAND NEAR THE MARKERS TAKING PICTURES OF THE CASINGS. FLASH . . . FLASH . . . FLASH.

A POLICE SIREN BLASTS THROUGH THE AIR AS DETECTIVES BEGIN CAN-VASING THE AUDIENCE THAT SURROUNDS THE SCENE. POLICE HAND THEM "HAVE YOU SEEN BOO CHARLES" FLIERS.

DETECTIVE 1
(*to audience*) Did you see anyone? Who had a gun? Sweets Walker? Boo? Which way did they enter the playground?

WITNESS 1
Like, YO, I seen Sweets. Looked like he was trippin and shit. He had a gun and shit. By the fence . . . All I heard was . . . bang-bang, pop-pop!

THE ENSEMBLE HAS BLENDED IN WITH THE AUDIENCE, STANDING AMONG THEM.

WITNESS 2
Bang-bang! Pop-Pop!

DETECTIVE
Sweets had on sneakers.

WITNESS 3
They was nice and shit!

DETECTIVE 3
What did you hear?

ENSEMBLE

(*softly*) BANG-BANG! POP-POP! BANG-BANG! POP-POP!

WITNESS 4

Boo had on a hoodie.

DETECTIVE 3

They were playing basketball?

WITNESS 5

Sweets shot Nina first . . .

WITNESS 1

He was trying to shoot Teela but missed.

WITNESS 2

Bullets flying . . .

ALL WITNESSES

Niggahs dyin . . .

THUGS

BANG-BANG! POP-POP! BANG-BANG! POP-POP! BANG-BANG! POP-POP! BANG-BANG! POP-POP!

DETECTIVE 2

Boo went lookin for Sweets?

DETECTIVE 3

Cause Sweets was after his sister?

THE POLICE CONTINUE TO TAKE PICTURES OF THE CASINGS.

WITNESS 3

After school they all came here.

WITNESS 4

They all had guns?

WITNESS 3

Someone had a gun!

WITNESS 2

Fuck, yeah . . .

WITNESS 5

Shooting each other . . .

WITNESS 1

Killing each other . . .

WITNESS 2

Bullets flying . . .

ALL WITNESSES

Niggahs dyin . . .

THUGS

BANG-BANG! POP-POP! BANG-BANG! POP-POP! BANG-BANG! POP-POP! BANG-BANG! POP-POP! "HE'S GOTTA GUN"—"HELP ME, HELP!" "NO!"—"STOP!"—"OH, GOD!"—"OH, GOD!"

KID BANG POUNDS DRUMS HARDER.

TEENS

RUN MUTHA FUCKER! RUN MUTHA FUCKER!
RUN MUTHA FUCKER! RUN MUTHA FUCKER!
RUN MUTHA FUCKER! RUN MUTHA FUCKER!
RUN MUTHA FUCKER! RUN MUTHA FUCKER!
RUN MUTHA FUCKER! RUN MUTHA FUCKER!
RUN MUTHA FUCKER! RUN MUTHA FUCKER!

POLICE

RUN! RUN! RUN! RUN! RUN! RUN! RUN! RUN!
RUN! RUN! RUN! RUN! RUN! RUN! RUN! RUN!

THE THUGS AND TEENS ENTER THE INNER CIRCLE CARRYING GUNS, BAS-KETBALLS, BACKPACKS. IN A CONTROLLED FRENZY. THEY REACT, AS IF BE-ING VIOLENTLY SHOT DOWN. THEY SPIN, TWIST, POP, FALL . . .

SIRENS BLARE, NOW MIXED WITH HELICOPTER NOISE AS THE THREE CHANTS SWELL ALONG WITH THE PHYSICAL MOVEMENT.

SILENCE—ALL IS STILL.

NO DRUMMING. NO HEARTBEATS.

THE ENSEMBLE DRIFTS BACK, SLOWLY BLENDING INTO THE CROWD.

DETECTIVE 1
(*to audience*) Did you know Boo Charles? Did you know Sweets Walker?

DETECTIVE 2
Who had a gun?

DETECTIVE 3
Five kids are dead! What did you see?

DETECTIVE 4
A lot of people died today . . . (*beat*) Probably over something stupid . . .

QUICK TO BLACK.

IN THE DARKNESS THE ENSEMBLE MOVES THROUGH AUDIENCE WHISPERING:

WHISPERS IN DARKNESS
Something . . . something stupid . . . something . . . something stupid.

PRINCIPAL IN DARKNESS
CLEAR THE HALLS PEOPLE! LET'S GO! HOME ROOM IS ABOUT TO BEGIN.

THE DRUMMING PULSATES AGAIN.

ON THE SCREEN—SHOTS OF NEWS TRUCKS THEN NEWS CLIPPINGS OF INNER-CITY GUN VIOLENCE IN MAJOR CITIES. THE SOUND OF A NEWS THEME IS HEARD.

2. ANOTHER TRAGIC STORY

TONI REED, A NEWS REPORTER, ZIG ZAGS HER WAY THROUGH THE AUDIENCE WITH A CAMERA OPERATOR BEHIND HER. THE GLARING LIGHT FROM THE CAMERA ILLUMINATES THE AUDIENCE.

JUAN GOMEZ, ANOTHER REPORTER, MAKES HIS WAY INTO THE AUDIENCE FOLLOWED BY ANOTHER CAMERA OPERATOR. THIS OPERATOR ALSO HAS A LIGHT MOUNTED ON THE CAMERA.

A THIRD SPEAKER, COUNCILWOMAN RUIZ (OR A LOCAL POLITICIAN), ALSO MAKES HER/HIS WAY INTO THE AUDIENCE WITH A CAMERA OPERATOR. A LIGHT FROM THE CAMERA LIGHTS HER AND THE SURROUNDING AUDIENCE.

TONI REED

Excuse me . . . excuse me. Three-One-Zero News. Excuse me. I need to get through. Sorry . . . sorry . . .

THE POLICE LET HER INTO THE INNER CIRCLE. NOW THERE ARE SEVERAL BODIES VISIBLE UNDER BLOOD-SOAKED SHEETS.

TONI REED

Thank, you. (*beat*) Okay . . . I'm good. Ready?

CAMERA OP

Yeah . . . 3-2-1 . . .

TONI REED

Toni Reed, for 3-1-0 News, here in East Brownsville, but I could just as easily be in Chicago, or D.C., Philadelphia, or Baltimore . . . where innocent people are too often touched by inner city gun violence.

SECOND REPORTER BEGINS OVERLAPPING TONI REED VIA IMPROVISED DIALOGUE.

(*beat*) This afternoon, five people were killed and a several more injured when gunfire erupted right here in this neighborhood playground. A place where teens normally spend their time playing basketball, riding bikes, or jumping rope.

TEELA CHARLES AND A TEEN EMERGE FROM THEIR BLOODY SHEETS. THEY PLAY SOME BALL. ANOTHER TEEN BEGINS JUMPING ROPE TO "MISS MARY MACK." THE SHEET ENLARGES, BECOMES A SCRIM, LIGHTING TEENS BEHIND IT.

TEENS BEHIND SCRIM

(*jumping rope*) MISS MARY MACK, MACK, MACK . . . ALL DRESSED IN
BLACK, BLACK, BLACK . . . WITH SILVER BULLETS UP AND DOWN
HER BACK, BACK, BACK

TONI REED

A fight that began earlier this morning in the hallways of Central High tragically
made its way to the streets of this nearby community. The first shooting, around
noon, left one teenager dead.

Then several hours later four more teens lost their lives including Boo Charles, the
older brother of Teela Charles, who came to the park looking for the suspect in the
first shooting.

JUAN GOMEZ

(*in Spanish*) An 18-year-old basketball star, Teela Charles, was gunned down in a
hail of bullets when a feud between her brother and Sweets Walker turned deadly.

(*in Spanish*) All of the Central High teenagers were pronounced dead at the scene,
right here on the basketball court where many of these teens would come to hang
out. Now it's a crime scene.

*A COUNCILMEMBER BEGINS TO SPEAK/IMPROVISE, OVERLAPPING THE
OTHERS.*

JUAN GOMEZ (CONT'D)

(*in Spanish*) Police continue to canvas the area for witnesses to see if any others
were involved but no arrests have been made. Law enforcement officials with close
ties to the investigation believe there is a link between the first shooting that took
place at noon in this very same neighborhood. I'm Juan Gomez, and this is
News50.

REVEREND WHITLOCK ENTERS.

REVEREND WHITLOCK

The recent deaths of these young people constantly remind us that the real issue is
guns. Here in East Brownsville gun-shots have become the norm. How did we let
this happen? Where do these kids get these guns? Why are guns in our homes, our
apartments, our schools, our streets? (*beat*)

REVEREND WHITLOCK (CONT'D)

I don't hear about shootings on Park Avenue or Morningside Heights up around Columbia University. Are Asian kids shooting each other in Chinatown? Do you see news trucks in Greenwich Village, by NYU? Where there's money, jobs, and opportunity do you find this? (*beat*) This mother, Rhonda Charles, lost her daughter today. She said goodbye to her in the morning and that's the last time she would see her child alive. Can you imagine that happening to you? Well, you should, because her child, all of these children who died today belong to all of us, not just their parents. Children are dead because we failed to keep them safe. Our community failed them. (beat) So now, as we stand here with Rhonda Charles, let us pray for her and the loss of her daughter, her son and for the other children.

REVEREND WHITLOCK PLACES HIS HAND TOGETHER

Pray with me, Reverend Whitlock, that we shall never let another child die from gun violence. (*beat*) Can I get an Amen!

ALL

AMEN!!!

LIGHTS FADE.

3. AMAZING

ENSEMBLE BEGINS TO SING "AMAZING GRACE." OTHER ENSEMBLE MEMBERS, ALSO SINGING, EMERGE WITH CANDLES, PHOTOS OF TEELA, AND FLOWERS.

THEY HAND THE CANDLES, PHOTOS, AND FLOWERS TO AUDIENCE MEMBERS AS THEY SAY "COME TO THE MEMORIAL"—"COME WITH US." THEN LOCK ARMS AND MOVE TOWARDS THE SCAFFOLDING.

A PLATFORM IS WHEELED IN PLACE, IN FRONT OF THE SCAFFOLDING STEPS, AS IF THEY ARE STEPS TO A BUILDING. THE STEPS ARE ALREADY DECORATED WITH CANDLES, FLOWERS AND CARDS.

ON SCREEN—WE SEE A SIMILAR GATHERING OF PEOPLE WITH CANDLES.

WHITLOCK/ENSEMBLE SING

Amazing grace how sweet the sound that saved a wretch like me
I once was lost but now am found, was blind but now I see . . .

WHITLOCK/ENSEMBLE

'Twas grace that taught my heart to fear and grace my fears relieved
How precious did that grace appear the hour I first believed
(*beat*)
Through many dangers, toils and snares I have already come
'Tis Grace has brought me safe thus far and Grace will lead me home
(*beat*)
The Lord has promised good to me, His word my hope secures
He will my shield and portion be as long as life endures
   (*beat*)
Yet, when this flesh and heart shall fail and mortal life shall cease
I shall possess within the veil a joy of life and peace
(*beat*)
When we've been there ten thousand years bright shining as the sun
We've no less days to sing God's praise then when we've first begun
(*beat*)
Amazing grace how sweet the sound that saved a wretch like me
I once was lost but now am found was blind but now I see . . .

ENSEMBLE GATHERS THE CANDLES BACK FROM AUDIENCE.

RHONDA

My two babies were alive 24 hours ago. Heard Teela and Boo carrying on like they always do every morning 'fore they head off to Central High. (*beat*) That was the last time I seen Teela, and Boo . . . alive. The very last time. Now I gotta bury both of my children.

LIGHTS FADE.

WINDOW SCENE A

BOO enters. He calls up to TEELA.

BOO

YO, Teela . . . come on! We gonna be late! First period be starting soon.

TEELA sticks her head out of the window.

TEELA

Quit all that damn yelling!

BOO

Well get your ass on up. Momma told me to wake you. Don't you got to read some damn poem today?

TEELA

Yeah, Mr. Todd got us reading and writing damn poems!

BOO

YOU KNOW HOW TO READ AND WRITE?

TEELA throws a book or two at him from the window.

TEELA

READ THIS!

BOO

I'm ah keep yelling 'til you come down!

NINA, MONIQUE, and JASMINE enter.

NINA

Where's your sister?

BOO

Upstairs sleeping.

NINA

TEELA . . . COME ON!

MONIQUE

Yeah, bitch, gonna make me miss free breakfast!

JASMINE

You eat that stuff? It's nasty!

MONIQUE

Your mother's nasty!

JASMINE

Well, your mother's a ho!

BOO

Damn y'all, just chill. Help me get Teela out of the house.

NINA

I know how . . . (*beat*) YO, TEELA . . . Tyson is looking for you. He wants to talk to you and shit!

BOO

Which knucklehead is Tyson?

JASMINE

The cute one!

MONIQUE

For real!

BOO

Who's that other fool always trying to get with Teela?

NINA

You mean, Sweets? That niggah's crazy. Ain't nobody wanna go out with him.

BOO

YO, TEELA!!! COME ON!

TEELA

I'M COMIN! YOU SEEN MY POETRY BOOK?

BOO

You threw it at me!

TEELA

Oh . . . right.

BOO

Here . . . give this to Teela. (*beat*) I wrote her a poem for Mr. Todd!

BOO hands NINA the book, then exits.

NINA

(*with a smile*) Bye Boo . . .

JASMINE

I think Boo's gay.

MONIQUE

Your mother's gay! And so are you!

JASMINE

Bitch, eat me and find out!

NINA

You know what I wanna eat, some Mickey Dee's. Who got some cash?

LIGHTS FADE ON THE GIRLS. BLACKNESS, THEN CHANTING, DRUMMING, WHISTLES, AND SIRENS ARE HEARD OFF STAGE. "STOP THE BULLETS NOW"

STOP THE BULLETS

THE ENSEMBLE ENTERS WITH BANNERS, POSTERS, PHOTOS, AND T-SHIRTS. THE T-SHIRTS, POSTERS, AND BANNERS ARE HANDED OUT TO AUDIENCE MEMBERS.

THE PLATORM IS WHEELED OUT. RALLY MEMBERS STAND ATOP THE PLAT-FORM CHANTING WITH THE OTHERS.

ENSEMBLE

(*chanting*) BULLETS FLYING, MOTHERS CRYING
WHY WE DYING, GOTTA BE SURVIVING
STOP THE MADNESS, STOP THE SADNESS
STOP THE MADNESS, STOP THE SADNESS

CHANTING fades.

SPEAKER 1

(*sings*) A 7-year-old boy who was watching fireworks with
his father was among several killed during a 4th of July
weekend in Chicago.

ENSEMBLE CHANTS AGAIN . . .

ENSEMBLE

STOP THE MADNESS, STOP THE SADNESS!

SPEAKER 2

(*sings*) A 16-year-old boy and a 15-year-old girl were shot
around 12:10 AM, Sunday, in the 1400 block of North
Hudson in the old town neighborhood.

ENSEMBLE

STOP THE MADNESS, STOP THE SADNESS!
STOP . . . STOP . . . STOP . . . STOP

SPEAKER 3

(*sings*) An annual firework display, along Lake Michigan,
ended when a boy was shot in the back of the head
when he was leaving the celebration to meet his
mother.

ENSEMBLE

STOP THE MADNESS, STOP THE SADNESS!
STOP . . . STOP . . . STOP . . . STOP

SPEAKER 4

(*sings*) A 12-year-old Hempstead, Long Island girl was
struck in the head by a bullet fired from outside
of her home while she was eating dinner.

SPEAKER 5

(*sings*) Three people were killed and 10 others wounded
in a wave of grisly unrelated shootings across
Philadelphia Saturday night!

ENSEMBLE

STOP THE MADNESS, STOP THE SADNESS!
STOP . . . STOP . . . STOP . . . STOP

RHONDA CHARLES TAKES THE STAGE WITH REVEREND WHITLOCK.

RHONDA/ENSEMBLE

MY BOY IS DEAD, MY GIRL IS DEAD
ONE SHOT IN THE BACK
ONE IN HER HEAD
MY BOY IS DEAD, MY GIRL IS DEAD
JUST WAITIN NOW TO BURY THEM
WAITING FOR DEATH'S BED
MY BOY IS DEAD, MY GIRL IS DEAD
ONE SHOT IN THE BACK
ONE IN HER HEAD

RHONDA/ENSEMBLE (CONT'D)
MY BOY IS DEAD, MY GIRL IS DEAD
JUST WAITIN NOW TO BURY THEM
WAITING FOR DEATH'S BED

REVEREND WHITLOCK

The Lord is my shepherd; I shall not want.

He maketh me to lie down in green pastures:

He leadeth me beside the still waters.

He restoreth my soul: He leadeth me in the

paths of righteousness for his name's sake.

Yea, though I walk through the valley of the shadow of death,

I will fear no evil: for thou art with me;

thy rod and thy staff they comfort me.

Thou preparest a table before me in the presence of mine enemies:

thou anointest my head with oil; my cup runneth over.

Surely goodness and mercy shall follow me all

the days of my life: and I will dwell in the house of the Lord forever

LIGHTS FADE.

WATER COOLER SCENE A

SWEETS

You tryin to play me?

TEELA

Get the fuck off me, Sweets. We're over!

SWEETS

Bitch! Your life will be over if you keep seein Tyson.

TEELA

Man, you'd better step the fuck off!

MONIQUE

Yeah, what's up with you?

NINA

Your shit is weak that's why Teela's hangin with Tyson.

SWEETS grabs TEELA by the neck.

SWEETS

You still gonna see Tyson? Huh, Bitch?

TEELA

Your mother's a bitch!

SWEETS

What did you . . .

BOO

YO, fool! You must wanna die! (*beat*) Now get your fuckin' hands off my sister!

SWEETS

My bad playa! No need to get Bad Boy and shit on me.

SWEETS lets TEELA go.

TEELA

Put your hands on me again and I'll fuckin shoot ya.

MR. TODD appears.

MR. TODD

Is everything all right, here?

SWEETS

It's all good. (*beat*) Just getting some water.

MR. TODD

After a visit to the principal's office, you can have all the water you want.

SWEETS

Why we got to see the principal?

BOO

Didn't you hear? We got perfect scores on our SATs.

They exit laughing.

MR. TODD

Ladies?

MONIQUE

What we do?

NINA

Yeah, why you got to be hating on us?

MR. TODD

Cause you're just asking for trouble with those two clowns.

TEELA

If they was white boys would you call them clowns?

TODD

Don't pull the race card on me, Teela.

TEELA

What, you think you're down because you read us poems by Langston Hughes or quote lines from The Autobiography Of Malcolm X.

NINA

You trippin, Mr. Todd!

MONIQUE

Yeah . . . no one got time to write poems when niggahs be runnin around these halls with guns.

JASMINE

A poem don't stop no bullets.

TEELA

For real . . .

The girls exit the platform.

LIGHTS FADE.

POEM 1

STUDENT

Yeah . . . I got my poem . . . right here. Quiet fool, where's your poem.
(*reads*) Lights fade, Lights go out
But from my window I can still
See the blinking, the twinkling, the shining

STUDENT (CONT'D)

I can see the police light tower

That don't ever fade

That don't ever go away

They say it's a good thing . . .

It's like when you keep the lights on . . .

When the lights on . . . people feel safe

Me? Do I feel safe?

Momma ask me that

The police ask me that . . .

Mr. Todd . . . Reverend Whitlock . . .

The Mayor . . . News reporters . . . they ask, and ask, and ask

I think it's a dumb question

Why do they have to ask me that

Why do they?

Shouldn't we be safe in the dark?

In the street?

At school?

At home?

In the playground?

At the corner store?

SAFE ANYWHERE IN THE WHOLE DAMN WORLD?

(*beat*) Sorry, I cursed . . .

But this way of living . . .

The light from the police tower

That ain't no real light, it's fake

That's why it ain't safe

That's why people are scared

Am I scared . . . Yeah . . . I guess I am

Who ain't afraid of the dark

When the lights go out, when the lights fade . . .

LIGHTS FADE.

WALKING DOWN THE STREET

VOICE

I'm walking down the street and I see . . .

VOICE

I see some Black kids . . .

VOICE

I see a white girl . . .

VOICE

And I'm thinking . . .

VOICE

Does she say I hate those Black kids . . .

VOICE

Does she see me, or my color?

VOICE

What does she see when she looks at us . . .

VOICE

What does she think?

VOICE

Should I keep my phone in my bag?

VOICE

Does she think we're gonna take her shit?

VOICE

They hate me . . .

VOICE

She's afraid of me . . .

VOICE

It's the newspapers . . .

VOICE

The TV . . .

VOICE

My parents, they never really had any Black friends.

VOICE

I never had a white friend . . .

VOICE

What's that bitch staring at!

VOICE

Are they staring at me?

VOICE

I'll fuck her up . . .

VOICE

I'll stare back . . . I'll look away.

VOICE

She thinks we're animals . . .

VOICE

They think, I think they don't exist.

VOICE

Why does she think that?

VOICE

Her parents? Grandparents?

VOICE

Fuck her . . .

VOICE

They hate me, I hate them.

VOICE

I hate that bitch, hate all of them!

ALL VOICES

HATE! HATE! HATE! HATE! HATE! HATE! HATE! HATE! HATE!

VOICE

I love them . . . maybe?

VOICE

Maybe she's different . . .

VOICE

You crazy?

VOICE

Am I crazy?

VOICE

If she takes out her phone . . .

VOICE

If I take out my phone . . .

ALL VOICES

Take out your phone, bitch! Take out your phone, bitch! TAKE OUT YOUR PHONE, BITCH! BITCH! BITCH! BITCH!!!

VOICE

(*shouts*) SO, I TOOK IT OUT . . .

VOICE

And nothing happened . . .

VOICE

Nothing happened . . .

VOICE

See?

VOICE

And nothing happened.

VOICE

So, it wasn't on the news or on the radio . . .

VOICE

And no one knew about the story . . . or heard about the time a white girl walked by some Black girls . . .

ALL VOICES

And nothing happened.

LIGHTS FADE.

Death of a Black Man (A Walk By)—police ask crowd if they know who did it.
Photo by Remy S.

Reverend Whitlock and Rhonda Charles at her son's funeral.
Photo by Remy S.

STREET SCENE 1

BOO

I tell you I'm gonna fuck Sweets up.

JEROME

Over Nina? Ain't worth it?

BOO

Niggahs on crack and shit.

JEROME

Let the police fuck him up.

BOO

He almost killed Teela.

JEROME

Still ain't worth it?

BOO

You tellin' me my sister ain't worth it?

JEROME

I'm just sayin if you do some mad crazy shit your life is over. You wanna go to the joint for that niggah?

BOO

You finish preachin, Reverend Whitlock?

JEROME

Yeah . . . I'm finished.

BOO

Cool . . . now go get me that piece like I asked you to.

JEROME

Just think you wrong, man.

BOO

Then don't think. Get me that fuckin gun and meet me over by the court. You feel me?

JEROME

Yeah . . . I feel you.

LIGHTS FADE.
SIRENS—POLICE CHATTER.

CHILDREN'S SONG

The TEEN girls enter playground with McDonald's bags, backpacks, etc. They CHANT, CLAP, AND DANCE PERFORMING A SHADOW SHOW BEHIND A SCRIM while they sing.

TEENS

(*sing*) Miss Mary Mack, Mack, Mack
All dressed in black, black, black
With silver bullets, bullets, bullets
All down her back, back, back.
She asked her kids, kids, kids
Where can he be, be, be
The naughty boy, boy, boy
Who shot at me, me, me
They ran so fast, fast, fast
To tell the cops, cops, cops
So that the shootings, shootings, shootings
Would finally stop, stop, stop
They told the cops, cops, cops
To look and see, see, see
Who had the gun, gun, gun . . .
That shot at me, me, me

TEENS

(*sing*) They put the boy, boy, boy
Inside a cell, cell, cell
Cause when you're bad, bad, bad . . .
Things don't end well, well, well
Cause when you're bad, bad, bad
Things don't end well . . .

LIGHTS FADE ON SCRIM.

WATER COOLER SCENE 2

TEELA

Homeroom's gonna be over soon. Better get goin'.

JASMINE

You just wanna hook up with Tyson.

MONIQUE

Yeah, bitch . . . be straight with us.

NINA

We always straight with you.

TEELA

Alright, if I tell y'all something you won't say nothing to nobody?

NINA

Cross my heart and hope to get booty implants.

TEELA

Alright . . . (*beat*) I like Taylor Swift!

TEEN GIRLS

OH, TIGHT!

GIRLS BREAK OUT into a Taylor Swift song (WITH SWIFT ATTIRE).

TEEN GIRLS

Cause baby, now we've got bad blood
You know it used to be mad love
So, take a look what you've done
Cause baby, now we got bad blood . . .

ENSEMBLE JOINS THEM IN BLACKNESS.

ENSEMBLE

Cause baby, now we've got bad blood
You know it used to be mad love
So, take a look what you've done
Cause baby, now we got bad blood . . .

SINGING FADES . . .

LIGHTS FADE.

POEM 2

A GIRL takes out her poem and reads.

GIRL

Okay . . . here's my poem, Mr. Todd. (*beat*) I call it Black/white . . .
(*reads*) My parents say Beyonce is black/white
Like, so they think she's alright?
Is that because she's like light?
But that doesn't seem really right
So, I screamed at my parents
BEYONCE IS NOT BLACK/WHITE!
(*beat*) Suddenly they got quiet, real polite
They questioned me,
Very worried about my sight
So, they began to show me pictures
Of her all day, and through the night
Like, were they right?
(*beat*) My parents say Beyonce IS black/white
Like, I tried to tell them different
But it gave them such a terrible fright
Now I find myself deeply troubled
When I think of their plight
How they need to see everything,
Anything, not in color . . .
But in black/white

LIGHTS FADE.

THE SHOOTING OF NINA

THE FOUR GIRLS MOVE THROUGH THE CROWD USING A SECTION OF A PLAYGROUND FENCE ON WHEELS. TEELA AND NINA MOVE WITH ONE FENCE. NINA AND JASMINE MOVE WITH ANOTHER. SWEETS AND JEROME MOVE WITH ANOTHER FENCE.

*ENSEMBLE MEMBERS HELP GUIDE THE FENCES THROUGH THE AUDIENCE.

TEELA

Jasmine?

JASMINE

Quiet, Sweets got a damn gun! He's looking for you, Teela.

ENSEMBLE

BANG-BANG! POP-POP! BANG-BANG! POP-POP!

NINA

Let's get back to school!

TEELA

You go! He's after me!

MONIQUE

I'm calling the police, Sweets!

SWEETS

GO AHEAD! YOU BE DEAD BEFORE THEY GET HERE!

ENSEMBLE

BANG-BANG! POP-POP! BANG-BANG! POP-POP!
BANG-BANG! POP-POP! BANG-BANG! POP-POP!

NINA

I'm scared! Why did we go out for lunch?

TEELA

Cause the school lunch <u>sucks</u>!

SWEETS

YOU ALWAYS BE PLAYIN ME, TEELA!

ENSEMBLE

They was playin' me . . .

ENSEMBLE

YO, you heard what dem bitches
Was sayin' bout me

SWEETS

NOT NO MORE!

NINA

WE GOTTA RUN!

ENSEMBLE

RUN MUTHERFUCKER, RUN!

SWEETS

You was playin' me
YO, I heard what you bitches
Was sayin' bout me

MONIQUE

WE GONNA RUN???

ENSEMBLE

RUN MUTHERFUCKER, RUN!

SWEETS

I'll shoot all you dead, word that's my philosophy
Don't care who it be . . . ain't feelin I love you
Or you love me

JASMINE

LET'S RUN!

NINA

I'M SCARED!

TEELA

RUN! RUN! RUN!

SWEETS

Gonna find your OB
In the Huffington Post
On Page Three

MONIQUE

RUN! RUN! RUN!

SWEETS

Yeah, I'm mad crazy B
Like after Hamlet seen a ghost
And rocked a fuckin tragedy

                    ENSEMBLE
RUN! RUN! RUN!

                    SWEETS

Y'all ain't gonna be happy
Cause a gun up in da hood
Brings nothing but calamity

                    NINA

NO!

                    SWEETS

Cause a gun up in da hood
Brings nothing but calamity

                    NINA

NO!

                    SWEETS

Cause a gun up in da hood
Brings nothing but . . .

SWEETS SHOOTS NINA . . . FLASH OF LIGHT.

                    ENSEMBLE

BANG-BANG!

NINA SLUMPS AGAINST THE FENCE.

LIGHTS FADE . . . SIRENS.

ALL STUDENTS

ANNOUNCEMENT 1

(*IN DARKNESS*) ALL STUDENTS, ALL STUDENTS WILL NOW LEAVE
THEIR 5TH PERIOD CLASSES AND REPORT TO THE AUDITORIUM.
PLEASE GO TO THE AUDITORIUM IMMEDIATELY.

LIGHTS UP.

HALLWAY SCENE

PRINCIPAL

LET'S GO PEOPLE! LET'S GO!

ASSISTANT

CLEAR THE HALLS!

ENSEMBLE BEGINS TO CHANT "Book, Backpack, Gun."

ANNOUNCEMENT 2

PRINCIPAL

Quiet down, people. Quiet! Please, we need your attention. Reverend Whitlock has joined us to help us heal in this moment of tragedy.

STUDENTS react.

PRINCIPAL

You see . . . we have received word from the local authorities that one of your classmates was killed not too long ago.

ENSEMBLE

WHO? WHO GOT KILLED? WHO DID IT?

TEELA

It was Sweets! He was looking for me, but shot Nina instead.

VOICE

That's fucked up!

VOICE

That's business!

TEELA

Fuck your business!

VOICE

FUCK YOU, TOO!

PUSHING AND SHOVING STARTS.

ASSISTANT

HEY! HEY! THAT'S ENOUGH!

PRINCIPAL

HOLD ON! THIS IS ABOUT NINA, NOT ABOUT YOU! NOW
REVEREND WHITLOCK IS HERE WITH US, SHOW SOME RESPECT.

REVEREND WHITLOCK

A lot of you know me, seen me around. I've been there for you, your families and
now, now I am here for you in your time of sorrow. So, let's not act a fool. Let us
bow our heads and say a prayer for Nina Perez. For her and her family. Our
Father, who art in heaven . . .

LIGHTS FADE.

ANNOUNCEMENT 3

IN THE DARKNESS.

PRINCIPAL

ALL STUDENTS WILL HEAD HOME DIRECTLY AFTER SCHOOL. I
REPEAT, ALL STUDENTS WILL HEAD HOME IMMEDIATELY AFTER
SCHOOL. ALL AFTERSCHOOL ACTIVITIES AND CLUBS HAVE BEEN
CANCELED DUE TO THE RECENT EVENTS. GRIEF COUNSELORS
WILL BE ON HAND ALL DAY TOMORROW TO HELP ANY STUDENT
WHO WOULD LIKE TO TALK ABOUT THE RECENT PASSING OF
ONE OF OUR OWN.

FACULTY ROOM

MR. TODD, PRINCIPAL, AND ASSISTANT PRINCIPAL STAND ON CUBES.

PRINCIPAL

Go ahead, Mr. Todd . . . tell Assistant Principal Johnson what you heard.

MR. TODD

I heard what you heard.

ASSISTANT

Sweets Walker shot Nina.

PRINCIPAL

And there's more, right?

MR. TODD

There's always more.

ASSISTANT

Like tests . . . there's always more testing that needs to be done.

MR. TODD

And evaluations. Don't forget those.

PRINCIPAL

Boo Charles is gonna take care of Sweets.

ASSISTANT

Boo . . . he's such a nice kid.

MR. TODD

So was Nina. Now she's a dead kid. One bullet in the back, one in the head.

VOICES

My boy is dead, my girl is dead
One shot in the back, one shot in the head.

MR. TODD

Shouldn't we do something?

PRINCIPAL

What should we do? Shoot them?

MR. TODD

Shoot them?

ASSISTANT

Test them? There's always more testing that needs to be done.

VOICES

Miss Mary Mack, Mack, Mack . . .
All dressed in black, black, black
With silver bullets, bullets, bullets
All down her back, back, back . . .

LIGHTS FADE.

WINDOW 2

JEROME calls up to the window. BOO appears at the window.

JEROME

YO, BOO!

BOO FROM WINDOW

WHAT?

JEROME

I GOT SOMETHING FOR YOU.

BOO FROM WINDOW

YOU GOT IT?

JEROME

MY BOY ROGER GOT IT!

BOO FROM WINDOW

WHERE HE AT?

ROGER appears.

ROGER

YO, LETS MAKE THIS SHIT HAPPEN QUICK! (*beat*) WHERE IS HE?

BOO FROM WINDOW

UP HERE!

ROGER

YOU WANT THIS SHIT OR NOT?

BOO FROM WINDOW

FUCK YEAH!

ROGER

LET'S GO, HOMIE! I GOT PLACES TO GO PEOPLE TO SEE . . . LOTS
OF WOMEN WHO WANT TO BE LOVED BY ME.

BOO FROM WINDOW

HOLD UP! I'LL BE RIGHT DOWN.

ROGER

Is he for real?

JEROME

Niggah tried to shoot his sister.

ROGER

Sweets? I heard.

NINA, MONIQUE, TEELA, and JASMINE appear in the audience.

NINA

WE GOTTA RUN!

MONIQUE

WE GONNA RUN?

JASMINE

LET'S RUN!

NINA

I'M SCARED!

TEELA

RUN! RUN! RUN!

VOICES

RUN! RUN! RUN! RUN! RUN! RUN! RUN!

BOO

And soon Sweets is gonna die!

BOO appears and takes the gun from ROGER.

LIGHTS FADE.

THE ENSEMBLE ENTERS WITH CANDLES—THEY FORM A CIRCLE LOOKING OUT TO AUDIENCE.

IN MY NEIGHBORHOOD

VOICE

In my neighborhood someone gets shot every day.

ENSEMBLE

BULLETS FLYING, MOTHERS CRYING

VOICE

Twice a day . . .

VOICE

People have guns . . .

VOICE

People die . . . people get shot.

VOICE

In the head, in the back, in the stomach . . .

VOICE

They bleed . . .

VOICE

They die . . .

VOICE

We leave candles . . .

VOICE

We buy candles and cards . . .

VOICE

We leave cards . . .

VOICE

They don't come back . . .

VOICE

We leave flowers and cards . . .

VOICE

I hate them . . .

VOICE

The guns?

VOICE

I hate the flowers, the fuckin cards, the candles . . .

VOICE

In my neighborhood there is a machine that can detect when a gun has been fired.

ENSEMBLE

BANG!

VOICE

In my neighborhood there is a tower with a camera that looks for people who fire guns.

ENSEMBLE

POP-POP!

VOICE

In my neighborhood there is a metal detector at Central High to find out if I am carrying a gun.

VOICE

But if I wanna gun . . .

VOICE

If I wanna kill somebody . . .

VOICE

Is there really anything?

VOICE

There's nothing . . .

VOICE

You can really . . .

VOICE

Nothing . . .

VOICE

You can . . .

VOICE

Really . . .

VOICE

DO!

VOICES

CAN YOU DO ANYTHING?

LIGHTS FADE.

POEM 3

ENSEMBLE CHANTS "Book, Backpack, Gun." MR. TODD stands on the platform. He takes out a poem.

TODD

Excuse me, class . . . hello? Ah . . . someone left this poem on my desk but there's no name. Anyone? No?
(*reads poem*)
Like ice, my heart is cold
So, I disrespect you, young and old
Black or white, yellow, brown
If I got no piece of the dream
Tear the muthafucker down . . .
(*beat*)
Whoever wrote this got an "A." What's that, your brother Boo wrote it? Tell him, tell Boo . . . I feel his poem.

LIGHTS FADE.

ANNOUNCEMENT

PRINCIPAL

(*IN DARKNESS*) ALL AFTERSCHOOL PROGRAMS HAVE BEEN CANCELED. THE CENTRAL HIGH BOYS BASKETBALL GAME HAS BEEN POSTPONED UNTIL NEXT WEEK.

LIGHTS UP.

THE DEATH OF A BLACK MAN

THREE FENCES/SECTIONS ON WHEELS ARE ROLLED OUT ALONG WITH THE BASKETBALL HOOP. THE THREE SECTIONS OF FENCE MOVE IN AND AROUND THE AUDIENCE. BOO AND JEROME ARE BEHINED ONE SECTION OF FENCE. SWEETS IS BEHIND ANOTHER SECTION WITH JASMINE. TEELA AND MONIQUE ARE BEHIND ANOTHER SECTION OF FENCE. THE ENSEMBLE STANDS/MOVES ALONG WITH THE BASKETBALL NET/HOOP.

JEROME

Heard Sweets was here in the playground.

BOO

Okay, your ass can go! GO ON NIGGAH!

JEROME exits into/through AUDIENCE.

SWEETS

YO, bitch . . . where they at?

SWEETS grabs JASMINE.

JASMINE

Let me go! I don't know nothing.

SWEETS puts a gun to her head.

JASMINE

Just that the cops are looking for you. For what you did to Nina!

SWEETS

You was there, weren't you?

JASMINE

I didn't see nothing.

SWEETS

You were there with Teela. You always running with her!

JASMINE

I . . . I wasn't! I SWEAR!

TEELA and MONIQUE move a section of fence, not too distant from SWEETS and BOO.

TEELA

BOO? BOO? MAN, FORGET THAT NIGGAH, SWEETS. BOO? YOU
HEAR ME?

MONIQUE

Quiet! You want Sweets to find us?

TEELA

Don't want him to find Boo.

SWEETS

COME ON, BOO! YOU AFRAID?

BOO

OF YOUR MOMMA? 'CAUSE SHE ONE UGLY HO!

TEELA

Did you get it?

MONIQUE

Yeah . . . took it from my brother.

MONIQUE hands a GUN to TEELA.

MONIQUE

BANG-BANG, POP-POP?

TEELA

BANG-BANG! FUCKIN' POP-POP!

SWEETS

BANG-BANG!

BOO

FUCKIN POP-POP!

JEROME

POP-POP?

TEELA

FUCKIN POP-POP!

SWEETS

FUCKIN POP-POP!

BOO

FUCKING POP-POP!

TEELA

FUCKIN POP-POP!

ENSEMBLE

POP-POP! POP-POP! FUCKIN POP-POP! POP-POP!
POP-POP! POP-POP! FUCKIN POP-POP! POP-POP!
POP-POP! POP-POP! FUCKIN POP-POP! POP-POP!
POP-POP! POP-POP! FUCKIN POP-POP! POP-POP!

THE FENCES MOVE CLOSER AND CLOSER AS TEELA, SWEETS, AND BOO

EXCHANGE STYLIZED GUNFIRE. LIGHTS FLASH AND DRUMBEATS POUND AS THE CHANTING AND GUNFIRE EXCHANGE COMES TO A DRAMATIC CLIMB, AND THEN . . . QUIET.

LIGHTS FADE.

LIGHTS UP.

THE FUNERAL

A COFFIN is wheeled in. The ENSEMBLE greets the audience handing them each a single rose, a large photo of BOO CHARLES is placed next to the coffin. SEATS, CHURCH PEWS, are also wheeled in for the audience members to briefly sit. REVEREND WHITLOCK enters.

REVEREND WHITLOCK

Boo Charles is the last child to be buried. We lost so many one week ago . . . Nina Perez, Monique James, Jasmine Weeks, Steven "Sweets" Walker, and Bernard "Boo" Charles. Let us pray . . .

WHITLOCK says a prayer, then . . .

REVEREND WHITLOCK

Principal Davis would like to say a few, brief words.

PRINCIPAL DAVIS enters.

PRINCIPAL

As a principal, you hope that each and every student who strolls down your school hallways has a chance to become anything they want. You imagine them graduating, then heading off to college, a good career, having a family . . . you never imagine this . . . bullets flying, mothers crying . . . You never imagine high schoolers turning a children's song into a song about death . . .

NINA, JASMINE, TEELA, MONIQUE APPEAR IN SHADOW . . . THEY SING "MISS MARY MACK, MACK, MACK . . . (2X)

TEEN GIRLS

(*sing*) Miss Mary Mack, Mack, Mack . . .
All dressed in black, black, black

TEEN GIRLS (CONT'D)

With silver bullets, bullets, bullets
All down her back, back, back . . .

PRINCIPAL

You never imagine the guns, the gangs, the graves they go to so early in their lives.
You imagine something beautiful for them, not something so dark, so hopeless.

REVEREND WHITLOCK

All rise please . . .

WHITLOCK SINGS "NEARER MY GOD TO THEE" AS THE AUDIENCE STANDS.
THE PEWS/SEATS ARE WHEELED OUT ALONG WITH THE PLATFORM. THE
COFFIN IS NOW PLACED ON A GURNEY AND MOVED INTO THE MIDDLE OF
THE AUDIENCE.

THE SCENE TRANSFORMS INTO . . .

THE CEMETERY

THE ENSEMBLE RAISES THEIR UMBRELLAS AS RAIN IS HEARD.

RHONDA CHARLES STANDS NEAR THE COFFIN AND READS A NOTE.

UMBRELLAS COVER AUDIENCE MEMBERS. ENSEMBLE MEMBERS WHISPER
"DID YOU KNOW BOO CHARLES?"—"DID YOU KNOW THE OTHERS?"

RHONDA

Reverend Whitlock said it might be easier for me if I wrote something first, but all
I got to say is already inside of me. Inside of my heart. (*beat*) A heart that weeps for
Boo, for my Teela . . . them others, y'all that come out here to the cemetery. But I
especially cry for my Bernard 'cause he was good. He worked hard at school,
teachers liked him . . .

VOICES

He's such a sweet boy.

RHONDA

. . . Was always looking after his sister. It was looking after her that got him shot.
He was trying to protect her but who was out here trying to protect him? To
rescue him? Which one of us came running to put out the fire. (*beat*) When there's
a fire the alarm rings, the firemen come . . . they try with all their strength God
gives them to put out that fire! All their strength. Sometimes the fire wins out. But

RHONDA (CONT'D)

they did not leave the house to burn down. We left the house. We just watch, like today, we stand in the rain and just watch. Hoping, praying that it will just go away?

VOICES

BULLETS, BULLETS GO AWAY
COME AGAIN ANOTHER DAY
LITTLE CHILDREN WANT TO PLAY

RHONDA

Will it just go away? Ask Boo, and my Teela . . . ask them if it will go away.

VOICES

WILL IT GO AWAY? WILL IT GO AWAY?
WILL IT GO AWAY?

RHONDA

I don't think so.

VOICES

BULLETS, BULLETS GO AWAY
COME AGAIN ANOTHER DAY
LITTLE CHILDREN WANT TO PLAY
(LOUDER) BULLETS, BULLETS GO AWAY
COME AGAIN ANOTHER DAY
LITTLE CHILDREN WANT TO PLAY

THE ENSEMBLE CONTINUES TO CHANT AS THEY USHER THE AUDIENCE TO EACH PLACE THEIR ROSE ON TOP OF THE COFFIN. ONCE THE ROSES HAVE BEEN PLACED THE ENSEMBLE EXITS, STILL CHANTING, LEAVING THE AUDIENCE STANDING AROUND THE COFFIN FOR A MINUTE, FIVE MINUTES, TEN . . . UNTIL THEY DECIDE TO EXIT.

A SPOTLIGHT REMAINS ON THE COFFIN.

THE SOUND OF RAIN SWELLS.

THE END

THEATER FOR THE NEW CITY

presents **Crystal Field Executive Director**

An Electric Black Experience

THE FACULTY ROOM

A Gunplays Series

WRITTEN & DIRECTED BY WILLIAM ELECTRIC BLACK

APRIL 13 TO 30, 2017

THEATER FOR THE NEW CITY
155 FIRST AVE. (AT E. 10th STREET)
THURSDAYS - SATURDAYS AT 8:00 PM
SUNDAYS AT 3:00 PM
$15 GENERAL ADMISSION
$12 SENIORS/STUDENTS, $10 GROUPS
BOX OFFICE: (212) 254-1109
www.theaterforthenewcity.net

Featuring: Brittney Benson, Mattie McMaster, Ann-Kathryn Mills,
Ciara Ramirez, Kaylin Reed, Sarah Q. Shah, Levern Williams

SET DESIGN: Lytza Colon and Mark Marcante
COSTUMES/PROPS: Susan Hemsley
LIGHTING DESIGN: Alexander Bartenieff
SOUND DESIGN: Jim Mussen
SOUND TECH: Alex Santullo
STAGE MGR: Megan Horan
PRESS REP: Jonathan Slaff

www.gunplays.org   www.williamelectricblack.com

The Faculty Room
Photo by RSFwolf Entertainment LLC / Courtesy Erikka James

The Faculty Room

a play by

William Electric Black

CAST

WILKINS: 50s, loves her boom box, many years on the job.

RAYLEE YOUNG: 17, streetwise, ball player at James Baldwin.

DONYA BANKS: 17, streetwise, ball player at James Baldwin.

MR. CUTTER: 60s, about to retire, history teacher.

COACH MOORE: late 20s, PE teacher/basketball coach.

JAYY SIMMONS: mid 20s, arts-in-ed drama teacher, hopeful.

SETTING

A Faculty Room. The faculty room sits in the center of the playing space. The audience sits within and around the furniture so in essence . . . they become part of the faculty in the room.

The set (faculty room) has an array of furniture—three tables, a refrigerator, xerox machine, two small round tables with chairs, a coffee machine, a bulletin board, a couch, floor lamps, a garbage can ALONG WITH seats for the audience.

There are also TWO WHITE BOARDS for classroom scenes, a team bench, and a half a dozen classroom desks and chairs.

PRESENT DAY—New York, the faculty room of James Baldwin High School. An urban school in the middle of urban gun violence. It could also be Chicago, Baltimore, Philadelphia, Newark, Hartford . . .

FLASHBACKS—Three Days Before and Yesterday

TIME—November, early morning

ACT I
1-LOCKDOWN

LIGHTS UP on HAROLD CUTTER, Black, well dressed, he carries a BOX OF DONUTS in one hand and a briefcase in the other. He gazes out seemingly lost. Mr. Cutter is about to retire. If it were up to him, it would be today. Perhaps it will be today.

MR. CUTTER

(*to audience*) You see . . . it's about taking action. Indeed, you've heard the commercials time after time. They say, get a colonoscopy. The idea is to discover something before it turns deadly. Polyps can be deadly so when they find them— poof! Removed. You go on about your business thanking God you have another day. (*beat*) That was a week ago. And in 30 or so more weeks I will retire. I'll say goodbye to the hallways and classrooms of James Baldwin High. A school filled with so many polyps the doctors have given up. Indeed, it is already dying and has no qualms about taking faculty and students with it. (*beat*) I am one of the lucky ones. When I retire, I look forward to spending time sleeping, reading, traveling . . . They can take this place and burn it. But they won't. That would cause outrage. More outrage in the Black community. We can't get enough of it these days so they package it up nicely and sell it to us with guns, gangs, drugs. (*beat*) Today, in the ill-fated halls of James Baldwin High someone is going to be shot. Students have books but they have more guns than books. Their role models have guns so they have them. Role models commit murder so, they, too, want to commit murder. (*beat*) Don't worry, they prepared us for this day. Over the loud speakers we will first hear ATTENTION, WE ARE NOW IN A HARD LOCKDOWN. TAKE PROPER ACTION, ATTENTION, WE ARE NOW IN A LOCKDOWN. TAKE PROPER ACTION. THIS IS NOT A DRILL. You have to move out of sight and be silent. Check the hallways then lock the door and turn off the lights.

ABRUPT TO BLACK.

MR. CUTTER

The darkness brings me back to my colonoscopy. I am not awake for it. I'm in the dark . . . waiting for some calming words to assure me that everything is okay. (*beat*) Then we wait for a first responder or these calming words THE HARD LOCKDOWN HAS BEEN LIFTED. OR, THE POLYPS ARE NOT CANCEROUS.

LIGHTS UP.

MR. CUTTER

But there's always the chance things will not be okay. The polyps were tested and the doctor calls to inform you that you have colon cancer. A student dies in the hallway. Gunned down by a shooter who was a student of yours. (*beat*) Sometimes . . . sometimes it's better to be in the dark. Better not knowing what terrible things lie waiting or dormant. Waiting to swallow you up . . . then spit you back out. It's the bitter taste of life that makes the beast crave something sweet. But sweet . . . we are not.

His PHONE RINGS as the stage lights fade.

2-DONUTS

A School Safety Officer, WILKINS, enters the faculty room and clicks on a lamp. In her hand is an old, worn BOOM BOX that plays some classic hip hop.

WILKINS makes her way to a coffee pot. She stares at it then looks at her watch. She looks away from her watch and looks back at the coffee pot.

WILKINS

What's this bullshit, no coffee? For 25 plus years, at 6:30am, there has been coffee in this pot. And next to the coffee, donuts. Not just any damn donuts . . . the ones I like. CHOCOLATE GLAZED! (*beat*) How can a Safety Officer do her job without a damn glazed donut and a cup of coffee. Mr. C ain't never missed a day a school let alone making the coffee and bringing in the donuts. (*beat*) There was that storm back in 08 but hell, no one expected coffee and donuts that day. But here he come. Covered with snow from head to toe, braving the elements just so's the good faculty of James Baldwin could have their donuts. (*beat*) Hell, I want Mr. Cutter on my side when the world comes to an end.

KNOCKS on BATHROOM DOOR, NO ANSWER. She goes to couch and sits.

Oh, it's coming! Make no mistake about it. These floods . . . these fires it's just a mutherfuckin' warning. I tell my fellow workers, hell I done told the faculty a few times . . . ain't nobody listening. They say Wilkins we don't want to hear that bullshit. So, to truly annoy them I turns up my boom box so's they can enjoy the finer things in life instead of my wisdom. Hell, the way I think, I should have been a teacher! Maybe teach history like Mr. C but teach the real deal. Not no bullshit

WILKINS (CONT'D)

about Columbus. (*beat*) Yeah, no kids be callin' me Uncle Tom behind my back. I be a straight up, kick some ass, in your face teacher! Kids, faculty, administrators . . . yeah, fuck this place! Hell with tenure! Wilkins would tell it like it is. But how can I do that without coffee and a glazed mutherfuckin' donut?

The faculty room door SWINGS OPEN and in walks RAYLEE, a high school teenager, holding a BASKETBALL. She is surprised to see WILKINS.

RAYLEE

OH . . .

WILKINS

Oh, hell is what you should be saying.

WILKINS turns off her boom box.

RAYLEE

I . . . I was looking for somethin' Coach Moore got of mine.

WILKINS

This early in the morning?

RAYLEE

Need it for practice.

WILKINS

Practice starts at 7. Y'all know you not supposed to be in the school before then. Who let you in?

RAYLEE

Miss Gwen.

WILKINS

She too damn soft! Told her she lets y'all get away with murder.

RAYLEE

No one usually gets away with murder.

WILKINS

You trying to be smart or something?

RAYLEE

No, just looking for what Coach took.

WILKINS

Guess it ain't that basketball. (*beat*) Toss it here.

RAYLEE

Why?

WILKINS

Why? 'Cause I got the uniform, the walkie, and damn badge. And if I ask you to do something, I expect you to do it. (*beat*) You know I could write your ass up for sneakin' into the faculty room.

RAYLEE

Ain't sneakin'.

WILKINS

Yeah . . . right. (*beat*) Toss me the ball. Not gonna keep it. I know a big, All City player like you is attached to the damn thing.

RAYLEE tosses WILKINS the ball.

WILKINS

Played me some ball when I went to James Baldwin.

RAYLEE

YOU?

WILKINS

Even started.

RAYLEE

Team was that good, huh?

WILKINS

You ain't funny!

RAYLEE

Can I see if Coach left it here.

WILKINS

Left what?

RAYLEE

My sneakers.

WILKINS

(*looking down*) Ain't you wearin' 'em.

RAYLEE

Not these. I got another pair that I play in. Mad expensive. Not like them skippys you used to wear.

WILKINS

Skippys my ass. Had me some real nice high top Converses.

RAYLEE

Like I said . . . skippys.

WILKINS

How much your sneakers cost?

RAYLEE

Enough.

WILKINS

Told you about being smart.

RAYLEE

It's my nature. You know . . . angry, belligerent, young Black girl just trying to get over. Trying to get her sneakers.

WILKINS

Yeah, I know about you being angry. Had to separate you and that damn Donya.

RAYLEE

Bitch be always up in my business. In the classroom, on the court . . .

WILKINS

Now I know you think you all that, but without Donya, who also made All City last year . . . y'all would not be shit.

RAYLEE

Whatever . . .

WILKINS

Not whatever. That's the problem with you fools. Whatever becomes your anthem to acting out, being disrespectful, shootin' one another . . . Whatever to rules, to discipline, to life . . .

RAYLEE

Life? What life I got living in the Tillman Houses.

WILKINS

Good people come out of there. Been lawyers, teachers, bus drivers, cops . . .

RAYLEE

Yeah . . . cops. Real good.

WILKINS fires the BASKETBALL back to her.

WILKINS

Without cops this jungle inside and outside of Baldwin would swallow you up little girl. There's bad folks and there's good folks. That's just how it is. (*beat*) Which one are you?

RAYLEE

On the court . . . I'm good. This ball, see, I can make it do anything I want. This bad boy will sing if I want it to . . . whoosh. Three points, no problem. (*beat*) After the game . . . after you become a lawyer, doctor, engineer . . . you still living in America where damn BS laws and BS amendments . . . set up by some tired old BS white people . . . end up putting us in BS prisons.

RAYLEE SNAPS the ball back to WILKINS.

RAYLEE

What? Ain't got nothing to say?

WILKINS

Think you so damn smart.

RAYLEE

Yeah, I am smart. Learned all that from Mr. Cutter. I pay attention in class so I can get out of here and get that basketball scholarship to UConn or Texas. (*beat*) Get me a nice job, some fly clothes and shit . . . so when this little girl gets swallowed up I'll go out in style. *SWOOSH!*

WILKINS

Mess up again in class and you can kiss them scholarships goodbye, 'cause I will personally make sure your butt is expelled. All City or All Gone . . . don't make no difference to me.

The door to the faculty room opens and in walks 25-year-old JAYY SIMMONS, teaching artist. A backpack hangs off one of her shoulders. She carries a few books in one hand and a cup of coffee in the other.

JAYY

Excuse me . . . is this the faculty room? There's like no sign on the door but I was told that . . .

WILKINS

Yeah . . . this is it.

JAYY

I'm Jayy . . . two "y's." Jayy Simmons. I was sent here by Teach Up to do a 12-week residency in drama?

WILKINS

I'm Wilkins, safety officer. You probably want the principal's office.

JAYY

I was there. Told me to hang out here until she arrives. Guess I came too early, but I wanted to get a feel for the students.

RAYLEE

Feel?

JAYY

Well, to see what they're like. What kind of mix the school has.

WILKINS

Black, Hispanic, and POOR. Ain't gonna find too many Asian kids here.

RAYLEE

Or white kids.

WILKINS

This is Raylee Davis. And she was just leaving.

RAYLEE

But I need to see Coach Moore.

WILKINS

Your morning practice starts in . . . (*looks at her watch*) . . . fifteen minutes. You can ask Coach for your sneakers during layup drills. Now let's go.

WILKINS tosses the ball back to RAYLEE.

JAYY

Raylee Davis? I read about you in the papers. What makes you so good?

RAYLEE

(*to Wilkins*) I don't wear cheap sneakers.

WILKINS

See you around, Jayy with two "y's." Don't take no crap from these kids. They can smell a teaching artist a mile away.

JAYY

Do we smell that bad?

WILKINS

Funny! But these kids ain't no joke. Especially this one who is going to follow me out. (*beat*) Right?

WILKINS exits. RAYLEE is halfway out the door when . . .

JAYY

So, do you like plays? Musicals? I saw The Color Purple and it blew me away.

RAYLEE turns back. SILENT.

JAYY

Movies? 12 Years A Slave? Precious?

RAYLEE

Movies cost money.

JAYY

Yeah, right, well . . .

RAYLEE

But Precious, I heard of that.

JAYY

Oh my God, a teenage girl who's about to have another baby, sexual assaulted at home, can barely read or write . . . I loved it. Didn't you?

RAYLEE enters back into the faculty room.

RAYLEE

Her life was horrible. Why would I love it?

JAYY

Not her life but her story. A young Black girl overcomes her obstacles and wins in the end! (*beat*) Applause! Cheers!

RAYLEE

Teaching artists are weird. (*beat*) I gotta go.

RAYLEE heads for the door.

JAYY

You gotta get your sneakers?

RAYLEE

What? Oh, yeah.

JAYY

Bet you'd be good in drama. I know you've got a character or a story you'd like to work on.

RAYLEE

When I was younger, I pretended to be Super Basketball Girl. She had a ball that had super powers.

JAYY

What kind of powers?

RAYLEE

Like it could fly out of her hands and knock a gang-banger out. Or if they shot at her she could spin the ball so fast that the bullets would bounce off, and head right back and kill them.

                          JAYY

I like Super Basketball Girl.

                        RAYLEE

But the real story I'd wanna act out is about a girl in high school who wants to shoot another girl.

                          JAYY

Well, ah, it needs a clear conflict. A beginning, middle, and end. (*beat*) See, a girl wants to shoot another girl . . . but why? What are the stakes? The consequences? How does their story start?

                        RAYLEE

It starts in history class.

                          JAYY

Okay . . . well, if you're in my drama workshop I hope we can turn your story into a play.

                        RAYLEE

Never been in a play before.

                          JAYY

Never been a teaching artist before. My acting career is kind of slow. (*beat*) Nice meeting you, SBG!

                        RAYLEE

SBG? Oh . . . Super Basketball Girl. (beat) Teaching artists are really weird.

LIGHTS FADE as RAYLEE exits.

3-HISTORY CLASS

THREE DAYS AGO. LIGHTS UP.

MR. CUTTER appears in the classroom setting, between the two white boards. RAYLEE enters and takes a seat in the class. DONYA enters and takes the other seat. Both girls are dressed in their BASKETBALL JERSEYS.

MR. CUTTER

(*to students/audience*) You see the founding fathers, James Madison, Patrick Henry and such, were not aware of the deadly cancer they were about to release.

RAYLEE

(*raising hand*) Cancer? That's a disease, right?

DONYA

Damn, bitch . . . everyone knows what cancer is?

RAYLEE

I know what kicking your ass is!

MR. CUTTER

Young ladies . . . this is a class not your locker room. Kindly refrain from using that language.

DONYA

My bad, Mr. C.

MR. CUTTER

Cancer . . . massive cell growth with no limits, no borders . . . dividing then consuming other cells.

MR. CUTTER writes C-A-N-C-E-R on the white board.

MR. CUTTER

And that is why we get check-ups. I recently went for one because if you detect the cancer early enough, one might have a fighting chance.

RAYLEE

(*raising hand, again*) What does this have to do with our history class?

MR. CUTTER

A great question.

DONYA

Really . . . that was great?

MR. CUTTER

The 2nd Amendment was ratified by these men and others to maintain and control the slaves, their labor force. Slave patrol militias were well armed for the sole purpose of keeping the slave population in check.

DONYA

YO . . . are you saying the slaves were like cancer?

MR. CUTTER

NO, I am saying giving these militias the right to bear arms and amending it as an affair of the state allowed and still does allow guns to consume us, to control us.

RAYLEE

The guns are the cancer. I get it.

DONYA

That's the only thing you get 'cause your ex, Drayton is riding my ass now.

RAYLEE

Fuck you!

RAYLEE stands and makes her way towards DONYA. DONYA stands ready to defend herself.

DONYA

Oh, you got something down there nice and hard for me.

MR. CUTTER

That's enough! Both of you sit down. (*beat*) NOW.

The girls sit.

RAYLEE

So, they got no kind of cure for cancer, right?

DONYA

What about breast cancer? Can't they like remove it?

MR. CUTTER

Some cancers they remove. Others require chemotherapy or drugs. But presently there is no magic pill.

RAYLEE

So, you're saying these guns, that was allowed way back, is why everyone can get one now?

DONYA

Why niggahs be shootin' each other?

MR. CUTTER

It's not just African Americans shooting each other. There are shootings everywhere . . . not just in the Tillman Houses.

RAYLEE

Man. That's messed up.

MR. CUTTER

Yes, it is. So, your assignment is to write a one-page essay on how you would imagine things would be without the 2nd Amendment. What do you think our society would be like without guns.

RAYLEE

That's a lot to imagine, Mr. C.

DONYA

Yeah, white people love their guns.

MR. CUTTER

Your assignment is to imagine what the United States of America would be like if folks could not get their hands on guns.

DONYA *stands, now heated.*

DONYA

Can I imagine the police won't be shooting us?

MR. CUTTER

Yes, if you want.

SILENCE.

DONYA

But that's not ever gonna happen.

                          RAYLEE

When is the paper due?

                       MR. CUTTER

In three days.

                           DONYA

Three days? How can I write a paper in three days?

                          RAYLEE

Yeah . . . it will take you that long just to write your name.

RAYLEE goes to the board and begins to spell as she speaks.

                          RAYLEE

(*writing on board*) B . . . I . . . T . . . C . . . H!

                           DONYA

Your mother!

                          RAYLEE

At least I got one!

                           DONYA

But I got Drayton. (*beat*) He said your legs was tighter than them laces on your
Nikes!

                          RAYLEE

Are they as tight as my hands around your neck!

RAYLEE charges DONYA and begins to choke her.

                       MR. CUTTER

I'VE HAD ENOUGH!

*MR. CUTTER exits the class as RAYLEE and DONYA continue to brawl. A beat, then
WILKINS rushes in and separates the girls.*

                          WILKINS

What the hell is going on here?

RAYLEE

We all got cancer, ain't you heard?

WILKINS

To the Principal's office. I think she got your cure.

WILKINS carts the two students away. A moment, then . . .

MR. CUTTER

Okay . . . now that things have settled down, here is what the 2nd Amendment says. Please listen carefully. (*reading from book*) "A well-regulated Militia, being necessary to the security of a free state, the right of the people to keep and bear arms, shall not be . . .

MR. CUTTER closes his book and looks up.

MR. CUTTER

. . . infringed."

LIGHTS FADE.

4-COACH

LIGHTS UP. JAYY sits on the couch reading a play. She writes a few notes down as she reads. COACH MOORE, basketball coach and PE teacher, enters with gym bag and a clipboard. She glances at the coffee table somewhat disappointed.

MOORE

(*to Jayy*) All the donuts gone? (*beat*) Damn.

JAYY

Ah . . . I don't know. I didn't see any when I got here.

COACH MOORE drops her bag and heads towards JAYY, extending a hand.

MOORE

Toni Moore . . . PE teacher, health teacher, coach . . . and a friend to the enemy.

JAYY

Enemy?

MOORE

Just messing with you.

They shake hands.

JAYY

I'm from Teach Up.

MOORE

Teach Up?

JAYY

They sponsor teaching artists. My specialty is drama.

MOORE

These kids don't need you for drama. They got plenty of their own.

JAYY

Yes . . . but I am here to focus that drama. Turn it into something productive.

MOORE

Is that right?

MOORE goes to the fridge and opens it.

MOORE

Damn . . . who's been eating my salad?

JAYY

Not me.

MOORE

Damn thieves! Got to put their hands on my shit.

JAYY

Is that a problem around here?

MOORE

Hell, yeah. So, if you put anything in this fridge be prepared for some fool to eat it.

MOORE closes the fridge and plops down next to JAYY on the couch. She looks over her clip-board and makes a few notes.

JAYY

Thanks for the warning. (*beat*) Anything else I should be worried about?

COACH MOORE puts down her clipboard and gives JAYY the once over.

MOORE

Where you from?

JAYY

I live in Harlem.

MOORE

No, where you <u>from</u>?

JAYY

Long Island.

MOORE

This your first artist-in-hell gig?

JAYY

Excuse me?

MOORE

You new at this, right?

JAYY

What does that have to do with where I grew up?

MOORE

Nothing . . . I didn't mean nothin'. (*beat*) I'm just pissed. There's no jelly donuts, someone ate my fucking salad. And my two best players are trippin'.

JAYY

Oh, you coach Raylee Davis? She was in here looking for you . . . about her sneakers.

MOORE

Her sneakers?

JAYY

She said you had her sneakers.

MOORE

These kids will say anything. So, first rule . . . don't believe shit they say. They gotta go to the nurse . . . they don't feel well . . . the principal wants to see them . . . NO! NO! NO!

JAYY

They have a big All City basketball game . . . ?

MOORE

Okay . . . you got me.

JAYY

What about trust?

MOORE

What about it?

JAYY

Don't you trust anyone in this school?

MOORE

I can't even trust these assholes from eating my salad.

SILENCE. JAYY takes out her cell phone.

MOORE

I didn't mean to say that. (*beat*) Sorry.

JAYY

Yeah . . . I get it. No donuts.

MOORE

I'm just saying trust is something you earn. You just don't let the next fool have it. And around here, there are plenty of fools. (*beat*) Maybe on Long Island it's different.

JAYY

Ah, I'm sorry but Long Island has its share of drugs, crime, single family homes, gangs, guns . . . you name it and it's out there, too. I'm not innocent or sheltered. I don't take shit . . . or eat other people's salads. And where's the principal? I'd like to get my damn schedule!

MOORE

There's a charter school three blocks over. They make you wait but you don't realize it because they manipulate your trust.

JAYY

Is that right?

MOORE

At private schools you pay for that trust.

JAYY

Ouch!

MOORE

I just tell it like I see it.

JAYY puts her phone away. A moment, then . . .

JAYY

I went to a private school.

MOORE

Knew there was something expensive about you. The cursing and getting mad at the principal was a good try.

JAYY

I have to trust someone here. 12 weeks is a long time. What about you? You don't trust anyone around here?

MOORE

This is my third year at Baldwin. Not sure who I should trust. But if I had to pick one person it would be Mr. Cutter, aka Mr. C.

JAYY

He was supposed to make the coffee and bring the donuts, right?

MOORE

Damn, word travels fast around here and it's not even first period.

MOORE picks up coffee pot, places it back down.

MOORE

(*beat*) He's never missed a day.

MOORE glances at her watch.

> **JAYY**

Maybe he's sick?

> **MOORE**

He's never sick. Man lives and breathes James Baldwin High. Not sure what he'll do after he goes and retires.

> **JAYY**

Probably die.

> **MOORE**

Die?

> **JAYY**

After my father retired from teaching, he died. Never even got to enjoy himself. That's why I'm never going to work somewhere for 30 years.

> **MOORE**

What . . . you plan to be a teaching artist for the rest of your life? Hop from school to school and only work 12 weeks out of 52?

> **JAYY**

I also plan to be a big TV star. Make a few films in between, and maybe sing on a record or two. (*beat*) How about you?

> **MOORE**

Hell, Beyonce, I'm gonna be your assistant. Ain't leaving my Black ass here with folks I can't trust!

The DOOR FLINGS open and WILKINS sticks her head in.

> **WILKINS**

Coach, Donya is waving a fuckin' razor in Raylee's face.

> **MOORE**

Damn it!

> **WILKINS**

NEED YOU IN THE CAFETERIA, RIGHT NOW!

WILKINS exits.

                    MOORE

Can I trust you?

                    JAYY

What?

                    MOORE

CAN I TRUST YOU?

                    JAYY

Ah, yes . . . why?

                    MOORE

In my bag there's a gun!

                    JAYY

WHAT?

                    MOORE

A GUN! Don't let no one near my bag.

                    JAYY

WAIT . . . WHAT?

WILKINS sticks her head back in.

                    WILKINS

COACH, NOW!

                    MOORE

I'M COMIN'!

WILKINS abruptly exits.

                    MOORE

I can trust you, right?

                    JAYY

Yes . . . YES!

MOORE bolts out the door. A look of panic crosses JAYY's face.

JAYY

Fuck!

JAYY grabs MOORE's gym bag and places it on the couch next to her. She stares at it. Thinks. She pushes the bag to the other side of the couch.

JAYY

FUCK!

SILENCE.

JAYY

Wait, is she messing with me? (*beat*) Great . . . White girl from Long Island falls for some faculty bullshit prank. (*beat*) She probably ate her own damn salad.

JAYY heads over to the bag. She starts to unzip it.

JAYY

What am I doing? I must be crazy!

JAYY zips the bag back up.

JAYY

Can I trust you? Can I trust you? I should have said no, goddamn it! Take your gun and get the hell away from me! SCREW THIS!

JAYY UNZIPS the bag and is about to reach inside when . . . WILKINS POPS her head back in.

WILKINS

Principal Brown wants to see you, <u>now</u>.

JAYY

NOW?

WILKINS

No, tomorrow!

JAYY

But . . .

WILKINS

LET'S GO, SHAKESPEARE!

JAYY grabs her book, backpack, and notebook and heads towards WILKINS. She glances back at the gym bag, then exits with WILKINS. SILENCE . . . for several beats. Then the door opens and RAYLEE takes a few steps into the room cautiously looking around. She sees the gym bag and makes a beeline for it. She slips her hand in, PULLS OUT A HANDGUN, then ZIPS IT SHUT. RAYLEE places the gun inside her backpack and heads to the door. She OPENS the door and comes face-to-face with MR. CUTTER who HOLDS a box of donuts in his hand and a briefcase in the other.

MR. CUTTER

I'm sorry . . . is someone confused?

RAYLEE

Ah . . . no, Mr. C. I'm not confused.

MR. CUTTER

Then maybe I have the wrong room? I must be confused.

RAYLEE

Ah, no, this is the faculty room.

MR. CUTTER

And why exactly are **you** in the faculty room?

RAYLEE

Coach Moore took something from me during morning practice, so I came in to get it 'cause I didn't want you to give me a zero.

RAYLEE opens her bag and pulls out her ESSAY.

RAYLEE

It's my essay on the 2nd Amendment. Remember you said it was due in three days?

MR. CUTTER

Yes, I remember.

RAYLEE

Well, today it's due. This is three days.

RAYLEE quickly hands him her essay.

RAYLEE

I have to go! Gonna be late for homeroom.

RAYLEE bolts out as Mr. CUTTER ponders over what just happened.

MR. CUTTER

(*reading*) Essay On The 2nd Amendment by Raylee Davis. (*beat*) Well . . . maybe there is hope after all.

MR. CUTTER places the box of donuts on a table next to the coffee machine. He places the essay in his jacket then walks over to a chair and sits. MR. CUTTER opens his briefcase and takes out a report from his doctor.

MR. CUTTER

(*reads*) Colonoscopy Report . . . Harold Cutter. (*beat*) Dear Mr. Cutter . . .

LIGHTS FADE.

5-UNZIPPED

LIGHTS UP. JAYY enters and sees the box of donuts. She stares at it.

JAYY

Donuts! Okay, maybe everyone will be fuckin' happy now.

She makes her way to the couch where COACH MOORE's bag sits. It's in the same place she left it. Hold on. There seems to be something not right.

JAYY

(*to gym bag*) Okay . . . you are zipped now but I left you unzipped? (*beat*) Or did I zip you on the way out? (*thinks*) LET'S GO SHAKESPEARE . . . said the big bad security officer.

JAYY reenacts her movement as she speaks . . .

JAYY (CONT'D)

So, I grabbed my book, notebook, my backpack . . .

SOUND of TOILET FLUSHING. JAYY stops her reenactment and looks towards the bathroom door as MR. CUTTER emerges. They exchange glances.

JAYY

Teaching artist.

MR. CUTTER

No, I'm a history teacher. There's a slight difference.

JAYY

No, silly . . . I was referring to me.

MR. CUTTER

And my name is Harold Cutter, not silly.

He sits back in his chair that he has known for many years.

JAYY

No, I was calling myself silly. (*beat*) Let me start over . . . I'm Jayy, with two "y's" and I'm here to work with the students for 12 weeks.

SILENCE.

JAYY (CONT'D)

Drama?

MR. CUTTER takes out RAYLEE's essay and looks it over.

JAYY

Thought I'd start off with A Raisin In The Sun by Lorraine . . .

MR. CUTTER

I know who wrote it. Save it for your students.

JAYY

I also thought about doing a few scenes from Hamilton. Talk about a history lesson, huh?

MR. CUTTER

(*unimpressed*) Ha . . .

JAYY

Did you see it?

MR. CUTTER

NO . . .

JAYY

YOU DIDN'T? I mean a multi racial cast using hip hop to tell the story of Alexander . . .

MR. CUTTER

An overpriced history lesson. Mine is free.

JAYY

Yes, but sometimes artists push for new and exciting ways to express . . .

MR. CUTTER

Exploitation. Oh, let's use rap and bring a unique experience to the suburban whites who belittle rap artists, rap culture, and rap music whenever they can. Not to mention their disdain for Black folks in general. But, hey . . . if we can make money from it . . . well, it's a masterpiece.

JAYY picks up the box of donuts.

JAYY

Ah . . . would you like a donut? They seem to have a calming effect.

MR. CUTTER

I buy them every day for the faculty but have never eaten one.

JAYY

There's always that first time. (*raps from Hamilton*) I'm not gonna . . .

MR. CUTTER

Please . . . I am trying to read an essay that one of my students wrote.

JAYY

Sorry, I'll look over my teaching schedule. Finally got one.

JAYY returns the donuts to the table. She finds a seat and begins reading her schedule.

JAYY

Hey, I have your class coming up.

MR. CUTTER

Excuse me?

JAYY

Mr. Cutter . . . first period.

MR. CUTTER

That can't be right.

JAYY

(*rapping again*) Alexander Hamilton . . .

MR. CUTTER makes his way to JAYY and grabs her schedule from her hand.

MR. CUTTER

This has got to be a mistake.

JAYY

Why?

MR. CUTTER

These students do not have time for drama, poetry, music, art . . . The world is leaving them behind. Knowledge is the revolution. Not guns, big booties, hip hop history, basketballs, nor fried chicken will open up any doors or knock down any walls for these kids.

JAYY

May I please have my schedule back, Mr. Grinch.

MR. CUTTER hands back the schedule.

MR. CUTTER

My classroom will not be part of your workshop.

JAYY

What's wrong with you? All of you? Don't you care about these kids? (*beat*) And by the way, artists have always been part of any revolution. Why do you think James Baldwin's name is stuck on the front of this school? I'll tell you why. He kicked ass. Told it like it was, and still is . . . told it like it should be told. (*beat*) You don't want me in your classroom because art knocks down those walls you mentioned. Kicks them down and exposes the truth. (*beat*) What . . . you're afraid that these kids will see the real you? The one that hides from the revolution? The one who gets his students to write an essay about history but not make it their own?

MR. CUTTER stares at JAYY.

MR. CUTTER

Teaching artists are weird.

JAYY

Yes, we are! And I will be in your class. And nothing you do or say will stop me.

MR. CUTTER

This is my school. Not yours Miss Artist who is a part-time, when you have time, teacher. (*beat*) Principal Brown respects my time here, my dedication to the job and my opinion that goes way beyond your small moment of enlightenment as a voice for the revolution. (*beat*) Alexander Hamilton? What about A. Philip Randolph, Harriet Tubman, Dr. Charles Drew? Now I'd spend $300 to see a show about them, would you?

MR. CUTTER exits. JAYY paces back and forth . . . pissed, she BOLTS over to her backpack, notebook, and book . . . then abruptly packs them up.

JAYY

I am out of here! THE HELL WITH THIS PLACE. (*beat*) I did not get a drama degree from Smith, learn to fold napkins, and drink tea with lactose intolerant, gluten-free, white bitches for this bullshit.

Starts to head out but STOPS in front of COACH MOORE's gym bag.

JAYY

And the bag was fucking unzipped! (*beat*) WHO FUCKING ZIPPED IT?

SUDDENLY . . . COACH MOORE enters followed by DONYA.

DONYA

YO, Coach Moore . . . why I gotta be expelled? Raylee said she was coming to school today to shoot my ass! You was there yesterday when she even said it. (*beat*) Damn it! It's not fair!

MOORE

It's out of my hands! You had a razor. You threatened another student.

DONYA

Bitch threatened me! Said she was bringin' a gun to school and was going to . . .

MOORE

I know what she said. That was yesterday and I took care of it! (*to Jayy*) You didn't leave my bag, did you?

JAYY

Ah, no . . . I was here. Mr. Cutter was also here.

LIGHTS FADE.

YESTERDAY. LIGHTS UP ON RAYLEE, in her TEAM uniform. In her hand she holds a TOWEL. LIGHTS UP on COACH MOORE as she confronts RAYLEE.

MOORE

(*calling*) Raylee . . . RAYLEE! You hear me?

RAYLEE turns towards COACH MOORE.

RAYLEE

WHAT?

MOORE

Why did you leave practice?

RAYLEE

Had to get my towel from the locker room. (*shows towel*) SEE!

MOORE

What's up between you and Donya?

RAYLEE

Got no beef with her!

MOORE

You're not passing her the ball off the screen.

RAYLEE

Took the shot instead.

MOORE

That's not the play.

                              RAYLEE

I ain't feeling her.

                              MOORE

And I'm not feeling this attitude.

                              RAYLEE

Whatever . . .

                              MOORE

Whatever? Okay, you can sit on the bench when we play on Friday.

                              RAYLEE

Yeah, right.

                              MOORE

You're not the whole team.

                              RAYLEE

A lot of colleges say I am.

                              MOORE

Then act like it. You wanna be the next Tina Charles, go pro, show me and
everyone else you got what it takes.

                              RAYLEE

Man, I hate Donya. (*beat*) She be hangin' with Drayton now, and all she does is rub
it in my face.

                              MOORE

You and Drayton are over?

                              RAYLEE

Yeah . . . we been over.

                              MOORE

So, move on. He's a punk and can't play ball half as good as you.

                              RAYLEE

Yeah . . . I know.

                              MOORE

And when you get to college the guys are gonna be all over you. Older guys . . .
not no teenage hood rats.

SILENCE.

MOORE

Now give it to me.

DONYA enters wearing her TEAM outfit. She holds a basketball.

RAYLEE

What?

DONYA

Bitch . . . you know what?

RAYLEE

Your mother's a bitch.

MOORE

HEY! THAT'S IT! You both want to sit on the bench this Friday?

DONYA

She's got a gun. Everyone in school knows she got a piece on her. Got it from that niggah, Sharod.

RAYLEE

I ain't got shit.

DONYA

What's in the towel?

RAYLEE

You ain't never seen a towel.

MOORE

Donya, go back on the court. Run some drills with the team.

DONYA

But Coach . . .

MOORE

DRILLS, DAMN IT!

RAYLEE

I'll see you in the cafeteria tomorrow, after morning practice. Gonna shoot your ass and settle this shit once and for all.

RAYLEE shapes her hand like a gun then points it at DONYA.

DONYA

Not if I settle it first.

DONYA exits.

MOORE

Where's the gun? (*beat*) Give it to me now and this is over. You don't get suspended, charged, or sent to jail. (*beat*) Is that what you want? All City . . . all gone?

RAYLEE unwraps the towel and reveals a gun.

MOORE

Give it here.

RAYLEE slowly approaches COACH MOORE and hands the gun over.

MOORE

What the hell were you thinking?

RAYLEE

I was thinking about cancer.

MOORE

What?

RAYLEE

It's true, you know.

MOORE

What's true?

RAYLEE

What Mr. C said. (*beat*) I think he's right.

LIGHTS FADE on flashback. LIGHTS BACK on COACH MOORE, JAYY, AND DONYA.

MOORE

You have to wait in the principal's office until your aunt comes.

DONYA

What about the gun?

MOORE

It wasn't in the towel and it wasn't in her locker.

DONYA

YOU LYIN'! I KNOW YOU ARE!

DONYA EXITS, violently KNOCKING THE DONUTS to the floor. A BEAT.

COACH MOORE heads to the couch. She takes her gym bag and places it on her lap. JAYY looks on, not knowing what to say. MR. CUTTER enters. He notices the donuts on the floor.

MR. CUTTER

Is anyone aware that there are donuts all over the floor? Anyone? That includes you, Jayy with two y's.

JAYY

A student came in. An unwanted student. She was asked to leave and on her way out . . .

MR. CUTTER

Thank you . . . I got it.

CUTTER picks up the donuts then tosses them in the trash.

MR. CUTTER

Maybe this is good. I'm about to retire so it's time for someone else to get the donuts. Coach Moore, what about you?

SILENCE, then . . .

MOORE

Did you say something to Raylee about cancer?

MR. CUTTER

In my class, a few days ago, I mentioned that the present day gun plague has infected us like a cancer would. Destroying a society that doesn't know how to fight back. (*beat*) Not yet.

JAYY

You said that in your class?

MR. CUTTER

It was part of my lesson on the 2nd Amendment. (*beat*) Raylee even wrote a paper about it. She was just in here. Gave it to me on her way out.

MOORE

(*concerned*) OUT?

MR. CUTTER

She was looking for you.

MOORE

(*to Jayy*) So, you were here. You saw her, too?

JAYY

No . . .

MOORE

(*alarmed*) NO?

JAYY

I mean . . . I saw her the first time.

MOORE

The first time?

JAYY

You had her sneakers.

MOORE

DID YOU LEAVE MY BAG? I TOLD YOU NOT TO TRUST THEM!

MOORE starts to FRANTICALLY unzip her bag as WILKINS RUSHES IN with a WALKIE TALKIE in hand.

WILKINS

(*into walkie*) ATTENTION! ATTENTION! WE ARE NOW IN A HARD LOCKDOWN! THIS IS NOT A DRILL.

COACH MOORE discovers the gun is missing, tosses bag to the floor.

MOORE

WATCH THE DAMN BAG! THAT'S
ALL I ASKED YOU TO DO! I SAID
DON'T FUCKIN' LEAVE IT!

JAYY

I'M SORRY! THE PRINCIPAL . . .
SHE HAD MY SCHEDULE. SO, I
WENT TO THE OFFICE.

WILKINS

ATTENTION! ATTENTION! WE
ARE NOW IN A HARD LOCK-
DOWN. TAKE PROPER ACTION.

RAYLEE

THE CANCER'S GOT ME! GOT
YOU! GOT ALL OF US!

MOORE

JUST WATCH MY FUCKIN' BAG!
I TRUSTED YOU! I FUCKIN'
TRUSTED, TRUSTED YOU, YOU.

JAYY

I'M SORRY! I THOUGHT YOU
WERE JOKING! MAKING FUN OF
ME . . . OF ME . . . OF ME . . . ME . . .
ME . . .

WILKINS

THIS IS NOT A DRILL! WE ARE
NOW IN A HARD LOCKDOWN!
THIS IS NOT A DRILL,
ATTENTION . . .

RAYLEE

THE CANCER'S GOT ME! GOT
YOU! GOT ALL OF US . . . ALL OF
US . . .US, US.

ABRUPT SILENCE.

DARKNESS, except for a solo SPOTLIGHT on MR. CUTTER.

MR. CUTTER

(*looking up from his report*) DEAR MR. CUTTER . . . YOU HAVE STAGE IV
COLORECTAL CANCER. YOUR CANCER HAS METASTASIZED TO
YOUR LIVER AND YOUR LUNGS.

He looks up . .

MR. CUTTER/ALL

It's the bitter taste of life that makes the beast crave something sweet. But sweet . . .
we are not.

LIGHTS FADE TO BLACK.

END ACT I

Levern Williams in the role of Mr. Cutter.
Photo by Jonathan Slaff

Ann-Kathryne Mills in the role of Safety Officer Wilkins.
Photo by Jonathan Slaff

Sarah Shah aka Tournesoul in the role of Donya.
Photo by Jonathan Slaff

Officer Wilkins, Coach Moore, and Mr. Cutter in the faculty room at James Baldwin High.
Photo by Jonathan Slaff

Sandra Bookman with Sarah Shah, Kalyin' Lavena, and William Electric Black.
Photo by Jonathan Slaff

ACT II
1-POW-POW

Lights up on RAYLEE, seated on top of one desk. DONYA is seated on the other desk. RAYLEE holds a gun, waving it into the air. DONYA holds a razor, ready to take on RAYLEE and the rest of the world. A lockdown siren is heard pulsating in the background.

RAYLEE

(*calling out*) Donya . . . BITCH. Where you at? I know you're in one of these hallways, one of these classrooms! (*beat*) Ain't no cops, no coach, no principal gonna save your ass! You hear me?

DONYA

(*calling out*) Bring it, bitch. You think they took away my only razor!

RAYLEE

I ain't afraid of you!

DONYA

I ain't afraid of you! Ain't afraid of the dirty looks, the name calling . . . the whips, the shackles, for coloreds only water fountains, bathrooms . . . You think you can back me into the back of the bus? Make me think I'm just 3/5's of a person. Lynch me if I don't jump when you say jump . . . walk when you say walk?

RAYLEE

Walk this way bitch and I got something for you? Got a gun up in this place, gonna shoot you in your face.

DONYA

Got a cross burning for me? Got a church bombing? Trying to take my life?

RAYLEE

Your life is mine!

DONYA

You don't own me, bitch. Tried to own my ancestors. Tried to Jim Crow them, slave ship them . . . but me, I got desire . . . got determination . . . got a damn destiny.

RAYLEE

Your damn destiny is a bullet with your fuckin' name on it. You can run . . . you can't hide. Might as well face the music.

                              DONYA

Like Aretha faced it? Billie Holiday? Nina Simone . . . Missy Elliot . . . Lauryn
Hill? (*beat*) Bitch . . . you can't kill the music.

                              RAYLEE

(*shoots into the air*) POW!

                              DONYA

My inner city blues!

                              RAYLEE

POW! POW!

                              DONYA

My boom box blasting James Brown.

                              RAYLEE

POW! POW! POW!

                              DONYA

The Tillman Houses are on fire. I took a molotov cocktail and burned the
mutherfucker down!

                              RAYLEE

You're goin' down, mutherfucker, down!

                              DONYA

I'm on fire!

                              RAYLEE

You're fucking dead!

                              DONYA

I'M ON FIRE!

                              RAYLEE

You're fucking dead!

                              DONYA

FIRE!

                              RAYLEE

DEAD!

DONYA

FIRE!

RAYLEE

DEAD!

DONYA	RAYLEE
FIREEEEEEEEE!	DEADDDDDDDDD!!!

SILENCE.

DONYA and RAYLEE hold their heads as they SCREAM. Then, police sirens fill the air.

LIGHTS QUICK TO BLACK.

2-IMAGINE

DARKNESS, then . . .

MR. CUTTER

Can we please turn the lights on? I have an essay to read?

LIGHTS UP in the faculty room.

MOORE

Now? You want to read some damn papers when there's a girl running around these hallways ready to blow another girl's head off.

MR. CUTTER

Raylee's essay might give us an explanation . . . some reason why she's doing this.

WILKINS

Reason? She's pissed off at Donya!

MOORE

Over some stupid ass boy!

JAYY

You think it's just about a boy? Does anyone know this girl? What her home life is all about? (*beat*) Hello? <u>Anyone</u>? Maybe she was abused at home . . . or maybe she's depressed or dealing with some tragic event that none of you apparently don't know a goddamn thing about. (*beat*) To you she's just some talented All City player. I think she's all hurt, all pain.

MR. CUTTER

Bravo! (*applauding*) The teaching artist has become a worthy addition to James Baldwin High.

MOORE

Yeah, right. She's the reason we're in this mess.

JAYY

Me? (*beat*) So, you think hiding a gun in your bag was a good idea? You did the right thing? You just took the gun and thought . . . hey, things are fine now. Raylee is cured.

MR. CUTTER

There is no cure and no one here is at fault. If the child didn't get her gun from Coach Moore's bag I am sure she would have acquired another one from elsewhere. (*beat*) Are we all in agreement?

SILENCE.

MR. CUTTER

I'll take that as a "yes."

JAYY

So, I guess you're not going out there?

WILKINS

Told you, we got procedures in place for this kind of thing and my thing . . . is staying alive.

JAYY

(*to Moore*) What about you? You're their coach. You got the gun once from her. Maybe . . . maybe you can do it again.

MR. CUTTER

And maybe she'll get shot trying to retrieve it.

WILKINS

I'm not going. Want my grandkids to enjoy themselves playing with me, not praying over me.

JAYY

Coach?

COACH MOORE gets up and walks towards MR. CUTTER.

MOORE

What BS did you fill her head with? I wanna hear her essay.

MR. CUTTER

Excuse me . . . but I teach history. And history my clipboard carrying, highly esteemed whistle blowing colleague, very often shows us the light. (*beat*) You messed up. That's the lesson to be gained from this. So, any blood that's about to be spilled is on your hands. Not on mine, or the artist, or on our Miss Wilkins, safety officer extraordinaire.

JAYY

(*to Moore*) So, what are you going to do?

WILKINS

Nothing. This is a hard lockdown and I can't let any of you go out. By now there are police outside ready to come in here and do what they gotta do.

JAYY

Shoot someone!

WILKINS

Worst case scenario.

MR. CUTTER

Is there another one?

JAYY

Super Basketball Girl.

MOORE

What?

SPOTLIGHT UP on RAYLEE wearing a CAPE, holding a GOLD basketball.

RAYLEE

FASTER THAN A ROACH WHEN YOU TURN ON THE KITCHEN LIGHTS! IT'S SUPER BASKETBALL GIRL!!

MR. CUTTER

Who on earth is Super Basketball Girl?

JAYY

She could stop this.

MOORE

The teaching artist is trippin'!

RAYLEE

I FLOAT LIKE A BUTTERFLY . . . STING LIKE A BEE . . . AND PUT A
WHUPPIN' ON YOUR ASS . . . LIKE MUHAMMAD ALI!

SPOT FADES on RAYLEE.

JAYY

Raylee never told you about her?

MOORE

Why don't you tell us?

JAYY

Raylee is Super Basketball Girl. Her secret identity to deal with all this.

MR. CUTTER

Can this Super Basketball Girl stop real bullets?

JAYY

(*to Moore*) Probably not. She's gonna need real help.

MOORE

OKAY, OKAY I'M GOING!

COACH MOORE starts for the door but WILKINS BLOCKS her path.

WILKINS

Stay the hell away from the door!

*COACH MOORE reaches for the chair wedged against the door but WILKINS quickly shoves
the chair back under the door handle.*

MOORE

Or what? You'll shoot me?

MR. CUTTER

Safety officers don't carry guns.

WILKINS

Because some foolish kid might get his or her hands on it. (*beat*) Now I don't wanna hafta say this again . . . back away from the fuckin' door. You go out there and you'll be puttin' all of us in danger.

MOORE

I already did.

JAYY

Finally . . . you own it.

MOORE

And you own it, too.

JAYY

Again? Blaming me?

MOORE

Look, I told you . . . (*beat*) Okay, I messed up. I take the blame. Is everyone happy?

MR. CUTTER

Ecstatic!

JAYY

Ditto!

WILKINS

You're probably gonna lose your fuckin' job over this shit.

MOORE

You're probably right. So, let me go out there and do what I gotta do.

WILKINS

I'm not gonna let you out of here.

MOORE

We'll see about that!

COACH MOORE goes for the chair, again, when suddenly . . .

MR. CUTTER

Coach, would you like to hear Raylee's essay?

MOORE turns towards MR. CUTTER.

MR. CUTTER
You said you wanted to hear it.

JAYY
I'd like to hear it.

MR. CUTTER
Are all the new teaching artists like you? Getting into business that is none of their business?

JAYY
I'm in a lockdown because a young, Black teenager is walking around with a gun. If she shoots my ass I wanna know fuckin' why.

MOORE hands the chair to WILKINS. WILKINS shoves it back under the door.

MOORE
Me too! But I'm still going out there after I hear this shit.

WILKINS
Fine! But once you leave, I'm not letting you back in.

SPOT UP on RAYLEE, still in super attire

RAYLEE
IMAGINE A WORLD WITHOUT GUNS . . . by Raylee Davis.

CUTTER takes out the essay and begins to read.

MR. CUTTER
I tried to imagine a world without guns. In this world . . .

RAYLEE
Martin Luther King Jr. would still be alive. So would Trayvon Martin . . . Sean Bell, that 12-year-old girl from Hempstead, Long Island and people from the Emanuel African Methodist Episcopal Church. And them cops ambushed in Dallas, and the two shot in Brooklyn, in their car.

MR. CUTTER

(*still reading*) I imagine them all sitting down . . . at a restaurant or something. Trayvon, church folks, and them cops probably be like, wow, we chillin' with MLK. Don't he have to lead a march or something.

RAYLEE

But suddenly my imagination stopped, like it froze. Because if I imagined they were alive, I'd have to imagine them kids at Columbine, Virginia Tech . . .

MR. CUTTER

. . . Sandy Hook . . . at that club in Orlando. I'd have to imagine everyone who got shot at a mall, on a college campus, or with their hands up in front of the police . . . all these people everywhere . . .

RAYLEE

. . . in every city were all still here, still alive. L.A., Baltimore . . . still alive. Philadelphia, Milwaukee, Detroit, alive . . . Memphis, Oakland, St. Louis, Newark, Kansas City . . .

MR. CUTTER

. . . ALIVE! But when I tried to imagine 64 people shot in Chicago, on a single, weekend, where . . .

RAYLEE

6 died . . . I could not, did not want to think about no more people coming back from their graves or coffins.

JAYY

10:56 pm, male, 25, Black . . . shot dead. 1:27am, female, 15, Hispanic . . . shot dead.

MR. CUTTER

I closed my eyes.

RAYLEE

My imagination, stopped, died . . .

MOORE

5:16 am, male, 25, White . . . shot dead. 5:18 pm, male, 27, Black . . . shot dead.

RAYLEE

I refused to imagine anymore. It's a crazy stupid essay. I'm not trying to bring no more dead people back. They are dead . . . and The United States of Guns made them that way.

VOICES

HELP, SUPER BASKETBALL GIRL! HELP! HELP! HELP!

WILKINS

11:00 pm, male, 39, Black . . . shot dead. 11:00 pm, male, 44, Black . . . shot dead.

RAYLEE/MR. CUTTER

So . . . in closing . . .

RAYLEE

I'd just like to say . . .

MR. CUTTER

I'm sorry . . .

RAYLEE

Sorry that the 2nd Amendment isn't going away. Sorry, I can't imagine that it doesn't exist.

(*beat*) You said it was ratified to protect and preserve slavery. I agree. I look around and see how folks in my hood have enslaved themselves with guns and bullets, bullets and guns . . . did someone imagine this would happen?

SILENCE.

MR. CUTTER

I think they did.

RAYLEE

In The United States of Guns there are more guns than people.

RAYLEE/MR. CUTTER

Imagine that?

SILENCE.

MR. CUTTER puts the essay away in his jacket. COACH MOORE, WILKINS, JAYY, and MR. CUTTER take a moment to let RAYLEE's essay sink in. THEN . . .

RAYLEE

Yeah, imagine that.

LIGHTS FADE on RAYLEE. LIGHTS FADE on the faculty room. DARKNESS.

VOICES

HELP, SUPER BASKETBALL GIRL! HELP US! HELP! HELP! HELP!

3-KNOCK-KNOCK

LIGHTS UP.

JAYY

How long do these lockdowns go on for? I called 9-1-1 again but . . .

MOORE

Told you . . . the charter school is up the way. (*beat*) You missed your chance.

JAYY

For what?

MR. CUTTER

Some say a better education. Or a better salary if you're in it for the money.

WILKINS

Or the pension. Yours must be pretty sweet. (*beat*) What are you gonna to do when you retire?

MR. CUTTER

Besides die?

WILKINS

No one said anything about dying. I was talking more about moving to that special place.

MR. CUTTER

So was I, heaven. Rumor has it you can put your feet up, read a good book, go fishing whenever you want . . .

JAYY

Sounds nice.

MR. CUTTER

Yeah . . . it does.

WILKINS

Hell, when I retire, I'm going south. Need to see me some trees, grass, a damn lake or something.

MR. CUTTER

And a few signs along the way that say Make America White Again? (*beat*) No thank you, I'll take heaven.

JAYY glances at her cell phone.

JAYY

It's been 50 minutes. Where are the police?

MOORE

In this neighborhood they're always here. It's like a bad marriage. Both parties can't stand each other but they got no choice, nowhere to go.

JAYY

So eventually, without a doubt . . . something bad is going to happen?

MR. CUTTER

Your first day here and you're already catching on.

MOORE

Gasoline on the fire. Who needs matches when everything's already burning.

WILKINS

Protocol calls for NYPD to assess the situation and then . . .

MR. CUTTER

WAIT.

WILKINS

By now some kids and faculty members are outside. They will explain or tell what they saw. If Principal Brown is outside she will also give them more information on Raylee's whereabouts. Other safety officers and staff will do the same . . . and so on and so forth.

MR. CUTTER

Like I said . . . <u>WAIT</u>.

JAYY

(*to Coach*) Okay . . . so while they wait you can do something. You said that after . . .

MOORE

I know what I said, damn it!

WILKINS

Maybe Coach changed her mind after hearing that essay about death.

MR. CUTTER

It wasn't about death. It was about our culture. A violent culture that promotes death and destruction. We are unraveling, people, we are becoming unglued, people . . . and all the king's horses and all the king's men will never be able to put us back together again unless we cast out the illness. And that is why Coach Moore is not sure if she wants to go out there. It takes a lot of strength to get rid of something like this. You can't call a play and win this one at the buzzer.

JAYY

(*to Moore*) You don't know until you try. And if you don't try it's over for them . . . it's over for all of us in here.

MOORE

You don't speak for me. And neither do you Mr. C. I do what I wanna do.

MR. CUTTER

Raylee discovered the ugly America. And today, we all see it. And I'm truly sorry about that.

MR. CUTTER walks to the couch and sits. He holds his head. WILKINS approaches.

WILKINS

You okay, Mr. C? You want some water or something? Seen a bottle behind the salad.

MOORE

So, you been eating my salad?

WILKINS

WHAT? NO . . .

MOORE approaches WILKINS.

MOORE

Then how do you know there's a bottle of water behind the salad?

WILKINS

I just know, that's all.

MOORE

You've been eating my damn salad, haven't you?

WILKINS

Hell, I ain't touched your lousy salad.

MOORE

If I ever catch you . . .

JAYY

ARE YOU GOING?

MOORE

Going where?

JAYY

You're arguing about a stupid salad when two kids are about to ruin their lives, forever!

MOORE

You so worried about them why don't you go out there and do something.

JAYY

Maybe I will!

MOORE

Well, go the fuck on!

JAYY

FUCK YOU! I WILL!

MOORE

FUCK ME? WELL, FUCK YOU FOR FUCKIN' UP!

WILKINS

HEY, KEEP QUIET BEFORE . . .

JAYY

YOU HAD THE FUCKIN' GUN, ASSHOLE! WHY DIDN'T YOU TURN IT IN?

MOORE

I DID HAVE IT UNTIL YOU FUCKED UP! UNTIL YOU . . .

POUNDING is heard on the door. Everyone is SILENT. The DOOR starts to move but the chair wedged against it keeps the door from opening.

WILKINS

Grab Mr. C! Everyone into the bathroom.

JAYY

Bathroom?

MORE POUNDING.

JAYY

WHY?

WILKINS

It's got a lock. Hurry up!

THE DOOR moves slightly.

MOORE

It could be the police.

WILKINS

Do you hear the police identifying themselves?

POUNDING.

RAYLEE (O.S.)

OPEN THE FUCKING DOOR! THAT DUMB BITCH IN THERE?

JAYY

Mr. Cutter, come on . . .

MR. CUTTER

What?

He drops his LETTER FROM THE DOCTOR.

JAYY

We need to go into the bathroom. It has a lock.

MR. CUTTER

We'll be safe there?

WILKINS

Safer than out here.

JAYY and MR. CUTTER enter the bathroom.

RAYLEE (O.S.)

I'LL BE BACK! IF I FIND OUT SHE'S IN THERE WITH Y'ALL I'M AH COME BACK AND FUCKIN' SHOOT ALL OF YOU! YOU FUCKIN' HEAR ME?

SILENCE.

WILKINS

Anyone want to be a hero? You can probably catch up to her if you hurry. But, once you leave the faculty room I'm not gonna open up the bathroom door no matter how much you beg me.

MOORE

Tell me the truth. You ate my salad, didn't you?

WILKINS

It wasn't that good. Hell, why didn't you put some avocado in it? Or some chicken?

MOORE

Fuck you!

COACH MOORE removes the chair and exits the faculty room.

WILKINS

(*calling after*) I AIN'T LETTIN' YOU IN THE BATHROOM. YOU HEAR??

WILKINS heads for the BATHROOM door. She stops to retrieve MR. CUTTER'S LETTER. She begins to read it.

WILKINS

Cancer? (*beat*) Ain't this some shit!

A FEW BEATS, she folds the letter and puts it in her pocket then heads inside the bathroom shutting the door behind her.

LIGHTS FADE.

4-THE FACULTY ROOM

LIGHTS UP. A little later. WILKINS emerges from the bathroom.

WILKINS

(*calling to the others*) JUST GETTING MR. C SOME WATER!

WILKINS takes out her walkie as she heads towards the fridge.

WILKINS

(*into walkie*) This is Safety Officer Wilkins . . . I'm in the faculty room with two others. Anyone copy? (*beat*) This is Safety Officer Wilkins . . . anyone copy?

WILKINS heads to the fridge and opens it. She inspects COACH MOORE's salad.

WILKINS

This is the worst fuckin' salad and she yells at me for eatin' it! (*beat*) Damn teachers!

MR. CUTTER emerges from the bathroom.

WILKINS

I'm just getting you a water. You seem . . .

MR. CUTTER

Distraught? Disillusioned? Dismayed? Dissatisfied?

WILKINS

Well . . . when you put it that way.

WILKINS removes MR. CUTTER's letter from her pocket and hands it to him.

MR. CUTTER

Did you read it?

WILKINS

Me?

MR. CUTTER

YOU. (*beat*) Anyone who eats another person's salad also reads other people's letters.

WILKINS

Okay . . . I read it. So, I get all of your distraught . . . dismayed stuff.

MR. CUTTER

I'm not referring to my cancer. I'm referring to this place. This faculty room, what it's done to me.

WILKINS

Yeah . . . guess there's more to it than donuts.

MR. CUTTER

We get a room like it's some very magical place.

MR. CUTTER (CONT'D)

(*beat*) There's a refrigerator . . .

WILKINS

Which keeps a water bottle nice and cold.

WILKINS hands MR. CUTTER a bottle of water.

MR. CUTTER

Microwave . . . coffee maker . . . an old computer. A copier but there's never any paper. (*beat*) I HATE THIS ROOM!

WILKINS

Yeah, it really needs a paint job and some new furniture. Then you might like it?

MR. CUTTER

Then I might like it? The point is I am not supposed to like it. I am supposed to hate it because if I get too comfortable, I'll forget about my Initial Planning Conferences, I'll forget about setting two, three, or four formative professional goals.

He sits on an old couch.

MR. CUTTER

If this were a brand new, spanking leather couch from Macy's . . . well, I'd put my feet up like this and tell Principal Brown, when she asked what the hell I was doing, that I am working on my self-assessment, but taking my damn sweet time so put that in my Measures of Teacher Practice and have a donut on the way out.

WILKINS

So, what are you gonna do?

MR. CUTTER

About my goals? About parent-teacher conferences? About . . .

JAYY enters from the bathroom.

JAYY

Am I the only one staying in the bathroom?

WILKINS

I came out to get Mr. C some water.

MR. CUTTER

And I came out because I am tired of hiding in this detestable place.

JAYY

You think we should leave?

WILKINS

Not until they come for us and the lockdown has been lifted.

JAYY

Wouldn't they be here by now?

WILKINS

These things take time.

MR. CUTTER

Like cancer?

MR. CUTTER holds out his letter. JAYY hesitates, then takes the letter and reads it.

MR. CUTTER

Slowly, it eats away at you then before you know it . . .

JAYY

OH MY GOD . . . you have stage IV cancer. How terrible.

WILKINS

Hey, Shakespeare . . . I think he fuckin' knows it's terrible. (*beat*) Give him some space, will you?

JAYY

God . . . I'm so sorry. I just . . .

COACH MOORE rushes in with DONYA.

MOORE

(*to Donya*) Sit over there and don't move!

DONYA

This is bullshit.

WILKINS

Now hold on! You can't . . .

COACH MOORE shoves a chair back under the door to the faculty room.

MOORE

I JUST DID!

JAYY

I remember you.

MR. CUTTER

Slowly at first . . . then it becomes aggressive. There's no stopping it.

MOORE

Stopping what?

WILKINS

She can't be in here!

DONYA

And I can't be out there, either. Raylee's looking for me and she's got a damn gun!

MR. CUTTER

Language, please.

WILKINS

This is the faculty room. She has to go!

MOORE

The police are sweeping the school. I've seen 'em. One room at a time.

WILKINS

I don't care. Take her outside and I mean now.

MOORE

If she stays in here with us, Raylee doesn't shoot her. She's safe. She'll walk out with us when the police knock. She walks out alive.

WILKINS

Let's go, Donya!

DONYA

Get the fuck off me.

MOORE

You send her out there and the police might shoot her by mistake.

WILKINS

I'll go with her.

MR. CUTTER

No, let me take her.

MOORE

Is anyone listening to me?

JAYY

I am. I say let her stay.

WILKINS

Child, get up! You ain't stayin' in here. You hear me?

DONYA

Yeah, I hear you!

MOORE

What the hell is wrong with you?

WILKINS removes the chair from the door. MOORE gets in her face.

WILKINS

What the hell is wrong with you? Who made you fuckin' king of the faculty room.

MOORE

Just 'cause you a fake cop you think you can tell us what to do.

WILKINS

Yeah . . . I can! And your ass is through here, anyway. So back the fuck off and let me take the girl outside.

WILKINS shoves COACH MOORE.

MR. CUTTER

Now there's no need . . .

MOORE

You back the fuck off!

COACH MOORE shoves WILKINS back.

JAYY

STOP IT! THIS IS UNACCEPTABLE!

MR. CUTTER

I'll take the girl. I'll . . .

MR. CUTTER holds his head.

DONYA

MR. C! YO, SOMETHING'S NOT RIGHT WITH MR. C.

WILKINS, COACH MOORE, and JAYY rush to MR. CUTTER's side.

WILKINS

Where's his water?

JAYY

I got it.

JAYY grabs his water bottle from the floor.

MOORE

Put him on the couch.

As they help MR. CUTTER, DONYA quietly moves to the door.

WILKINS

Drink some water. You haven't been looking well since you got here.

JAYY

We should find the police.

MR. CUTTER

I'm okay. Just haven't had anything to eat all morning.

WILKINS

You're not okay.

MOORE

What's wrong with him? (*beat*) Hello? I asked a question.

MR. CUTTER

I have cancer. It's . . . it's too far along to do much. I know, and the cancer knows, that I'm dying.

MOORE

That's messed up.

DONYA

(*exits unnoticed*) Fuckin' trippin'.

MR. CUTTER

Yeah . . . that's messed up.

JAYY

(*looking up*) Hey . . . she's gone.

MOORE

FUCK!

WILKINS

She wasn't supposed to be in here.

MOORE

Will you let it go.

MR. CUTTER

She did. Took matters into her own hands.

JAYY

Because we couldn't.

WILKINS

What are you saying?

JAYY

She could have stayed. But why would she? You were all screaming and fighting. The girl probably sees enough of this at home. And she knows when she sees it that no one cares about her. No adult cares about her. (*beat*) At least Raylee cares. Yeah, she's got a damn gun but at least there's someone out there trying to make contact with her. It's fucked up out there and there's no difference in here.

MR. CUTTER

You're gonna make a really good teacher one day. I'm sure you'll have a dozen goals to share at your Initial Planning Conference.

JAYY

My what?

MR. CUTTER

Not important. What is important is that we save those two girls.

MOORE

I just had one of them.

WILKINS

You had a gun, too. Lost both of them.

MOORE

Had a little help losing them.

MR. CUTTER

Now you are going to have help saving them.

DISTANT KNOCKING IS HEARD.

> MOORE

Better go now. Sounds like the police are getting close. I'll take upstairs.

> WILKINS

I'll take the first floor.

> JAYY

What do you want me to do?

> WILKINS

You and Mr. C hang out here as long as you can. The girls might come back. They both been here once before.

> JAYY

But I want to do something!

> WILKINS

Keep an eye on Mr. C.

> MR. CUTTER

I'm fine.

> WILKINS

Said the man with a terminal illness.

> MOORE

(to *Wilkins*) You coming?

> WILKINS

If you find them bring them back here.

> MOORE

Can they stay this time?

> WILKINS

Yeah . . . smart ass!

COACH MOORE and WILKINS exit.

> JAYY

You know, folks think a lot about you.

> MR. CUTTER

It's all about the donuts. (*beat*) Especially the chocolate glazed.

JAYY

Yeah . . . I'm down with chocolate glazed myself.

SILENCE.

JAYY

So . . . do you think a lot about dying since . . .

MR. CUTTER

Since Donald Trump got elected?

MR. CUTTER (CONT'D)

Yeah . . . I thought about sticking my head in the oven or jumping off the roof of my building when I first heard the news. Then I said . . . it's a calling, a sign. Time to rise on up, be strong, fight the demons that are now walking among us.

JAYY

So, you don't think about dying?

MR. CUTTER

Truth keeps marching on. Like these kids will. But they just don't see it. That's why I teach history.

JAYY

That's why Momma wanted to move.

MR. CUTTER

Momma?

JAYY

In A Raisin In The Sun. Their house was choking them. She needed to show them a different way.

MR. CUTTER

Guess you won't be able to share that wisdom with your students today.

JAYY

Maybe tomorrow. (*beat*) Truth keeps marching.

MR. CUTTER

Yes . . . yes it does.

JAYY

What's it like?

MR. CUTTER

Having cancer?

JAYY

No . . . teaching for so long?

MR. CUTTER

With all its ups and downs . . . I always feel blessed to be able to stand in front of a classroom and elicit thoughts . . . provoke change . . . enlighten minds . . .

JAYY

What a piece of work is man . . . How noble in reason, how infinite in faculty.

MR. CUTTER

In form and moving how express and admirable.

JAYY

In action how like an angel, in apprehension, how like a god.

JAYY/CUTTER

The beauty of the world, the paragon of animals—

JAYY

And yet, to me . . .

MR. CUTTER

. . . what is this quintessence of dust? (*beat*) See, I do like arts. Even sing in my church's choir. But I still think Hamilton cost too damn much.

JAYY

Maybe I'll treat you to a ticket.

MR. CUTTER

I'll take the money instead.

MR. CUTTER holds out his hand.

JAYY

On what a teaching artist makes, it might be years from now before I have that kind of cash.

MR. CUTTER

I'll wait. I'm not planning on dying right away.

JAYY

Didn't think so.

JAYY heads to the door.

JAYY

They didn't come back with the girls, so I think we should go look for them.

MR. CUTTER

Was thinking the same thing, myself.

JAYY

I came here today to make a difference and, well . . .

MR. CUTTER

Like I said, you're gonna make one hell of a teacher. (*beat*) You'll be poor, but hell if you ain't gonna change some lives. (*beat*) You already changed mine.

JAYY

You sure you feel up to this?

MR. CUTTER

Sure? What can one ever be sure about other than life and death. In between, it's gray . . . no color. So, we try desperately to fill in the blank canvas the best way we can. (*beat*) Teachers? We are the guideposts along the way like family, friends, neighbors . . . clergy . . . unsure of ourselves at times so we reach for a . . . a partner . . . a prayer . . . a prophet. (*beat*) The darkness is always present. WHERE IS MY GOD? GOD IS NOT DEAD! But if you dare to think so . . . then you reach for drugs . . . the guns . . . the alcohol. You lose faith . . . you lose sight . . . you lose hope. (*beat*) The beauty of the world is inside of us. ALL OF US! SO, HOLD FAST! HOLD FAST! HOLD FAST! DEAR LORD, HELP US TO HOLD FAST!

MR. CUTTER grows silent.

MR. CUTTER

This morning, on my way here, I received a call from my doctor. And I am trying to hold fast.

JAYY

Man delights me not, nor woman neither, though by your smiling . . .

MR. CUTTER looks up at JAYY.

JAYY/CUTTER

You seem to say so.

JAYY EXITS the faculty room. MR. CUTTER follows but turns back . . .

MR. CUTTER

(*sings*) When the Lord gets ready . . .
(*speaks*) You gotta move.

MR. CUTTER exits the faculty room.

LIGHTS FADE.

The SOUND OF GUNSHOTS. POLICE RADIOS crackle.

5-NO CURE

LIGHTS UP. Moments later. The faculty room is empty for several beats . . . then . . .

RAYLEE rushes in with a GUN in one hand. BLOOD covers the PALM of the other hand.

RAYLEE

Fuck! FUCK! FUCKKKK!

She quickly SHUTS the door behind her. She surveys the room . . . EMPTY. RAYLEE makes a dash into the bathroom and CLOSES the door behind her. SILENCE. Then SEVERAL MORE beats. MR. CUTTER enters the faculty room pulling DONYA along with one hand. He uses his other hand to keep pressure on a gunshot wound to his stomach.

MR. CUTTER

Now just sit down and keep quiet. (*beat*) Don't say a word.

DONYA

Did you see 'em?

MR. CUTTER

I said sit down and keep quiet!

DONYA

They got shot! Officer Wilkins . . . Coach Moore . . .

MR. CUTTER

They got shot trying to keep you alive!

DONYA starts pacing back and forth.

DONYA

IT WASN'T MY FAULT! RAYLEE WAS SHOOTIN' . . . THEN THE
POLICE STARTED SHOOTIN' . . .

MR. CUTTER

(*calming her*) I KNOW! I KNOW!

CUTTER guides her to a seat.

MR. CUTTER

The chaos . . . calamity . . . conflict, it was here long before you were born. Long
before . . .

*LIGHTS FADE. DAYS BEFORE. A SCHOOL BELL is heard. LIGHTS UP on the TWO
white boards. MR. CUTTER walks over to one and writes WAR on one board, then he walks to
the other and writes PEACE. DONYA and RAYLEE take seats in the classroom.*

MR. CUTTER

Can we ever find peace in a country that has advocated war since its birth?

CUTTER/VOICES

King Philips's War . . . King William's War, Queen Anne's War, King's George's
War, French and Indian War, The American Revolution, War of 1812 . . . Does
anyone have an educated guess? A thought?

DONYA raises her hand. RAYLEE also RAISES her hand.

DONYA

Within ourselves?

RAYLEE

Within other people?

MR. CUTTER

Yes, two excellent answers. Find peace within yourself, then go make peace within others.

DONYA

But what if you can't find it?

DONYA glances at RAYLEE. The SCHOOL BELL rings. WE ARE BACK TO SCENE. LIGHTS CROSS FADE as MR. CUTTER and DONYA return to the couch. RAYLEE returns to the bathroom where she continues to hide.

DONYA

Mr. C, what if you can't find that peace?

MR. CUTTER is silent. HIS EYES CLOSED.

DONYA

Mr. C?

MR. CUTTER

Then you become a very minor, mundane, meaningless person.

DONYA

Ain't feelin' you?

MR. CUTTER

You become nothing . . . you vanish . . . you don't exist.

MR. CUTTER is silent. He struggles with the pain from his gunshot wound.

DONYA

I'M SOMEBODY! I'M NOT NOTHIN'! I'M RIGHT FUCKIN' HERE!

RAYLEE BOLTS out of the bathroom.

RAYLEE

AND SO AM I, BITCH!

DONYA backs away.

DONYA

YO, you don't have to do this!

RAYLEE

I don't have to, but I'm going to.

DONYA

Me and Drayton are over. Said he didn't wanna have nothin' to do with two crazy females.

RAYLEE

He said that?

DONYA

Look at my phone if you don't believe me. Or go ahead and shoot me, bitch. But after you shoot me ya gotta help Mr. C. He's been shot.

RAYLEE crosses to MR. CUTTER and stares at him.

RAYLEE

What did he ever do for me? (*beat*) For you?

DONYA

Came to one of our games. That time we played Saint Anthony.

RAYLEE

Yeah, right . . .

DONYA

Only stayed for the first half but I seen him. Dressed in one of his fancy ass suits.

RAYLEE

YO, that was a mad crazy game!

DONYA

You passed me the ball off the screen and I scored the layup and got fouled.

RAYLEE

Made the foul shot and we beat them niggahs by one point. Now that was some All City shit.

DONYA

For real . . .

MR. CUTTER opens his eyes.

MR. CUTTER

That's what Super Basketball Girls are supposed to do.

DONYA

What's he sayin'?

RAYLEE

Who told you about that?

MR. CUTTER

Teaching artist told me before she went out of that door and gave her life to save yours.

RAYLEE

FUCK! Nobody told her to do that.

RAYLEE, agitated, sits, resting the gun on a nearby table.

DONYA

Yeah . . . that dumb shit was on her.

MR. CUTTER

And Miss Wilkins? And Coach Moore? Had nothing to do with their deaths either?

RAYLEE

If I shot them, I didn't mean it. Cops was shooting, too. Maybe <u>they</u> killed Coach and the rest of 'em.

DONYA

Yeah . . . the shit ain't all on her.

RAYLEE

Yeah, it ain't all on me.

MR. CUTTER

Indeed, it's on all of us.

DONYA

It's fucked up, though. I seen 'em all lyin' on the floor. Could have been me lyin' there, too, if Mr. C didn't grab me.

DONYA shakes her head as she crosses to the fridge. She opens it and looks inside.

DONYA

Damn, they got sodas in here. (*to Raylee*) You want one?

RAYLEE

Yeah . . . what you think?

DONYA

Bitch, I ain't no damn mind reader.

RAYLEE

Yeah, bitch . . . I want one.

BEAT.

DONYA

YO, give me the piece.

RAYLEE

What?

DONYA

Give me the damn gun. I'm gonna hide it.

RAYLEE

Or shoot me.

DONYA

Ain't gonna shoot your ass. Give me the damn piece.

RAYLEE crosses to DONYA and hands her the gun.

RAYLEE

Where you gonna hide it?

DONYA

Inside this damn salad.

DONYA places the gun inside the salad.

RAYLEE

Man, I hate salad.

DONYA hands RAYLEE a can of soda. The girls open their sodas and start to drink.

KNOCKING IS HEARD on the faculty room door.

MR. CUTTER

Girls . . . the door.

DONYA

You think they still gonna let us play this Friday?

RAYLEE

Fuck, yeah . . . we got a disease. (*beat*) This ain't on us.

MORE KNOCKING.

MR. CUTTER

(*faintly*) Answer the door.

DONYA

Yeah . . .

RAYLEE

We got cancer . . . right, Mr. C?

MR. CUTTER

Cancer . . . yes. And it has metastasized to our homes, our streets, to our schools . . .

RAYLEE

We just tell the police, the judge, the fuckin' Mayor that we got cancer and there ain't no real cure.

DONYA

Yeah, it can come back even after you have that chemo and shit. Happened to my aunt.

MR. CUTTER

Chaos . . . calamity . . . conflict . . .

RAYLEE

You want a soda, Mr. C? (*beat*) Mr. C?

SILENCE. Then . . .

MR. CUTTER

A donut. (*beat*) Think I'd like a chocolate glazed donut.

MR. CUTTER shuts his eyes. RAYLEE and DONYA sip their sodas. RAYLEE looks up.

RAYLEE

You hear that?

DONYA

Bitch, I don't hear nothin'!

RAYLEE

Thought I heard someone callin' for help.

DONYA

Help?

RAYLEE

Yeah . . . (*loudly*) . . . HELP!

LIGHTS FADE TO BLACK. KNOCKING . . . KNOCKING . . . KNOCKING . . .

VOICES

HELP, SUPER BASKETBALL GIRL! HELP US! HELP! HELP! HELP!

FLYING SOUND then: SPOTLIGHT—SUDDENLY SUPER BASKETBALL GIRL AP-PEARS as the faculty room door flings open. She spins the basketball on her finger as the SOUND OF BULLETS ARE HEARD RICOCHETING off it.

BLACKOUT.

THE END

Theater for the New City Presents **Crystal Field Executive Director**

An Electric Black Experience   **A Gunplays Series**

SUBWAY STORY (A SHOOTING)

Written & Directed by William Electric Black
February 22 - March 18, 2018

THEATER FOR THE NEW CITY
155 FIRST AVE. (AT E. 10th STREET)
THURSDAYS - SATURDAYS AT 8:00 PM
SUNDAYS AT 3:00 PM
$15 GENERAL ADMISSION
$12 SENIORS/STUDENTS, $10 GROUPS
BOX OFFICE: (212) 254-1109
WWW.THEATERFORTHENEWCITY.NET

Featuring: Sebastian Gutierrez, Shyla Idris, Jeremy Lardieri, Mohamed Madboly, Natalie Marie Martino, Brandon Mellette, Jacqueline Nwabueze, John Patterson, Yessenia Rivas, Tournesoul, Camille Upshaw, and Levern Williams. Cast understudy: Ann-Kathryne Mills.

SET DESIGN: Lytza Colon & Mark Marcante
COSTUMES/PROPS: Susan Hemley
LIGHTING DESIGN: Alexander Bartenieff
SOUND DESIGN: James Mussen
SOUND TECH: Alex Santullo

STAGE MANAGER: Megan Horan
PROD. MANAGER: Dylan Vaughn Skorish
PERCUSSION ADVISOR: Jacob Shandling
PRESS REP: Jonathan Slaff
SOCIAL MEDIA: Ryan Leach

For tickets visit smarttix.com

gunplays.org   williamelectricblack.com

Subway Story (A Shooting)
Courtesy Erikka James

Subway Story
(A Shooting)

a play by

William Electric Black

A POLICE BAG CHECK table is present as the audience enters. Audience members should randomly be checked as they enter the theater. As they take their seats RANDOM HOMELESS PEOPLE with various signs sit in the stairs of the theater. There are subway signs (A TRAIN, 1 TRAIN, L TRAIN, ETC.) scattered about the theater. Signs are also present indicating assorted subway stations or stops. There might be a magazine stand—a drummer bangs on buckets as the audience enters or a guitar player strums a tune hoping to fill his suitcase with dollar bills. An MJ DANCER (Michael Jackson Impersonator) does his thing then disappears.

THE SOUND OF subway trains rushing along fills the air. Maybe a garbled announcement comes over the PA—there's train traffic up ahead, we'll be moving shortly . . .

An MTA WORKER sporting an orange vest, lantern, and orange helmet appears from time to time. Another garbled announcement comes over the PA—we are sorry for the delay . . .

THE STAIRS—seated on both sides of the audience serve as the stairs used by various assorted PASSENGERS rushing to get onto their trains or rushing to exit.

THE PLATFORM—becomes a platform or the interior of a train.

A SUBWAY CAR—behind the platform is used for assorted car scenes. Audience members ARE SEATED in this area as if in the car.

LIGHTS UP.

PROLOGUE

GOD, mid 20s, enters holding a sign: God Bless. A used CIGARETTE dangles from his lips. He is dressed in 70s GLAM ATTIRE.

GOD

And God shall wipe away all tears from their eyes and there shall be no more death, neither sorrow, nor crying, neither shall there be any more pain: for the former things are passed away.

ROCK MUSIC BLARES as PEOPLE scurry up and down subway stairs (audience stairs). DREAMER enters with a sign. He rushes off into the darkness. A HOMELESS GIRL sits on the steps, not moving. MTA HARDHAT WORKER with a lantern walks down the stairs and disappears into the darkness. More PEOPLE rush about. MJ DANCER dances a sec. MTA CONTROLLER enters with a flashlight. The CONTROLLER waves a flashlight then disappears. As the ROCK MUSIC reaches a climax the PEOPLE jam themselves into a subway car with GOD, cigarette still in his mouth.

GOD

Excuse me, can GOD get a damn seat?

BLACKOUT.

CHAPTER 1 . . . COME BACK HERE

LIGHTS UP on a SUBWAY PLATFORM BOOTH. BOOTH TELLER is on her cell phone.

BOOTH TELLER

(*on phone*) Yeah, girl . . . I even had to spell it out for him. I know, right. Is it worth it? HELL NO, his ass ain't! These men out here, I don't have to tell you. All they wanna do is get over and get some. Am I right? (*beat*) So, I'm like C . . . O . . . M . . . and he's like what are you doing?

CUSTOMER approaches.

CUSTOMER

Can you put 10 dollars on my card?

BOOTH TELLER does so. CUSTOMER exits.

CUSTOMER

Thanks . . .

BOOTH TELLER

I'm like I've been trying to tell you in so many ways but you ain't getting it. He's like . . .

BOYFRIEND 1 on stairs . . .

BOYFRIEND 1

Getting what?

BOOTH TELLER

That's when I says . . . getting no more of this until I get something on my finger. He's like . . .

BOYFRIEND 2 appears.

BOYFRIEND 2

Yeah, right.

BOOTH TELLER

Look, I <u>been</u> committed. When there's a kale recipe on The Chew I'm like HELLO, it's on his plate. And when Leon wanted to watch that Game of Thrones BS I gave the fool my HBO GO password. Talk about commitment.

CHEVONN enters. BLACK TEEN—her hand is bandaged and stays that way until the end of the play.

CHEVONN

Don't have my MetroCard.

BOOTH TELLER

And then for his birthday who got him Amazon Prime? Oh yes, I did.

CHEVONN

I gotta write a story . . . my teacher said . . .

BOOTH TELLER

Hold on . . . (*beat*) What are you saying girl?

CHEVONN

I don't have my MetroCard.

BOOTH TELLER

You kids always forgetting your card.

CHEVONN

Someone stole it.

BOOTH TELLER

Well, you got a problem, don't you?

CHEVONN

That's why I need you to please let me through.

BOOTH TELLER

What you gonna do tomorrow, and the day after that? (*back to phone*) Girl, I'm still here. Got some crazy teenager done got her card stolen. So, she says.

CHEVONN

YO, I'm telling the truth.

BOOTH TELLER

So, you say . . .

MUSLIM WOMAN enters, approaches booth.

MUSLIM WOMAN

Excuse me, the World Trade Center? I want to see the names . . . so many people died there.

CHEVONN jumps the turnstile.

BOOTH TELLER

HEY, COME BACK HERE. HEY . . . DAMN KIDS.

MUSLIM WOMAN

Excuse me, what train do I take?

LIGHTS FADE on booth. LIGHTS UP on the platform—MR. EVERS, high school teacher. He holds a composition book. He opens the book and begins reading.

*MEANS MR. EVERS IS READING DIRECTLY FROM THE NOTEBOOK—WHEN NO (*) IT'S AS IF HE HAS MEMORIZED WHAT HE IS READING SO HE CAN SPEAK CHEVONN'S WORDS DIRECTLY TO THE AUDIENCE WITHOUT READING THEM.

*MR. EVERS

SUBWAY STORY (A SHOOTING) by Chevonn Johnson. (*reading from book*) I jumped the turnstile because the Booth Lady wouldn't let me through. It's 7:30, the next morning after you threatened me. (*looks up*) Chevonn, I did not threaten you.

SCENE RESETS at booth. CHEVONN jumps the turnstile.

BOOTH TELLER

HEY, COME BACK HERE. HEY . . . DAMN KIDS.

MUSLIM WOMAN

Excuse me, what train do I take?

LIGHTS FADE on booth.

CHAPTER 2 . . . THE ASSIGNMENT

CHEVONN APPEARS on the SUBWAY PLATFORM.

CHEVONN

Are you threatening me?

MR. EVERS appears on the platform holding a blank composition book.

MR. EVERS

Chevonn, your journal is empty.

CHEVONN

Like my stomach . . .

MRS. JOHNSON appears on the stairs, CALLING OUT FROM A WINDOW.

MRS. JOHNSON

Chevonn . . . you play my numbers yet?

CHEVONN

There's nothing to eat.

MRS. JOHNSON

That money I give you ain't for food. It's for my Lotto tickets.

CHEVONN

Whatever . . .

MRS. JOHNSON

I know you ain't talkin' to me that way.

CHEVONN

There's no milk . . . no cereal . . . no bread . . .

MR. EVERS

You were supposed to write a non-fiction story last year to be promoted to 12th grade. That was our agreement.

CHEVONN

I got mad busy. I had other stuff to deal with.

MRS. JOHNSON

If you don't play my numbers I got something up here waiting for you.

MR. EVERS

Like what?

MTA CONTROLLER

DO NOT BLOCK THE DOORWAYS WHEN PASSENGERS ARE
GETTING ON AND OFF THE TRAINS.

*MRS. JOHNSON and PASSENGERS rush onto platform behind CHEVONN with irons in
their hands.*

MRS. JOHNSON

Child . . . this will teach you TO NEVER forget to play my numbers.

*THEY engulf CHEVONN, pressing their HOT irons into her body. SHE SCREAMS and the
sound transforms into a RUSHING TRAIN while LOUD BUCKET DRUMMING fills the
air.*

*OTHER PASSENGERS begin to rush up and down the stairwells. Some carry strollers, some
carry handbags, or backpacks, some have iPads, iPhones, shopping bags, food bags, dog carriers,
shopping carts, a bike, a box, food, sports equipment, gym bags, shoulder bags, e-readers—some
wear headphones, hats, caps, suits, T-shirts, dresses, skirts, sports gear . . .*

THEY RUSH UP AND DOWN finally cramming into the subway car.

PASSENGER

I'm eating pizza . . .

PASSENGER

Texting my lawyer . . .

PASSENGER

Playing Angry Bird . . .

PASSENGER

Playing with my angry child.

PASSENGER

Reading a comic . . . Spiderman!

                         PASSENGER

Taking up two seats.

                         PASSENGER

Excuse me, you're taking up two seats.

                         PASSENGER

Yes, I am.

                         PASSENGER

Asshole!

                         PASSENGER

I'm late.

                         PASSENGER

I'm early.

                              GOD

I'M GOD! YEAH . . . that's right.

                         CHEVONN

I haven't eaten.

                         ROCK ON

I have no place to crash.

                         PASSENGER

She's hot.

                         PASSENGER

He's hot!

                         PASSENGER

Damn it's hot in here.

                         PASSENGER

Can you move your bag?

                         PASSENGER

Can you move in?

PASSENGER

I was going to sit there.

PASSENGER

I'm looking at her ass.

PASSENGER

Did you touch my ass?

PASSENGER

DON'T TOUCH ME!

PASSENGER

GET THE FUCK OFF ME.

BAD KID 1

YO, LOOK AT THAT FREAK.

EMMETT

I'M NOT A FREAK!

ANNOUNCER

THIS TRAIN IS OUT OF SERVICE.

ALL

AHHHHHHH . . .

PASSENGER

Getting off.

PASSENGER

Is this train out of service?

MR. EVERS

If you don't hand in the assignment you will have to repeat 11th grade.

CHEVONN

I'm not repeating no damn 11th grade.

MUSLIM WOMAN

So many people . . .

PASSENGER

God, there are so many people on this train.

GOD

Yes, I know. I know everything.

PASSENGER

You want a seat?

PASSENGER

Take my seat, you're pregnant.

PASSENGER

Guess this I'm pregnant button really works.

ALL

I'M GETTING OFF.

PASSENGER

Is he jerking off?

PASSENGER

HEY . . .

PASSENGER

Hey . . .

PASSENGER

Fuck you!

PASSENGER

FUCK YOU!

ARMY

FUCKING HOT SUBWAY! IT'S LIKE IRAQ.

PASSENGER

It's like a zoo.

PASSENGER

ZOO STORY!

MR. EVERS

Write a story and you can stay in 12th grade.

DREAMER

Can I stay in America?

PASSENGER

Dreamer . . .

PASSENGER

GETTING OFF.

PASSENGER

GETTING ON.

PASSENGER

There's no room.

PASSENGER

There's room.

PASSENGER

MOVE IN.

PASSENGER

MOVE BACK WHERE YOU CAME FROM.

MTA WORKER

BACK AWAY FROM THE PLATFORM EDGE.

DREAMER

I'M NOT GOING BACK.

ARMY

I'M NOT GOING BACK.

CHEVONN

FUCK THAT, I'M NOT GOING BACK TO 11TH GRADE.

MR. EVERS

Then write something.

ANNOUNCER

THERE'S A SICK PASSENGER ON THE TRAIN IN FRONT OF US. WE
WILL BE MOVING SHORTLY.

ROCK ON

(*sings*) Get back . . . get back . . . get back to where you once belonged . . .

ALL

SORRY FOR THE DELAY.

LIGHTS BEGIN TO FADE.

ALL

SORRY FOR THE DELAY.

AND MORE . . .

ALL

SORRY FOR THE DELAY.

BLACKOUT—SUBWAY SOUNDS.

CHAPTER 3 . . . WRITE SOMETHING

LIGHTS UP on the platform.

CHEVONN

Okay, I'll write something . . .

MR. EVERS

And I want it by tomorrow.

VOICES

TOMORROW?

CHEVONN

So, I didn't go to school the next morning. I didn't eat no breakfast . . . and I didn't play Lotto for my mother.

MRS. JOHNSON appears in the window.

MRS. JOHNSON

Eat at school! Just go play my numbers.

CHEVONN

My story was going to be about shooting my mother. But I didn't have a piece. Gotta have some bank for a piece. Hell, I didn't even have enough for an egg sandwich.

ROCK ON

Excuse me . . .

ARMY

Excuse the interruption . . .

DREAMER

I don't mean to bother you . . .

GOD

I ain't no thief, I'M GOD! You are my children and God needs a new pair of sequin shoes.

ARMY

I'm a Vet! In Baghdad a 50 cal was my best friend. Over here, ain't got no friends.

ROCK ON

I'm a fuckin' rock star. Folks don't know it yet. BUT I FUCKIN KNOW IT. Wanna be my groupie?

DREAMER

I'm a Dreamer. President Trump wants to send me back to Mexico. I need money for Movimiento Cosecha!

ARMY

Need money for a MetroCard so I can ride the subway to forget the war. Riding makes me think I'm going somewhere.

GOD

HOW ABOUT HEAVEN?

ROCK ON

I'M A ROCKER and I need money to pay for musicians, studio time, clothes, booze, blow, women . . . what no sympathy for the devil?

CHEVONN

I need money to buy a gun.

MRS. JOHNSON

I always keep me a hot iron by my bed so you better just forget about breakfast and play my numbers.

CHEVONN

Fucking hate her . . . you would too. So, I'm gonna do two things. I am gonna write a story and . . .

*MR. EVERS

(*reading*) Get a gun and kill my mother. I don't know how it's gonna end, but this is how it starts. If I do what I say I'm gonna do, well, it's not really your fault. You're a good teacher, but I ain't such a good student. You wanted something true. Well, this is all I got.

CHEVONN

Excuse me, pardon me folks, sorry for the interruption . . . I just need some money to buy a gun so I can kill my mother . . . (*beat*) Anyone? Can anyone help me? Got any change?

PASSENGERS enter with subway maps, interacting with the audience.

PASSENGERS

Change at 14th Street for the L . . . for the F . . . Change at Union Square for the 6 . . . for the R . . . Q . . . Change at 59th St. for the A . . . D . . . 1 Train. Change at 125th for the C . . . Change at Grand Concourse for the 4 . . . Change at West 4th for the E. Change at Grand Army Plaza for the 2. Change at Hoyt for the G. Change at Forest Hills for the M. At Jamaica Center for the Z. At Broadway Junction for the J. Change at Grand Central for the 5. CHANGE . . . CHANGE . . . CHANGE.

They put away their maps and take out cans filled with change. They RATTLE the cans while they say . . . CHANGE. They enter a subway car. GOD enters the car.

GOD/PASSENGERS

. . . CHANGE . . . CHANGE . . . CHANGE . . . CHANGE . . .

THEY ALL KNEEL and begin to sing the National Anthem.

GOD/PASSENGERS

Oh, say can you see, the NFL take a knee . . .

THEY QUICKLY STAND.

CHEVONN

ANY DAMN CHANGE?

BLACKOUT.

SOUND OF SUBWAY CARS rushing along, then . . .

CHAPTER 4 . . . MTA ANNOUNCEMENT

LIGHTS UP. MTA PLATFORM CONTROLLER appears.

MTA CONTROLLER

SERVICE CHANGE . . . QUEENS BOUND LATE NIGHT E TRAINS STOP HERE AND RUN VIA THE F TO ROOSEVELT AVENUE. NO F TRAINS AT THIS STATION. F TRAINS ARE REROUTED VIA THE Q BETWEEN LEXINGTON AVE./63RD ST AND DEKALB AVE.—AND VIA THE D TO/ FROM STILLWELL AVE. FOR QUEENS F SERVICE, TAKE THE L TO 14TH ST./UNION SQ. AND TRANSFER TO THE F AT THE Q PLATFORM.

LIGHTS FADE . . .

CHAPTER 5 . . . NO ONE TOOK ME SERIOUSLY

LIGHTS UP on MR. EVERS, reading from the composition book.

*MR. EVERS

No one took me seriously.

RIDER

She can't be serious.

WOMAN

She's crazy.

GUY

CRAZY BITCH.

*MR. EVERS

In every car I went into . . .

PASSENGERS *change their stance as if on another car, then another* . . .

CHEVONN

No one took me seriously. (*beat*) Change? Anybody? I'm trying to get me a piece so I can shoot my mother.

MOTHER

You need help!

MAN 2

Girl needs help.

PERSON

Maybe it's a cry for help.

WOMAN 2

Does someone need help? Should I pull the emergency brake?

GUY

ARE YOU CRAZY? You never pull the emergency cord on a subway train when there's an emergency.

CHEVONN

There's no emergency brake on the 20th floor of the Thurgood Marshall Houses—2C.

MRS. JOHNSON

Chevonn . . . you hear me talkin' to you? Are you listening to me?

*MR. EVERS

In the last car that I went into . . .

CHEVONN

It was really hot.

MTA WORKER

Man, it's hot.

MUSLIM WOMAN

They said it was hot that day. Was it this hot?

ALL

SORRY FOR THE DELAY . . . there's a train crossing in front of us . . .

MR. EVERS

. . . I asked for money, to buy a gun, to shoot my mother just like I did in the other cars.

OLDER WOMAN

Shouldn't you be in school?

CHEVONN

Yeah, but I'm excused today because my teacher wants me to write a story . . . a real story. So, I'm writing it now.

MAN

Crazy Black girl . . .

LADY

Does your mother know you want to kill her?

CHEVONN

She ain't dumb. She knows.

EMMETT

Hey . . . you wanna gun?

*MR. EVERS

Some crazy white kid came up to me.

EMMETT

Hey, you want a gun or are you just frontin'?

CHEVONN

Now I know he's crazy. Tryin' to act Black. Talk Black.

ALL

Yeah, girlfriend! Uh-huh, I feel you. What? WHAT? SHAKE THAT BOOOOOTYYYY.

MRS. JOHNSON

You know your mother's crazy, Chevonn, so you better not be messin' with me.

*MR. EVERS

Whenever my mother said that . . . I left her alone.

CHEVONN

Do I know you?

EMMETT

You want a gun or not?

CHEVONN

Everyone in the train was silent.

ALL

We were silent.

CHEVONN

But I know they heard him. I heard him.

MAN

We didn't know what to say.

PASSENGER

What to do?

ANNOUNCER

42ND STREET . . . change here for the 2-3, R, N, W, Shuttle Train . . . the 7, with connections to the A . . . C . . . . DO NOT BLOCK THE DOORS. LET PASSENGERS OFF.

ALL EXIT the platform. CHEVONN and EMMETT stare at each other.

EMMETT

I have a gun inside my backpack. You want it?

CHEVONN

He didn't sound Black anymore. He sounded alone.

*MR. EVERS

Just like me.

ROCK ON appears with a guitar case. He takes out the guitar, places his case down, tosses a few dollars into the case. HE SINGS.

ROCK ON
WHEN I SEE KIM KARDASHIAN AND ALL THEM
OTHER DAMN KARDASHIANS ON TV
I WANT TO KILL MYSELF
WHEN STARBUCKS RAISES THE PRICE OF THEIR
ALREADY EXPENSIVE LATTES
I WANT TO KILL MYSELF
WHEN I SEE ANOTHER SUPERHERO MOVIE
STARRING ROBERT DOWNEY JUNIOR
I WANT TO KILL MYSELF
WHEN THEY PUT A SHITTY CITIBIKE RACK
RIGHT IN FRONT OF MY SHITTY EAST VILLAGE
APARTMENT BUILDING
I WANT TO KILL MYSELF OR GET A NEW APARTMENT

ROCK ON keeps strumming.

CHEVONN
What are you doing with a gun?

EMMETT
Was going to kill some assholes today. They did some shit to me, bad shit.

BAD KID 1
What's your problem trans kid? Your father wanted a boy so you became one.

BAD KID 2
You getting a sex change, or what?

EMMETT hands CHEVONN a backpack with a gun in it.

CHEVONN
Was gonna kill them?

EMMETT
I'm Emmett, no longer Emily. No longer trying to be what others want me to be . . . to do . . . to say. No longer being referred to as the strange kid. The odd kid. The lost kid.

BAD KIDS enter stairwell, house right.

BAD KID 1

YO, there goes that freak! The one that wants to be a dude and shit.

BAD KID 2

What we did to you was just the beginning.

BAD KID 1

You feel us?

*MR. EVERS

Emmett told me they all went to the same high school and every day they made his life a living hell.

BAD KIDS

FREAK! QUEER! SICK BITCH!

MR. EVERS

So, Emmett wasn't going to school today. Today . . .

EMMETT

I was going to kill them . . . then myself. Now just me. Will you do it?

CHEVONN

He wanted to die.

ARMY enters the other stairwell.

ARMY

Can anyone swipe me? Anyone?

ANNOUNCER

Stand clear of the closing doors.

MR. EVERS

They were coming towards us.

BAD 1

GET THE FREAK!

BAD 2

HEY, FREAK!

CHEVONN

. . . so, I grabbed Emmett, and we ran onto the 2 train.

ANNOUNCER

STAND CLEAR OF THE CLOSING DOORS.

DOORS CLOSE.

BAD KID 1

YO, we gonna get your ass!

BAD KID 2

Don't think you can get away!

BAD KID 1

Yeah, bitch!

BAD KIDS

YOU HEAR? YOU HEAR? YOU HEAR US?

BLACKOUT.

SPOTLIGHT up on MRS. JOHNSON at her window.

MRS. JOHNSON

CHEVONN? CHEVONN? Now I know that damn girl did not go out of here
and forget to play my numbers?

BLACKOUT.

CHAPTER 6 . . . THE REQUEST

SUBWAY CAR . . . RUMBLES ALONG.

*CHEVONN and EMMETT sit. CHEVONN looks inside the bag. She takes out her composi-
tion book and starts to write as PASSENGERS enter.*

PASSENGERS

I looked inside the backpack.

CHEVONN

There was a gun. (*to Emmett*) Is it real?

                              EMMETT

Fuck yeah, it's real.

                              CHEVONN

Where did you get it?

                              MR. EVERS

I asked?

                              PASSENGERS

Guns are everywhere?

                              EMMETT

It wasn't hard.

                              PASSENGERS

Lots of guns, so many guns . . .

                              CHEVONN

For real . . .

                              EMMETT

So, you really wanna kill your mother?

                              *MR. EVERS

He didn't believe me.

                              CHEVONN

What the fuck? You don't think I'm gonna do it.

                              EMMETT

Sorry, I didn't mean anything . . .

                              CHEVONN

Take your damn gun. Blow your own fucking brains out.

                              PASSENGERS

Getting off at the next stop.

                              EMMETT

I want you to have it.

CHEVONN

Don't want it.

PASSENGERS

Are you sure?

CHEVONN

Can get my own damn gun.

EMMETT

I can't do it.

ANNOUNCER

Next stop . . . Union Square.

PASSENGERS

He couldn't kill himself.

*MR. EVERS

He needed me. No one ever needed me before.

GOD wanders onto the train.

GOD

Excuse me, God's just strolling through. I'm in disguise. Undercover God. Trying to make sure you good folks know what truly matters.

*MR. EVERS

And then I realized what truly mattered.

GOD

Does Zero Coke matter? What Beyonce's dropping matter? Do you really give a shit if they have no more avocado toast or who the hell is Dancing With the Stars? OH, GOD, NO WI-FI SERVICE! Please stop calling my name out loud over bullshit.

EMMETT

Will you do it?

MR. EVERS

Emmett needed me.

PASSENGERS

Kill me then go kill your mother.

GOD

KILLING ME SOFTLY WITH HIS LOVE . . .

EMMETT

What do you think?

CHEVONN

I thought he was crazy.

EMMETT

Please, we'll find a place. I need your help; you need my gun.

MR. EVERS

The train pulled into the next station.

PASSENGERS

A lot of people got off.

PASSENGERS exit.

CHEVONN

But we stayed on. And so did God.

GOD

If I, GOD, gave you a billion dollars would you help the flood victims, the fire victims? Would you help a starving civilization, a drought plagued nation? Or would you say, fuck this shit, I'm getting me a Maserati, a mansion, and a mountain of mushrooms. PEOPLE, WHO ARE YOU?

BLACKOUT.

CHAPTER 7 . . . SCHEDULE CHANGE

CHEVONN

(*reading from her book*) Got off at the next stop so Emmett could get a map. That's when I saw Army, again. Rock On was counting his bank on the platform, nearby.

ROCK ON

(*strumming/humming*) Who are you—doot-doot-doot-doot. (*looks inside case*) Three dollars, what the fuck. Where's the love, people? Where's the love?

MRS. JOHNSON appears on the platform.

MRS. JOHNSON

Don't look to me for love, Chevonn. Ain't none here. My Momma took away most of it and your father took the rest. Especially after . . .

ROCK ON

A Canadian dollar? Damn it!

He KICKS his guitar case.

*MR. EVERS

Rock On is a regular down here. Seen him on the A-train, the E, even the 2-3. Candy Kid is also another subway fixture.

CANDY KID appears. He sells candy on the platform and continues selling to the audience.

CANDY KID

Got Sour Patches, M & M's, Twizzlers . . . two for a dollar.

CHEVONN

And Brother Drum? Man gives you a history lesson same time he be playing.

BROTHER DRUM appears. He drums.

BROTHER DRUM

The Djembi comes from the old Mali Empire. It is a hand drum made from a solid log of wood, laced with rope, and covered with a goat skin, and hollow on the inside.

*MR. EVERS

And them singing dudes . . . you know they go from car to car singing Swing Low Sweet Chariot, or some whack 50s tune no one ever heard of.

SINGERS/BUSKERS appear. They sing.

BUSKERS

SWING LOW, SWEET CHARIOT . . . DOO-WHOP-SHE-WHOP.

BROTHER DRUM, CANDY KID, BUSKERS exit.

CHEVONN

Once, I saw Army in the tunnel. The one that goes from 7th Avenue to 6th, where you catch the L Train. Army was just sitting there . . .

EMMETT

We need a map.

CHEVONN

I'm writing something.

*MR. EVERS

What, Emmett asked me.

ARMY

Need to get on the train. I was already on the C, but I had to get off and get my bag. See? Got it right here.

ARMY shows BOOTH TELLER his army bag.

BOOTH TELLER

Yeah, I see it.

ARMY

So, can you let me through?

EMMETT

What are you writing?

CHEVONN

A story about how one day I shot my mother. And about all the other mad crazy folks that I seen along the way.

BOOTH TELLER

Are you crazy?

ARMY

For going to war? For serving this country? Guess that's what I'm trying to figure out. So, can you let me through the damn gate?

BOOTH TELLER

And lose my job over some BS?

EMMETT

Can I get a map?

ARMY

Hey, I'm talking.

CHEVONN

She was talking.

ARMY

I'm dealing with things . . . bad things that I don't wanna deal with.

CHEVONN

Like what?

*MR. EVERS

I wanted him to tell me.

EMMETT

Me, too . . .

CHEVONN

Found out there are lots of people riding the subway dealing with stuff.

MR. EVERS

Not just me.

ARMY

FUCK IT . . . I'll get someone to swipe me.

ARMY slings his bag over his shoulder and storms off.

EMMETT

I'll get a map from some other booth. You coming?

EMMETT exits. CHEVONN turns and bumps into MUSLIM WOMAN.

MUSLIM WOMAN

Excuse me, I am looking for the World Trade Center. No one will tell me. They are afraid of me. I fly here from Canada just to visit the site. On the plane I heard

MUSLIM WOMAN (CONT'D)

whispers. People did not want me on board. They said horrible things to me. Do you want to hear what they said?

CHEVONN

So, I listened. And so did God.

GOD enters the platform.

GOD

I'M WALKING INTO THE FIRE. WHO WILL WALK WITH ME?

MUSLIM WOMAN

I AM ALWAYS WALKING INTO THE FIRE. (*beat*) MY FEET . . . MY FEET . . . THEY BURN.

CHEVONN

Just like my hand.

CHEVONN shows the MUSLIM WOMAN her bandaged hand. A Muslim PRAYER is heard in the distance.

LIGHTS FADE.

CHAPTER 8 . . . THE FIRE

A RED WASH fills the theater. VOICES HUMM . . .

GOD

I saw the dust, the debris, the flames . . .

MUSLIM WOMAN

They say there are new towers now, and a museum.

CHEVONN

Did you ever talk to people in the subway, Mr. Evers?

*MR. EVERS

Did you ever walk into the fire with God?

GOD

There was a flash . . . we never thought they would launch a missile.

MUSLIM WOMAN

Two planes that day . . . no one suspected.

CHEVONN

The iron . . . so hot . . .

GOD

When it came . . .

MUSLIM WOMAN

When they hit . . .

CHEVONN

When she pressed it on my hand . . .

MUSLIM WOMAN

Can you imagine?

GOD

No one imagined the destruction . . . that came with the fire.

CHEVONN

The heat . . .

MUSLIM WOMAN

So hot the beams, the concrete, glass . . . all melted.

CHEVONN

My hand, the skin . . . my flesh melted.

GOD

The people, dying . . .

MUSLIM WOMAN

Screaming . . .

CHEVONN

I'M SCREAMING STOP! STOP! WHY ARE YOU DOING THIS? WHY?

MUSLIM WOMAN

WHY?

GOD

WHY SO MUCH DEATH? WHY SO MUCH PAIN? WHY SO MUCH FIRE?
LOOK AROUND. CAN YOU SEE THE FIRE? TOUCH IT! TOUCH IT!
LET YOUR TEARS FALL INTO IT.

CHEVONN

My tears?

MUSLIM WOMAN

My tears?

GOD

YOU can put out the fire. YOU can stop the burning.

MUSLIM WOMAN

Buildings burning . . .

CHEVONN

My hand is burning . . .

GOD

Walk into the fire with your tears.

CHEVONN is lifted into the air.

MR. EVERS

So, I did. And my body went up, into the air, over the turnstiles, over the stairs and
out onto the street—up to the 20th floor, 2C, into my mother's bedroom where I
saw the fire.

CHEVONN

She held the iron on top of her hand, turned towards me and said . . .

MRS. JOHNSON

My mother put an iron on my hand and said, Girl . . . this world out here is
hurtful. You just got to take the hurt. No tears, you hear me? My child will not
drown in no tears. So, you listen up, Chevonn. Do not cry in my house. I NEVER

MRS. JOHNSON (CONT'D)
CRIED IN MY MOTHER'S HOUSE SO, THERE WILL BE NO CRYING
IN MINE.

MRS. JOHNSON exits.

CHEVONN
I flew back over street corners where gang drive-bys shoot down my hopes and dreams, while on their way to buy more guns and drugs and guns and drugs . . . I flew by a mixed tape my dad once gave me, now tossed down a drain. Back, I flew, down into the subway and landed onto the train platform.

CHEVONN is lowered to the ground.

*MR. EVERS
I turned to God and said . . .

CHEVONN
I've never cried in my life.

MR. EVERS
And God said . . .

GOD
Then cry now . . .

CHEVONN
Cry now and put out the fire.

MUSLIM WOMAN
But cry she could not.

BLACKOUT.

CHAPTER 9 . . . CRY SONG

ROCK ON enters subway car STRUMMING on his guitar.

ROCK ON
YOU EVER SEE ANYONE CRY ON THE SUBWAY
YOU EVER SEE THEM CRY AND WONDER

ROCK ON (CONT'D)
WHAT BROUGHT ON ALL THE PAIN . . .
A BREAK-UP, A DEATH, AN ILLNESS
JUST LOST A JOB, THEIR HOME, NOW
THEY'RE STUCK ON THIS DAMN TRAIN
WITH PEOPLE STARING AT THEM, BUT
THEY JUST STAND AND KEEP . . .
(*beat*)

SILENT . . .

LIGHTS FADE.

Chevonn asks passengers for change so she can buy a gun to shoot her mother.
Photo by Jonathan Slaff

MTA Worker (Sebastian Gutierrez) shines light during blackout.
Photo by Jonathan Slaff

MTA Worker (Jeremy Lardieri) dances with passengers.
Photo by Jonathan Slaff

CHAPTER 10 . . . CHEVONN WRITES

LIGHTS UP on CHEVONN sitting on the subway stairs writing in her book.

CHEVONN

Emmett was looking for me. I forgot he went looking for a map.

LIGHTS FADE.

CHAPTER 11 . . . ARMY UNRAVELS

BOOTH TELLER sits at her window on the phone. PASSENGER approaches.

PASSENGER

Do you have a subway map?

BOOTH TELLER

No.

PASSENGER exits.

BOOTH TELLER

(*on phone*) Leon, I've been calling you all morning. Why you just picking up the phone now? (*beat*) You were busy? Busy doing what?

EMMETT enters.

EMMETT

Excuse me, did you see my friend? I thought she was going to follow me to get a map.

BOOTH TELLER

What does she look like?

EMMETT

Well, she's Black.

BOOTH TELLER

That's all you got for me? You know how many Black women take the subway?

EMMETT

No.

BOOTH TELLER

Neither do I but there are lots and lots, so you are gonna hafta do better than Black. (*beat*) Come back when you got a better description.

EMMETT exits.

BOOTH TELLER

Leon, you will not believe what just happened. A white kid just asked me if I had seen a Black girl down here in the subway where there's thousands of us. Leon? LEON? Oh no, he did not hang up on me.

ARMY enters.

ARMY

Can you let me in the gate. I'm a Vet. I was here before.

BOOTH TELLER

I know who you are. And my answer is still NO.

ARMY

NO?

ARMY reveals an automatic weapon from his bag.

ARMY

OPEN THE FUCKING GATE, NOW!

BOOTH TELLER

Okay . . . just go on through. Don't hurt . . .

ARMY

NOW I CAN GO THROUGH? NOW IT'S, OKAY?

VOICES

NOW . . . NOW . . . NOW . . . NOW . . . NOW . . . NOW . . .
KILL . . . KILL . . . KILL . . . KILL . . . KILL . . . KILL . . .

The sound of a TRAIN ROARING BY, BUCKET DRUMMING, the RATTLING OF LOOSE CHANGE in cup.

BLACKOUT.

CHAPTER 12 . . . MTA ANNOUNCEMENT

MTA PLATFORM CONTROLLER appears.

MTA CONTROLLER

FARE EVASION IS DEFINED UNDER PENAL CODE 1050.4. NO PERSON
SHALL USE OR ENTER UPON THE FACILITIES OR CONVEYANCES
OF THE AUTHORITY, FOR ANY PURPOSE, WITHOUT THE PAYMENT
OF THE FARE OR TENDER OF OTHER VALID FARE MEDIA USED IN
ACCORDANCE WITH ANY CONDITIONS AND RESTRICTIONS
IMPOSED BY THE AUTHORITY.

LIGHTS FADE.

CHAPTER 13 . . . WALKING WITH GOD

*PASSENGERS CHANT "KILL . . . KILL . . . KILL . . . KILL . . . KILL" AS THEY RUSH
UP AND DOWN the stairs finally cramming into the subway car. THE SOUND OF
DRUMMING AND ELECTRIC GUITAR RIFFS. CHANTING AND SOUNDS STOP,
THEN . . .*

CHEVONN

So, I walked with GOD. He didn't pay his fare . . . just went right through them
security gates like he didn't give a damn. So, I followed.

*MR. EVERS

And no one said nothing. Besides . . . what can you really say to God. I mean—
GOD???

CHEVONN

His sermon on the train was . . .

GOD

DO NOT! DO NOT! DO NOT! DO NOT! DO NOT!

CHEVONN

I looked around and realized there are a lot of DO NOT do this, and DO NOT
do that signs in the subway. But there wasn't one that said DO NOT SHOOT
YOUR MOTHER.

PASSENGER

DO NOT ENTER OR CROSS ONTO THE TRACKS.

PASSENGER

DO NOT SMOKE.

DREAMER appears on the train with his DACA PROTEST SIGN.

DREAMER

DO NOT PLAN AHEAD. Your future has been destroyed. The program known as DACA will no longer protect 800,000 undocumented immigrants from being deported. You are not safe . . . no longer secure. Your jobs, homes, family are truly, just a dream. DO NOT PLAN ON STAYING HERE. DO NOT PLAN ON GOING TO COLLEGE. DO NOT PASS GO. DO NOT COLLECT $200.

PASSENGER

DO NOT BLOCK THE DOORS.

PASSENGER

DO NOT HOLD THE DOORS . . .

PASSENGER

DO NOT PLAY LOUD MUSIC . . .

BLARING LOUD MUSIC is heard. PASSENGERS cover their ears.

MUSLIM WOMAN

DO NOT BE AFRAID OF MY BURKA.

PASSENGER

DO NOT SIT WITH YOUR LEGS SPREAD.

PASSENGER

DO NOT LEAN ON THE DOORS.

MJ DANCER

DO NOT DANCE DOWN THE AISLE.

MJ DANCER does a move, then suddenly STOPS. MRS. JOHNSON appears.

MRS. JOHNSON

DO NOT FORGET TO PLAY MY NUMBERS. HEAR ME?

PASSENGER

DO NOT EAT FOOD.

GOD

DO NOT PULL THE EMERGENCY BRAKE . . . UNLESS YOU'RE GOD.

BAD KID 1

DO NOT SPIT ON THE FLOOR.

BAD KID 1 spits on floor.

ROCK ON

DO NOT PANIC IF YOU ARE STUCK IN THE
SUBWAY FOR HOURS. I'LL PLAY FOR YOU.

PASSENGERS panic. They SCREAM as ROCK ON strums.

BOOTH TELLER

DO NOT GIVE UP YOUR HBO GO PASSWORD IF THE FOOL WON'T
COMMIT.

BAD KID 2

DO NOT CROSS IN BETWEEN CARS WHEN THE TRAIN IS MOVING.
YEAH, RIGHT!

PASSENGER

DO NOT URINATE IN BETWEEN CARS.

BAD KIDS 1 & 2

YEAH, RIGHT.

ARMY

DO NOT GO INTO A MILITARY SHOWER, IF YOU ARE FEMALE,
WITHOUT YOUR WEAPON.

PASSENGER

DO NOT BLAME EVERYTHING ON OBAMA.

MTA CONTROLLER

DO NOT BE AFRAID TO TAKE THE SHUTTLE BUS.

PASSENGER

DO NOT CUT ME WITH YOUR RAZOR.

PASSENGER

DO NOT ALLOW <u>THEM</u> TO TAKE AWAY BIRTH CONTROL.

EMMETT

DO NOT ALLOW <u>THEM</u> TO KEEP A TRANSGENDER PERSON FROM JOINING THE MILITARY.

PASSENGER

DO NOT ALLOW THEM TO STOP PEOPLE FROM VOTING.

DREAMER

DO NOT BUILD A WALL.

MTA CONTROLLER

DO NOT JUMP THE TURNSTILE.

MRS. JOHNSON

DO NOT SHOOT YOUR MOTHER.

PASSENGER

DO NOT LITTER.

CHEVONN

DO NOT CUT SUBSIDIES TO HEALTH CARE.

PASSENGER

DO NOT PANHANDLE.

GOD/VOICES

DO NOT. DO NOT. DO NOT. DO NOT. DO NOT.

PASSENGER

DO NOT DESTROY SUBWAY PROPERTY.

MUSLIM WOMAN

DO NOT BAN MUSLIMS FROM TRAVELING HERE.

BAD KIDS

DO NOT SHOOT ME! MY HANDS ARE UP.

CHEVONN

DO NOT MAKE ME WRITE A DUMB STORY.

GOD

DO NOT. DO NOT. DO NOT. DO NOT. DO NOT.

MTA CONTROLLER

DO NOT MAKE YOURSELF A TARGET OF OPPORTUNITY.

MR. EVERS

CHEVONN . . . YOUR STORY OR NO 12TH GRADE.

MRS. JOHNSON

CHEVONN . . . PLAY MY LOTTO OR YOU KNOW WHAT.

EMMETT

CHEVONN . . . SHOOT ME OR I'LL JUMP.

ALL (REPEAT 4X)

IF YOU SEE SOMETHING . . . A SUSPICIOUS PACKAGE . . . A PERSON
AT RISK . . .

GOD

WHAT IF YOU SEE GOD?

DREAMER

WHAT IF YOU SEE THEM DRAGGING YOUR NEIGHBOR AWAY? HER
CHILDREN CRYING? HER HUSBAND POWERLESS TO DO
ANYTHING. THE COMMUNITY POWERLESS TO STOP THE
AUTHORITIES FROM SENDING YOU AWAY.

ARMY

WHAT IF YOU SEE A SOLDIER WITH HIS LEGS GONE, HIS BRAINS
RIPPED AWAY BY MORTAR SHELLS, HIS BODY SENT HOME IN A
COFFIN WITH A FLAG DRAPED OVER IT.

BOOTH TELLER

WHAT IF HE WON'T COMMIT TO LOVE, TO CARING, TO
GOODNESS, TO KINDNESS, TO COMPASSION, TO
UNDERSTANDING . . .

MUSLIM WOMAN

WHAT IF THE TOWERS NEVER FELL. WHAT IF A FAMILY NEVER
LOST A LOVED ONE ON THAT DAY?

ROCK ON

WHAT IF BOWIE AND PRINCE, TOM PETTY, MICHAEL JACKSON, JAMES BROWN, JANIS JOPLIN, JOHN LENNON, AND BOB MARLEY WERE STILL ALIVE AND PLAYING TONITE AT MSG. HELL, I'D EVEN PAY TO SEE THAT SHIT.

CHEVONN

WHAT IF WHEN YOU LOOKED UP GOD WASN'T THERE.

MR. EVERS

The train stopped at West 4th Street and God left with everyone else.

PASSENGERS exit the car.

CHEVONN

Just like that night in Chicago . . . when God left my cousin Jay D.

PHONE RINGS. SPOT hits MRS. JOHNSON as she answers her cell phone.

MR. EVERS

It was Aunt Mary. She didn't stay on long, but I knew . . .

CHEVONN

Something was wrong.

MR. EVERS

Heard a crash from my mother's bedroom.

MRS. JOHNSON knocks over the IRONING BOARD, then . . .

MRS. JONHSON

OH GOD! OH, GOD! GOD NO!

CHEVONN

There was lots of screaming . . .

MRS. JONHSON/ALL

OH GOD! OH, GOD! GOD NO!

CHEVONN

She just kept on screaming, even after she dropped the phone.

MR. EVERS

So, I picked it up. HELLO?

VOICE

Chevonn? That you, Baby?

CHEVONN

Cousin Jay D.'s been what?

*MR. EVERS

She told me Jay D. had been . . .

VOICE

He got shot, Baby. Jay D. is dead. Him and 100 other folks got shot over the weekend.

MRS. JOHNSON/ALL

GOD, OH GOD. GOD . . .

MR. EVERS

God left Chicago . . .

CHEVONN

Now I know why my mother dropped the phone. I'm sure there were others who dropped their phone after they got the same news.

PASSENGERS appear on the stairs and drop their phones.

ALL

Phones dropping in Las Vegas . . . Orlando . . . Sandy Hook . . . Virginia Tech . . .

MRS. JOHNSON

OH, GOD! OH, GOD! GOD, NO!

ALL

Phones dropping in Chicago . . . Baltimore . . . Oakland . . . New York . . . Newark . . .

The ENSEMBLE drops more phones. Then SILENCE.

CHEVONN

On the stairs to the F train, I saw Emmett.

CHEVONN and EMMETT meet on the stairs.

                         EMMETT

Where the hell have you been?

                         CHEVONN

I lost God. Have to find him. Have to ask him why he left. Why he's always leaving.

                         EMMETT

Left?

                         CHEVONN

Don't you get it?

                         *MR. EVERS

Did he get it?

                         EMMETT

God? Yeah, I get it. Things are terrible. For you, for me . . . (*beat*) What if I shoot God?

EMMETT takes his backpack.

                         CHEVONN

Shoot God? Then I would have to kill you.

                         EMMETT

I was hoping you would say that.

EMMETT exits.

                         CHEVONN

He headed for the F train looking for God.

                    CHEVONN/MR. EVERS

I HAD TO STOP HIM.

SOUND OF TRAINS roaring by.

BLACKOUT.

CHAPTER 14 . . . MTA ANNOUNCEMENT

MTA PLATFORM CONTROLLER appears.

MTA CONTROLLER
PLEASE STAND AWAY FROM THE PLATFORM EDGE WHEN THE
TRAIN IS PULLING INTO THE STATION. IN 2015, THERE WERE 172
INCIDENTS INVOLVING CUSTOMERS WHO CAME IN CONTACT
WITH TRAINS. 50 PEOPLE DIED. LET'S TRAVEL TOGETHER, SAFELY.

SUBWAY SOUNDS . . . BLACKOUT.

CHAPTER 15 . . . THE GOD AND THE BAD

*SFX: TRAINS RUSHING. MJ DANCER appears for a moment, then GONE. PASSEN-
GERS FLOOD the stairs with cardboard signs. They RUSH up and down and up and down.*

HOMELESS
CAN ANYBODY SPARE ANY FOOD . . .

HOMELESS
GOD, BLESS.

HOMELESS
HELP ME, GOD.

HOMELESS
HELP, PLEASE.

HOMELESS
GOD, PLEASE.

HOMELESS
HAVE MERCY, GOD.

HOMELESS
PITY.

HOMELESS
I'M DIABETIC.

HOMELESS

I HAVE HIV. GOD BLESS.

HOMELESS

I LIVE IN A SHELTER.

HOMELESS

THE STREET.

HOMELESS

SO HUNGRY. GOD HELP ME.

HOMELESS

I HAVE CANCER. GOD, PLEASE.

The HOMELESS repeat the above lines directly to the audience.

*MR. EVERS

Mr. Evers, did you know there are a lot of people who believe in God. My mother used to take me to church when I was little . . . I even sang in the choir for a while.

CHEVONN enters the stairs. She sings softly.

CHEVONN/MR. EVERS

(*sing*) Amazing Grace
How sweet the sound . . .
That saved a wretch like me
I once was lost, but now am found
'Twas blind but now I see

The HOMELESS join her.

ALL

(*sing*) Amazing Grace
How sweet the sound . . .
That saved a wretch like me
I once was lost, but now am found

The HOMELESS continue humming.

CHEVONN

But life changed after my father left. And when we did try to go to church one Easter Sunday we found out someone had turned our church into some condos. God had moved on up to Harlem and was now drinking Pinot Grigio, sporting an Armani suit, and walking his French bulldog in Marcus Garvey Park.

GOD

And God goes to the Red Rooster on Jazz Nights to hear a sweet trumpet blow and a mean bass go boom-boom, boom-boom . . .

HOMELESS

Boom-boom, boom-boom . . . Boom-boom, boom-boom . . . Boom-boom, boom-boom . . .

EMMETT enters and stands on the edge of the tracks. CHEVONN writes.

CHEVONN

When I got to the F train platform Emmett was standing on the edge . . . making people very nervous.

MR. EVERS

(*reading*) A man yelled at her.

MAN/MR. EVERS

HEY! HEY, YOU! MOVE BACK.

CHEVONN

EMMETT, WHAT THE HELL ARE YOU DOING?

EMMETT

God's down there on the tracks. I know he is.

CHEVONN

What are you talking about?

EMMETT

If I go down there . . . I'll find him.

CHEVONN

God is not real. He's just some guy walking through the subway cars.

                          EMMETT
But you saw him. You said . . .

                          CHEVONN
I know what I said.

                          EMMETT
It's the only way . . . then I know you'll do it.

                          VOICES
STAND BACK FROM THE PLATFORM EDGE.

GOD appears.

                          GOD
He wants to walk into the fire. Can't stop the music.

                          EMMETT
I stood here before.

                          MR. EVERS
I didn't know what he was talking about.

                          CHEVONN
On the edge?

                          EMMETT
After that day at school. The day they grabbed me.

BAD KIDS 1 and 2 appear. They grab EMMETT.

                          CHEVONN
Emmett said they stripped him naked.

                          MR. EVERS
Then they tied his hands behind his back.

BAD KIDS mime stripping EMMETT then tying his hands.

                          EMMETT
Stop . . . what are you doing?

                    BAD KID 1
We want everyone to see the real you!

                    BAD KID 2
See what you really are.

                    CHEVONN
They took out a can of spray paint . . .

                    *MR. EVERS
And sprayed the word FREAK on Emmett's arms . . .

BAD KIDS mime spraying EMMETT.

                EMMETT/MR. EVERS
STOP.

                    BAD KIDS
LEGS.

                EMMETT/MR. EVERS
DON'T.

                    BAD KIDS
ARMS.

                EMMETT/MR. EVERS
STOP.

                    BAD KIDS
FACE.

                    EMMETT
HELP ME! SOMEONE HELP!

                    CHEVONN
And then left Emmett in the hallway, naked.

ENSEMBLE gathers around EMMETT. They take out their phones.

                    EMMETT
Kids laughed . . . took videos . . . photos . . . posted them.

CHEVONN

Finally, a teacher came and covered him up.

TEACHER covers EMMETT with a coat. The STUDENTS move away.

EMMETT

That very same day I came here . . . I came to the edge looking for God. Just like you did.

*MR. EVERS

You see, he said. I know God's down there. He lets bad things happen to me, so I have to find him and shoot him.

EMMETT

I have to.

EMMETT steps closer to the edge about to go over . . . A TRAIN ROARS CLOSER.

VOICES

STOP! DON'T! MOVE BACK! MOVE BACK! MOVE BACK!

CHEVONN

WAIT . . . STOP! I'LL FUCKIN' DO IT! (*beat*) I was assaulted, too.

SILENCE.

*MR. EVERS

He stepped back.

A TRAIN roars into the station. LIGHTS FLICKER.

EMMETT

You too?

CHEVONN

Me too. By my father . . .

LIGHTS FADE.

CHAPTER 16 . . . MTA ANNOUNCEMENT

FLASHLIGHTS flicker in the darkness.

ANNOUNCEMENT

THIS TRAIN IS OUT OF SERVICE. PLEASE EXIT THE TRAIN. THERE
ARE NO TRAINS AT THIS STOP. PLEASE EXIT THE STATION

The FLASHLIGHTS go BLACK.

CHAPTER 17 . . . WHAT'S GOING ON

LIGHTS UP.

PASSENGERS are jammed onto the subway platform. Very upset.

PASSENGER

Does anyone know what's going on?

PASSENGER

There are no trains.

PASSENGER

I bet it's the Russians.

PASSENGER

Maybe ISIS?

PASSENGER

What about the Long Island Railroad?

PASSENGER

There's no Long Island Railroad. No Metro North.

PASSENGERS

WHAT THE . . . ? THIS IS CRAZY! THIS IS BS! SHIT!

CHEVONN

There were no trains and people were getting mad pissed.

MR. EVERS

Nobody could get uptown, downtown . . . even New Jersey Transit was shut down.

PASSENGER

Hey, my phone says there's someone in the subway with a gun.

                    PASSENGER

A gun?

                    PASSENGER

IS THIS FAKE NEWS?

                    PASSENGER

Maybe North Korea's missiles have launched?

                    PASSENGER

I'm sure the police have it under control.

                    PASSENGER

Is the person Black? I hope it's not a Black person.

                    PASSENGER

What's the difference?

                    PASSENGER

They shoot first!

                    PASSENGER

That's not fair.

                    PASSENGER

Is it fair that Black folks keep getting shot by the police?

                    PASSENGER

Maybe they deserve to get shot.

                    PASSENGER

And maybe white supremacists deserve to open up charter schools. ALT RIGHT
SUCCESS ACADEMY where we learn our A-B-C's along with our K-K-K's!

                    PASSENGER

Hey, fuck you!

                    PASSENGER

Fuck you and your Christopher Columbus statues!

                    PASSENGER

Well fuck Obama! Fuck the Mexicans! The Muslims! Jews!

PASSENGER

Ah, you forgot the Asians!

PASSENGERS begin yelling, pushing, shoving, brawling . . . POLICE SIRENS, WHIS-TLES fill the air. The PASSENGERS continue fighting but in slow motion as THE SOUND OF MARCHES, PROTESTS, fill the air. SPOTLIGHT up on ROCK ON. With guitar. HE SINGS.

ROCK ON

GOT THE WHITE HOUSE BLUES
SOMEBODY PLEASE HELP ME
GOT THE WHITE HOUSE BLUES
LORD, SOMEBODY PLEASE HELP ME
CAUSE WE'RE THE UNITED STATES OF HATRED
ONE NATION UNDER RACISM AND BIGOTRY . . . .

The brawling PASSENGERS now join in singing along with ROCK ON.

ROCK ON/PASSENGERS

GOT THE WHITE HOUSE BLUES
SOMEBODY PLEASE HELP ME
GOT THE WHITE HOUSE BLUES
LORD SOMEBODY PLEASE, PLEASE HELP ME
CAUSE WE'RE THE UNITED STATES OF HATRED
ONE NATION UNDER RACISM AND BIGOTRY . . . .

They go back to yelling, fighting, shoving, cursing . . .

LIGHTS FADE.

CHAPTER 18 . . . MTA ANNOUNCEMENT

LIGHTS UP.

MTA CONTROLLER

THERE ARE NO TRAINS RUNNING AT THIS TIME. PLEASE EXIT THE STATION.

LIGHTS FADE.

CHAPTER 19 . . . THE SUBWAY TUNNEL

CHEVONN and EMMETT now stand in an abandoned WORK TUNNEL.

*MR. EVERS
There was so much pushing and shoving going on no one noticed when we jumped down onto the tracks and just started walking.

EMMETT
I heard people live down here.

CHEVONN
And die down here.

EMMETT
Yeah . . . I'm ready to die.

*MR. EVERS
I didn't say anything.

CHEVONN
(*writing in composition book*) In fact, we were both silent for a while. Like we were waiting for something or someone.

*MR. EVERS
Remember when we watched West Side Story, Mr. Evers? And at the beginning of the movie Tony was waiting for something.

EMMETT
I'm not afraid. I want you to do it.

CHEVONN
I didn't say you were afraid. It's just that if I do this, what happens to me?

VOICES
BLACK GIRL SHOOTS WHITE KID IN SUBWAY TUNNEL.

CHEVONN
No one will understand.

EMMETT
No one ever understands. (*beat*) But maybe after they read your story they will.

CHEVONN

My story's not finished.

EMMETT

So, finish it.

*MR. EVERS

He handed me the backpack with the gun still inside it.

EMMETT

Finish it. Finish the damn story.

CHEVONN

The story's about my mother. Not about you.

EMMETT

You hate her. She let your father do horrible things to you.

CHEVONN

And you let some thugs rip your clothes off and spray paint you. Why don't you shoot them?

EMMETT

Fuck you, I didn't let them do it.

CHEVONN

Fuck you, I didn't let my father rape me.

EMMETT

I'm tired of this! JUST DO IT. DO IT NOW!

EMMETT takes the gun out of the bag and places it in CHEVONN's hand. EMMETT tries to force CHEVONN to shoot him but is suddenly frozen by ARMY's entrance from the darkness. He aims his weapon at both of them.

ARMY

The dead can only shoot the dead.

CHEVONN

I asked him what he meant. He replied . . .

ARMY

Can't you see I'm already dead.

VOICES IN THE DARK

KILL-KILL-KILL-KILL . . . KILL . . . KILL . . .

HELICOPTER/JET FIGHTER SOUNDS.

LIGHTS FADE.

CHAPTER 20 . . . MTA ANNOUNCEMENT

In the DARKNESS flashlights flicker. ANNOUNCEMENT is heard.

ANNOUNCER

THERE ARE NO TRAINS BETWEEN 241ST AND SOUTH FERRY. DUE TO AN EARLIER INCIDENT FREE SHUTTLE BUSES WILL OPERATE BETWEEN 241ST AND SOUTH FERRY.

FLICKERING FLASHLIGHTS FADE.

CHAPTER 21 . . . BOOTH TELLER

LIGHTS UP on booth.

BOOTH TELLER

(*on her phone*) He was right in front of me, Leon. He was right there and I thought . . . oh, my God. He's going to shoot me and I am going to die right now. Then I thought about you. What would you say when you heard the news that I was shot. Yeah, they told me that I could go, but . . . but I can't move. I've just been watching hundreds of police run by me. They got all these weapons and I'm thinking that poor soldier don't stand a chance. He comes back from war, and he gets this? It's my fault, though. He asked me to let him through the gate and I didn't. I was trying to be some big shot, someone who thinks she's all that. But I'll tell you something, I ain't all that, Leon. Right now, I ain't nothing. (*beat*) Why did I call you earlier? It wasn't important, Leon. It was nothing. Nothing at all.

SOUND OF POLICE RADIOS/SIRENS.

LIGHTS FADE.

CHAPTER 22 . . . TUNNEL OF HELL

CHEVONN, EMMETT, and ARMY are where we saw them last. ARMY continues to hold his automatic weapon on them.

CHEVONN
(*writing in her book*) Can't you see? I'm already dead.

ARMY
What the hell you doing?

EMMETT
She's writing a story that no one will ever read.

CHEVONN
My teacher, Mr. Evers, he'll read it.

EMMETT
He's not going to read it.

ARMY looks up.

ARMY
He'll read it if I'm in your story. No one passes up a chance to meet death. I didn't.

SOUND OF HUMVEES/CONVOY rolling along. HEADLIGHTS appear in the stairways. JAMES BROWN music mixes in during the following . . .

ARMY
I was leading a convoy to Baghdad. Lt. knew it was a road to hell because insurgents had launched several rocket-propelled grenades at other convoys just days ago.

*MR. EVERS
He said 5.56 mm. rounds hit them like . . .

ARMY
. . . A James Brown rhythm section. BAM. And when several pressure plated IEDs exploded they made a noise 100 times louder than any shriek the Godfather of Soul could ever make.

A James Brown shriek is heard along with . . .

> **VOICES**
> . . . . AHHHHHHHHHHHHHHH

> **ARMY**
> My Humvee took a hit . . .

EXPLOSIONS rock the tunnel. POLICE RADIOS get louder. The HEADLIGHTS (FLASHLIGHTS) shake, move about.

> **MR. EVERS**
> He said the brains of his gunner splattered across his face.

> **VOICES**
> THIS IS THE NYPD . . . DROP YOUR WEAPON.

> **ARMY**
> I grabbed hold of that 50 cal. and started lighting them insurgents up like they was some alien creatures in a video game. (*beat*) Yeah, thank you America for making me a violent Black man in your land of I ain't free and the home of unequal rights.

> **VOICES**
> TAT-TAT-TAT-TAT-TAT-TAT-TAT . . .

MORE EXPLOSIONS, MACHINE GUN FIRE, POLICE SIRENS/RADIOS . . .

> ***MR. EVERS**
> The police were coming down the tunnel.

> **VOICES**
> THIS IS THE NYPD . . . DROP YOUR WEAPON.

> **CHEVONN**
> Army was right . . .

> **VOICES**
> TAT-TAT-TAT-TAT-TAT-TAT-TAT . . .

> **MR. EVERS**
> Death loves an audience, and an audience loves death.

ARMY

DEATH IS HERE.

VOICES

TAT-TAT-TAT-TAT-TAT-TAT-TAT . . .

EMMETT

CHEVONN?

CHEVONN

EMMETT?

ARMY

GONNA LIGHT YOU UP MUTHERFUCKERS.

VOICES

RUNNNNNNNNNNNNNNN!!!!

HUGE, TOWERING EXPLOSION. RAPID GUNFIRE. FLASHES . . .

BLACKOUT.

CHAPTER 23 . . . CHEVONN RUNS

SPOTLIGHT up on CHEVONN.

CHEVONN

So, I crawled out of the tunnel as fast as I could.

VOICES

STUMBLING, FALLING, TRIPPING . . .

SPOTLIGHT up on MR. EVERS (READING).

*MR. EVERS

I don't know what happened to Emmett. To Army . . . to God . . .

CHEVONN

All I remember is that Army started firing. And the police fired back.

*MR. EVERS

I crawled underneath the platform. In the darkness, feeling my way . . . cuts, bruises . . . then an MTA worker grabbed me and said . . .

MTA WORKER

WHAT ARE YOU DOING DOWN HERE?

CHEVONN

I didn't hear what he said. I just ran.

MR. EVERS

Past . . . YouTube, Snapchat, Facebook, Twitter . . .

CHEVONN

Past . . . CVS, Starbucks, Chase, Chipotle, McDonald's, Starbucks, Subway, Bank of America, Starbucks, Chase, Duane Reade, McDonald's, CVS, Starbucks . . .

MR. EVERS

I kept running . . . thinking them bullets . . . might find me . . . like they found my cousin Jay D. causing one more death of a Black man.

CHEVONN

So, I kept running . . .

*MR. EVERS

Past the best sellers, best dressed, best educated, best dead rap artist of the year . . . Tupac, too soon.

CHEVONN

Tripped over a guy dealing loose cigarettes.

GUY

What the fuck . . .

CHEVONN

Bumped into a girl popping Vicodin while maxing out her credit cards.

GIRL

You bitch . . .

CHEVONN

I ran for 12 years but white people still think I'm a slave . . .

MR. EVERS

I ran, ran, ran . . .

CHEVONN

Ran by Black boys dying on street corners and Black boys locked up in prisons, only to be the flavor in a NY Times Op-Ed column . . . or a PBS documentary.

VOICES

RUN! RUN! RUN!

CHEVONN

RUNNING HOME TO MY MOTHER, GLORY JOHNSON.

*MR. EVERS

Running by cops profiling me. Thinking I stole my freedom . . .

CHEVONN

Running by Hollywood movies trying to see me . . . but they never get me right.

MR. EVERS

I called to my mother as I raced up the stairs. FLOOR AFTER FLOOR CRUMPLING BENEATH MY NIKES LACED UP REAL TIGHT TO KEEP ME FROM FEELING MY EMPTY STOMACH.

CHEVONN

BURN ME! I DON'T WANT TO REMEMBER MY FATHER RAPING ME. BURN ME MOMMA! BURN ME! I WON'T CRY! I CAN'T CRY!

MRS. JOHNSON appears. She wraps her arms around CHEVONN.

MRS. JOHNSON

I got you . . . I got you, Chevonn. Your father ain't never gonna hurt you again. And neither am I. (*beat*) Ain't gonna study war no more, ain't gonna study war no more. Gonna lay down my burdens . . .

*MR. EVERS

And I thought everything was going to be alright. But I thought wrong.

*EMMETT suddenly appears. He pulls a **gun out** of the backpack **AND POINTS** it at MRS. JOHNSON.*

EMMETT

(*to Mrs. Johnson*) Are you God?

*MR. EVERS

Emmett had followed me home.

CHEVONN

I didn't run fast enough.

BLACKOUT. MR. EVERS *sings "down by the river side."*

SQUEALING BRAKES. THE SOUND HURTS OUR EARS.

CHAPTER 24 . . . CHEVONN'S EARTH—EPILOGUE MUSIC—EARTH SONG

MJ DANCER appears in spotlight—he dances then lights fade.

LIGHTS UP on . . .

CHEVONN stands ON TRAIN PLATFORM with composition book in hand. HER BAN-DAGE IS GONE. The ENSEMBLE enters. They fill the theater. Some stand in the stairwells, some on the platform, and some in the subway car area.

CHEVONN

It's been a year since I haven't been afraid of a hot iron. No more bandages. But I still got the scars. And my story . . .

CHEVONN thumbs through the pages of her notebook.

CHEVONN

Mr. Evers read the whole thing. But it took him a few weeks. Guess he couldn't read it right away because of Emmett shooting my mother and it being all over the news and stuff.

MR. EVERS

I'm sorry, Chevonn. So sorry. If there is anything I can do . . .

CHEVONN

Can you erase that day?

MUSLIM WOMAN

WHAT IF THE TOWERS NEVER FELL? WHAT IF A FAMILY NEVER LOST A LOVED ONE ON THAT DAY?

ARMY

I was leading a convoy to Baghdad. Lt. knew it was a road to hell because insurgents had launched several rocket-propelled grenades at other convoys just days ago.

CHEVONN

Erase the fear?

DREAMER

WHAT IF YOU SEE THEM DRAGGING YOUR NEIGHBOR AWAY? HER CHILDREN CRYING? HER HUSBAND POWERLESS TO DO ANYTHING. THE COMMUNITY POWERLESS TO STOP THE AUTHORITIES FROM SENDING YOU AWAY.

BOOTH TELLER

WHAT IF HE WON'T COMMIT TO LOVE, TO CARING, TO GOODNESS, TO KINDNESS, TO COMPASSION, TO UNDERSTANDING . . .

CHEVONN

Erase the suffering?

GOD

WHY SO MUCH DEATH? WHY SO MUCH PAIN? WHY SO MUCH FIRE? LOOK AROUND. CAN YOU SEE THE FIRE? TOUCH IT! TOUCH IT! LET YOUR TEARS FALL INTO IT.

CHEVONN

Never saw God before or after that day. Haven't seen Mr. Evers since graduation.

CHEVONN	MR. EVERS
I wonder if Mr. Evers . . .	If Chevonn ever thinks about me.

MR. EVERS

I always think about what Chevonn wrote.

CHEVONN

About the pain? There's so much pain.

MRS. JOHNSON

My mother put the iron on my hand and said Girl . . . this world out here is hurtful. You just got to take the hurt. No tears, you hear me? My child will not drown in no tears. So, you listen up Chevonn . . . do not cry in my house. I NEVER CRIED IN MY MOTHER'S HOUSE SO THERE WILL BE NO CRYING IN MINE.

CHEVONN

I always think about Emmett and what had happened to him.

The BAD KIDS grab him. They spray paint him (mime).

EMMETT/MR. EVERS

STOP.

BAD KIDS

LEGS.

EMMETT/MR. EVERS

DON'T.

BAD KIDS

ARMS.

EMMETT/MR. EVERS

STOP.

BAD KIDS

FACE.

EMMETT

HELP ME! SOMEONE HELP!

CHEVONN

He needed someone to help him. I couldn't back then, but maybe now . . .

MTA CONTROLLER

IF SOMEONE'S AT RISK OF FALLING ONTO THE TRACKS . . .

CHEVONN

Or crying . . .

ROCK ON (SPOKEN)
YOU EVER SEE ANYONE CRY ON THE SUBWAY YOU EVER SEE
THEM CRY AND WONDER WHAT BROUGHT ON ALL THE PAIN . . .
A BREAK-UP, A DEATH, AN ILLNESS, JUST LOST A JOB, THEIR HOME,
NOW THEY'RE STUCK ON THIS DAMN TRAIN WITH PEOPLE
STARING AT THEM, BUT THEY JUST STAND AND KEEP . . .
(*beat*) SILENT . . .

PASSENGERS gather. They stand SILENTLY for many beats, and then . . .

PASSENGERS
42ND STREET . . . change here for the 2-3, R, N, W, Shuttle Train . . . the 7,
with connections to the A . . . C . . . DO NOT BLOCK THE DOORS. LET
PASSENEGERS OFF.

PASSENGERS EXIT leaving CHEVONN. She reads from her notebook.

CHEVONN
(*reading*) The police came and took Emmett away. I held my dying mother in my
arms. I didn't want anyone to move her. I touched her lips as life walked away from
her. And for the first time . . . I cried. I cried into the fire.

*A RED WASH fills the theater. PASSENGERS SCURRY up and down the stairs. Where are
they going? What do they want? Who are they? The people we see, but we don't know them.*

GOD/PASSENGERS
And God shall wipe away all tears from their eyes; and there shall be no more
death, neither sorrow, nor crying, neither shall there be any more pain: for the
former things are passed away. For the former things, for the former things, for the
former things . . . .

PASSENGERS stand still. MR. EVERS stops singing.

CHEVONN
Are passed away.

CHEVONN closes the book.

SILENCE.

MR. EVERS sings "AMAZING GRACE."

MR. EVERS

Amazing Grace
How sweet the sound . . .
That saved a wretch like me
I once was lost, but now am found
'Twas blind but now I see

LIGHTS FADE TO BLACK.

THE END